NOVICE
NUMBER NINE

A Novel by

Anne Overland

PublishAmerica

Hardcover 9781456085254
Softcover 9781456085247
PUBLISHED BY PUBLISHAMERICA, LLLP
www.americastarbooks.com

The Lord God is my strength;
He will make my feet like deer's feet,
And He will make me walk on my high hills.

Habakkuk 3:19

For my parents...

SPECIAL THANKS TO:

Mrs. Ruth Herbert, whose assistance and
support made this book possible

NOVICE
NUMBER NINE

CHAPTER

1

The concept of spirituality in the desert seems like a good idea in the light of day, I thought, as the headlights flashed repeatedly on tall profiles and dark silhouettes of cacti lining the highway. If it was only the desert I feared.

I looked anxiously at the dark rolling hills we were paralleling. With my hand on the lock I was learning the hard way traveling from Tucson with a complete stranger is a bad idea any time, it's especially true at night. Surrounded by six windows of ice cold glass, I was chilled inside the yellow cab and pushed the top button through a hole in my dark green coat.

My shivering wasn't entirely due to the weather, but by the thought of being left on a doorstep like a baby to start my new life. It took the encouraging words of Saint Anthony urging me to find a new identity after losing the old one to keep me in my seat. Now that I was actually here, I wondered if I could handle the void.

The deeper we went into the threatening desert, the more misgivings I had. Who knows what snares the taxi driver has in the undergrowth of his imagination waiting to entangle the unwary? A host of perilous possibilities came to me on the wind whistling through the uneven windows, none of which I wanted my thoughts preoccupied with. I leaned away from the driver on shiny gray upholstery which years of rips had custom designed.

I avoided the static pull drawing the driver's carelessly flicked ashes toward me like floating sackcloth by waving my new tan cowboy hat at them in defense. I couldn't dodge the driver's surly voice though, "Boars, yep, boars. Twenty years ago this land was teeming with them, but too many hunters have cut their numbers. It's the high price of an expanding civilization."

I took a sweeping look at the desolate surroundings: at the sword-like long-limbed cacti, the butchered remains of rocks littering the desert floor like body parts, at the clouds smothering everything; dark forces I felt were keeping me from my destination. He was right though, I didn't see any boars.

I felt as crowded and wedged in as one of the tamped out cigarettes in the taxi's tiny ashtray. What *was* he talking about? I hoped he didn't want to start a running conversation with me now, when I wanted time to think.

"The Javelina, or skunk pigs," the driver started again, "are known as peccaries. You probably know them as boars. A peccary is a medium-sized animal that have a strong resemblance to pigs with tusks." Now every passing car had hideous reflections of hogs, tusks protruding from their bristled faces. I could almost see their hot slobbering breath fogging the windows, leaving wet nasal imprints to interfere with the view for the remainder of the ride.

I was working up a strong dislike for this man who was keeping me from my deliberations. The cabby wasn't finished yet. "Boars have a snout and small beady eyes and use only two digits for walking. The tusks are for defending against predators, and by rubbing the pointy projections, they make a chattering noise that warns predators not to get too close. They usually live in pairs, so if you hear clicking while out walking, run in the other direction. They've been known to kill people."

If he was trying to scare me, it was working. I slid as as far away as possible from his deadly intimations, all the way inside my parent's garage. I was standing in the dim wattage of a naked yellow bulb looking through streams of unsettled dust where I spied a box full of shabby old books. I was surprised. I thought I was aware of any new item introduced among the familiar. Yet, here was this recent addition of a worn cardboard box full of faded dog-eared books.

Holding on the seat in the cab, I recalled how I didn't go to the box immediately. I was savoring the odd feeling that this difference had somehow been slipped into the garage without my knowing. An impending shift in my father's temperament was why I left the house in the first place; hard liquor has an unpredictable effect on most people. I was still in college. I wasn't about to look for another place to live like he ordered. It had taken *years* of practice, but I had learned not to take his boorish behavior any more seriously than a wrong phone number.

I peered out the window beside me at the passing cacti while the cabbie rambled on. "Boars have dark grey skin which is both both ridgid and strong, as well as soft and supple, making it ideal for leather gloves…"

I wasn't listening. I was still in the garage stunned at my father's directive until I remembered people who drink too much have their own problems. I didn't let his outburst spoil that evening. Instead, I reached down and shuffled through the dusty books that included Taylor Caldwell's *Dear and Glorious Physician*, and a quintology of comparative religions held together by a black cardboard case. These five books had never been used and their newness was very appealing, enticing me with their 'new print' smell. The hardback titles included *Judaism, Buddhism, Protestantism, Hinduism,* and *Catholicism.* The box also held Saint John of the Cross's *Dark Night of the Soul,* and Saint Teresa of Avila's *Interior Castle.* They described a different kind of wildness.

The book that made a lasting impression on me was *The Sign of Jonas* by Thomas Merton. Inside the hard cover was a black and white photograph of a solitary man strolling around a lake among stark and barren trees in an outfit I wasn't familiar with. I studied the picture a long time and could almost hear his shoes kicking the thick leaves and cracking dead branches.

I peered distractedly out the window remembering. How different Merton's meditative walk was in comparison to the frenetic atmosphere I'd left in my parent's house. I don't know how many books I mentally devoured in the following months, but when I had finished, Merton the monk had instilled in me a love of cloisters, solitude and the Cistercian lifestyle. I longed to embrace the aloneness he was experiencing; it made me spiritually envious to a physical degree. So here I was, taking drastic steps to emulate Merton's life, confident the mixed reactions of being raised in a drinking environment wouldn't interfere with my present endeavor.

"They have claws. You know, fused foot bones used for running down their prey. These hogs are good huntin', but don't go near them. Their teeth are like blades. Javelina can eat prickly pear cactus, spines and all," the cabbies' words broke into my thoughts.

Good God, I thought, when his reminicing began again. Now every passing car threw up hideous reflections of wild beasts; demons with cloven hooves. I could almost see their hot slobbering pig breath fogging the windows, leaving wet nasal imprints to interfere with the view for the remainder of the trip. I wished he'd just stop talking.

"Half the time they don't even chew their food," he continued. "They can snap off a piece…"

"Like my hand?" I finished for him. I was I no mood to hear the gory details of him shooting a wild boar and skinning it with his favorite knife.

He glanced at me over his shoulder with an accusing look of 'So *you're* the one who readjusted my site to the left, aren't you?'

I didn't mean to override his descriptive account of taking down dangerous game but I had heard enough. There was no need to continue with the bloody details. Couldn't he tell I was already on the edge of my seat as it was?

I sat back expunging images of predatory animals, mouths drooling, pawing their way after us gaining ground. As a passenger during the one hour taxi ride from Tucson airport, I wanted to use this remaining time for some last minute thinking, not listening to adventures of some white bwana's former hunting stories. Maybe I was making him as uneasy as the emptiness was making me. I certainly wasn't a typical fare, and this wasn't an average destination; single women don't ask to be dropped off in the desert in the middle of the night.

Talking is familiar so in he charged again with the boars, this time more animated, as if he had narrowly escaped landing on bamboo shoots at the bottom of a pit himself. Trapped inside this rolling metal ice box with him, my imperceptible nods instead of replies seemed to be enough contribution to keep up his one-sided conversation.

We were traveling under the auspices of a full moon that left forms distorted in the night. Shapes had a menacing feel in the shadows and I pressed my nose against the glass for a better look.

I strained to see the lingering spirits of Indians and missionary explorers moving from cactus to cactus, vanishing the moment I studied their trails of invisibility. Darkness, moonlight and the sparseness of winter all made the trip a caricature of the bright desert I spent as an 'observer' the previous August.

We had been driving countless miles on level ground in air with no humidity. The inside of my nose felt raw and my nostrils were a conduit of pain with every breath. All I needed was a nosebleed. I shook the image off of me arriving covered in blood and made a conscious effort to breathe through my mouth from then on.

My cautious entrance under cover of night may have been the unconscious reason I booked a late flight, so I could sneak in undetected. Laying low felt right to me.

The driver slowed his speed, pulled to the right, and exited the uncongested freeway this time of night. He joined a two lane highway aimed at a low mountain range, like a demarcation separating me from my past. He used the bright setting on the headlights for the remainder of the trip.

This was no longer straight monotonous freeway driving, this was much different. We were now driving gradually uphill over low undulating hills more like how I thought a high desert should look with shrubby cactus. The higher we climbed, the smaller the desert flora became along the road, going from distinctive forms of tall cacti with almost humanlike shapes, I was convinced were from prehistoric times, to low spiny plants. With the subtle change in landscape, I noticed the driver had changed his talking too and went from highly charged speaking in slow regular speech as if the beauty of the smaller vegetation had affected him too.

With the headlights scattering more light briefly on the surrounding countryside, I knew I was really in the desert now, the one sketched in my mind filled with deep peace and quiet, where the only sounds are explosions of color on wildflowers in the spring, and blooms bursting to life in the summer.

As a sightseer looking intently at the landscape for more than an hour, I spotted a handmade wooden sign on the shoulder of the highway like a grave marker for an animal that didn't make it across the road.

It was hewn with a directional arrow pointing off the highway to a dirt road. A part of me was elated we found our turn, while another part was hoping we had overshot the way in and we're on our way to Mexico.

Trembling slightly from fear of the unknown as much as from the cold, I pulled the ends of my coat together. The cabby turned right on the untraveled weedy dirt road. Where the paved highway had been dark even in the moonlight, we didn't have the occasional passing headlight to aid us now. This was a buckboard ride, bumpy and slow, an obstacle course of erosion with a bad planning design like that of a string of black pearls someone had carelessly tossed on the blueprint, if it had a blueprint at all.

Suddenly the driver stopped the car. Alarms went off in my mind. Why is he stopping way out here? I pulled my cowboy hat in front of me like a shield.

He turned on the interior light, and hung his elbow on the bench seat so he could face me. I scanned his face and saw that like the sign, it too looked as if had been hewn out of rough wood, chiseled and pockmarked with an old scar etched deep in his right cheek. I wanted to ask if it had been punctured by the claw of a trapped boar, or a cornered passenger who refused to keep up his conveyor belt conversation, but I didn't want to reopen an old wound. In an impatient voice, he said, "This can't be the way; it looks more like a firebreak than a road. Maybe the sign was turned the wrong way."

"No, this has to be the right way."

He grunted his annoyance but went back to following the road that led into a depression I remembered was a dry river bed. With the headlights sparkling stones like they were drops of water, the taxi acted like a gush of water splashing bits of sand, drenching us in dust; our car awash in dirt.

Running along the edge of the road was a collection of last years' growth of disintegrating tumbleweed, dead bushes, and particles of bark blurring the windows like disturbed pollen. Or an embalmer's mixture, preparing me for God knows what waiting at the end of the road.

We forged our way through the rough that was terrain scratching and scraping the cab's side panels. I tried not to let my nerves get the better of me and trained my eyes on a clean spot on the windshield, hoping the taxi would keep running and dust wouldn't clog the engine. Radioing for help would be poor this far out of the city, if we were able to make any contact at all. I wasn't wearing heels, but still, I'd hate to have to fight my way through this sticky terrain looking for help in any shoes.

By the shimmering light of the moon, we drove out of the wash relieved the car made it. We were now driving on a road that was gutted with chuckholes and ruts, jostling us about the cab like lottery balls. My eyes opened wide seeing it lead up a short but steep hill curving right at the top out of sight. There were no road signs to mark the way; no assurance we were heading in the right direction, only this unfamiliar road, almost impassible, taking us deeper and deeper into this dark night.

We drove over bumpy cattle guards grouped to defend the higher ground by keeping untamed beasts from continuing their upward ascent. I sensed this was the last hill before reaching the journey's end. With the steep incline directly in front of us now, hearing the tires slipping in the dirt, the driver gunned the engine. I held my breath as he attempted to make it up on the first try with a running start. We shot up the hill and stopped briefly at the top, stunned, anxiously looking around, like we made it to the top of the world.

As strangers in this strange new landscape, I looked with interest on the elevated tract of level land. Our headlights gleamed over the empty dirt surface, on a small cared-for green leafed tree on the left side of the road, at the bumpy yellowish crab grass covering the land on the right, and at a mountain range over my left shoulder miles away.

Even in the dark, clarity hung over it all, a purity I could feel letting me know I had reached hallowed ground that was so different from the confused tangle of weeds we just left. While I was sure it was an anticlimactic end for the driver, it was the beginning of an exciting adventure for me.

The driver moved cautiously over the plateau in the moonlight while I searched the foreground through the clean spot in the bug-splattered windshield. My attention was drawn to a few walled structures at the other end barely distinguishable in the darkness I knew had to be the knot on the end of the road.

I moved closer to the driver on the bench seat and told him, "This is far enough; you can let me out right here." He cocked his head at an angle and looked at me with a puzzled expression. There was something protective about his gesture, for after all, we were in the middle of nowhere, and I didn't have his expertise of the high country. I assumed hadn't noticed the buildings ahead yet.

Catching his perplexed look in the rear view mirror, I heard him mutter "Crazy broad" under his breath, and avoided making any further eye contact."Yes, this is far enough, I want to get out," I said again, ignoring another disapproving look. He stopped the car anyway and put on the emergency brake.

I was in no hurry. I wanted to walk the rest of the way to prolong my arrival as long as I could. I thought by walking the last stretch I would have more time to quell my buoyant resurgence of doubts and maybe the exercise would help curb my nervousness. I pushed my way from the dusty yellow cab and stepped into the carbon blackness dragging my suitcase and holding my cowboy hat.

For the last hour, as his captive audience, I heard all about boars and what beautiful country this is and how much the driver missed driving out this far. This was the same person now complaining he had to drive all the way back alone holding out his hand for a tip.

"Just enjoy the beautiful scenery," I said, meaning it, handing him some money. He thanked me and got back in his cab doubling back over the plateau with me half wishing I was going with him. That's when it hit me; there was no going back now. Standing alone on the plateau watching the lights from the cab filter away, I shifted uncomfortably.

I heard the trailing sound of the tires crunching the gravel for a long time, and then was left in darkness. I stood in the dirt next to my luggage inwardly reveling in the quiet, letting it soak in as much as it could. I stood dumbfounded, for I had forgotten what absolute quiet felt like. As I waited in the moonlight, it was slowly sinking in where I was—on a five thousand foot mountain that turned into rolling hills at the bottom with a magnificent mountain range capped in snow for a backdrop. There was a definite chill in the air, but no there was snow on the plateau. And it was oh, so quiet.

With a quick slap of cold across my face I was reminded this was the middle of December and pulled my coat tighter to me. I fastened the top button and put my cowboy hat on. I picked up my bag, and started walking toward the dark buildings startled by the loudness of my own steps. The ground was so cold it sounded brittle. The closer I came, the slower I walked.

I sized up the one story red brick building. I found the front door and sidled up knocking with the reserve of someone who really wasn't sure they wanted someone to answer. I leaned over brushing the dust off my new loafers with my hands and stepped back. There was no response. I knocked harder, and began feeling the stucco exterior for a doorbell. I was in luck and pushed the button. I stepped back, stood straighter, and waited. I didn't hear a buzzer, chimes and or people rushing to answer, so I pushed it, again and again.

To the right of the door were a couple of low windows and I peered in the interior of each. But the rooms were cark and empty. After pounding loudly on each, I walked to the end of the porch where I saw a detached wing with many doors a couple hundred feet away, but it too was dark so I didn't bother looking closer. I was relieved to see at least they weren't boarded up.

Where could they all be? It must be at close to two o'clock by now. I walked back to the front door debating what I should do next.

It didn't take long for the coldness to become a bone chilling stiff breeze that blew through me to my marrow. I knew I had to do something to keep warm or I would be in real trouble. The porch was long and narrow with no lawn chairs or benches. I paced back and forth looking for the best place to sit. Freezing on a porch was no way to start my new life, I mumbled to myself.

I placed my suitcase and hat on the porch under a small window too high for me to look into. Choosing a spot against a door, I awkwardly sat on the cold cement next to a welcome mat. Realizing the desert is full of all kinds of threatening species, some which I didn't want to know about, out of desperation, I pulled the welcome mat over my legs regardless of what was underneath: scorpions, black widow spiders or snakes. Because it was dark and I couldn't see underneath, the mat felt safe. Right now I needed to keep warm no matter what. My personal revulsion to long-legged, slithering; perhaps poisonous crawling creatures would have to be disregarded.

As my eyes grew accustomed to the darkness, forms began taking shape in the moonlight. Miles away I could make out a snow topped mountain range, and directly in front of me was a small square rock garden sparsely planted with cacti between strategically placed rocks. While studying the closest outlines, I heard the stuttering hoot of an owl and raised my eyes to follow the silent flap of wings taking flight off the roof disappearing almost immediately in the darkness.

A chill went though me hearing the unmistakable yelping howls of a pack of wild coyotes somewhere in the distance making their eerie presence known. They were far enough away I knew I wasn't in any danger, but gave their passage through the open countryside my respectful concern.

I was so cold now there wasn't a chance of me falling asleep shivering, with my head against the the door.

All of a sudden a loud machine started up inside breaking the silence with its jolting mechanical noise. I straightened up stiffly and stood on my toes trying to see if I could see if anyone came into the room. No one! I waited a minute before crawling back under the mat. Apparently, the temperature kicked the heater on, I reasoned, but figuring this out didn't make me feel any warmer.

Undoubtedly this was cruel; sitting on a cold cement porch, freezing, looking down at a large **WELCOME** across my legs, forced to listen to a heater turning on and off. "Well, I wanted more time to think," I thought sarcastically.

I had lost track of time, but by now I was so cold, it didn't matter. The periodic on-again motorized workings of the heater brought me back to the reality of the cold porch time after time. I crossed my legs and kept my hands wedged under the stiff blanket and stopped getting up to check if anyone was in the room every time the heater turned on. I resigned myself to wait for the break of day.

I kept going over and over my reasons for being here. With my imagination vividly working overtime, I was actually grateful for having this extra time to myself. This restive waiting was worthwhile because I was filled with heightened anticipation that flooded me with warmth from worry every time the thought came to me, 'This is not a visit. This is *it!* I blew on my hands repeatedly trying to thaw my fingers to ward off hypothermia. A chilly taxi ride, now an hour in this icy cold, a picture of me covering the patio with germs from a sneeze was forming in my mind.

Nevertheless, with all my anxious nerves, worry and self-doubt was the realization there was nowhere else in the world I would rather be, than sitting alone, deep in the night, atop a 5,000 foot hill at the base of a southern Arizonan mountain range. I knew that at precisely this moment in time, this was where I needed to be.

With a slight sense of annoyance I noticed a light filtering down from the little window above me, its soft steady glow illuminating the **WELCOME** across my legs. Rising to my feet, I gathered my courage, swallowed hard, and knocked on the door.

A framed face of a woman wearing dark rimmed glasses appeared at the glass, her eyes peered out uneasily into the cold inhospitable night searching the dark patio for unwanted intruders. Cautiously, the door opened a crack, and with a puzzled look the woman asked, "Are you *Anne*?"

All pleasantries aside, through chattering teeth, I heard myself blurt out, "Yes. Could I come in?"

"By all means," the lady replied, and with a gracious sweep of her arm, watched as my shadow moved into the light.

CHAPTER

2

The décor inside a Trappistine monastery is exactly what one would expect; less is more. With my hunched body unfurling as it warmed, I realized I had been leaning against the church door. Pews were a welcome sight along with the wave of warmth that had a slight scent of incense.

Glancing around, it felt like I had stepped into a wonderland where things were somehow different now they were steeped in tradition and antiquity; they had meaning.

I followed the sister, who wore a long white robe and short black veil, along an isle past several pews. My low peripheral glance saw kneelers that had padding, but the rows of pews had padding, but the rows of pews were hard wood without cushions. The brick walls of the chapel were painted white with dark wooden beams interconnecting the roof, giving it the impression we were walking under the skeletal structure of a whale. I couldn't help comparing myself to Jonah and hoped I would be disgorged unharmed too.

The chapel was constructed in the shape of an 'L', with the visitors' chapel on one side, and the sisters' section on the other. A raised altar, noticeably barren of flowers, candles, or books was positioned at an angle in the center. A plain white cloth stretched flat, had a stained glass crucifix in the center that was mounted on a beautiful piece of sculptured driftwood. The work of art was the focal point of the chapel. A gold metal case containing the Eucharist had been secured on the back wall of the sanctuary where a small candle was burning.

I followed the sister's slow deliberate steps as she lowered the small chain marking the visitors' side of the chapel. She led me between a dozen green high-backed chairs, six on one side and six on the other. They were pulled close to the walls so the sisters could face each other. This was the sisters' choir with the organist's station in back. In front, a large red candle was burning its vigil in stillness.

The sister opened the back door and we walked into a little foyer with a small table holding a couple books. In two steps she turned right and walked along a wall to a long hallway marked with intermittent nightlights casting yellowish hues the length of the corridor. Dragging my suitcase and holding my hat, I followed the sister into her office. She turned on a light and reintroduced herself as Reverend Mother Esmeralda. She told me how surprised she was to see me arriving at such a late hour. I apologetically explained I hadn't taken into consideration flight delays, long cab rides, and the hour's difference when crossing a time zone.

I don't know what I was expecting to find in the office of a Superior of an abbey: a large print displaying the Last Supper covering an entire wall, maybe; or a reproduction of archangels on swirling clouds painted on the ceiling. But there were no pictures of rosy cheeked cherubic angels to greet me. I didn't even see a dog-eared copy of Butler's *Lives of the Saints*, open and lying flat, its spine broken from use waiting for her return.

Gratefully, she didn't engage me in a long conversation, but saw how tired I was. In a quiet voice she told me I could sleep as late as I wanted the first night. "Let's get you settled in."

We went back into the hallway where she stopped midway in front of my bedroom and pushed the door open. I felt for a switch and flipped on a light. She said goodnight, closed the door, turned, and was swallowed in the yellow darkness.

It was not much of a room; purely functional. I swung my suitcase on the bed, hung my jumper and blouse in the closet and tossed my brown cowboy hat on the top shelf. I checked out the modern looking bathroom that had a shower, sink and a toilet. I was very happy seeing bathrooms here weren't large barrack-like latrines. I noticed a small mirror over the sink right off, even though I had a hunch I'd have a uni-brow in no time.

I was exhausted. Trading my jeans for pajamas, I crawled into bed at the end of my long journey. As I did, I wondered if the cabbie had made it back to the highway yet.

I lay utterly exhausted in the strange new darkness. The last thing I remember before falling asleep was the rumbling of the heater and its pleasant warmth gliding over my face from the vent overhead.

When I woke, I couldn't distinguish where anyone was because the sisters had taken a vow of silence and no one said anything. I was looking forward to not talking knowing it would open a whole new depth of spirituality. The whole building seemed deserted and felt solemnly serious. It is definitely a shock to suddenly have to squelch familiar verbal responses and it wasn't easy. I found myself covering my mouth with my hand as a reminder not to talk, even to myself.

The room was so small, in two steps I was standing next to the drapes covering a glass slider. I gave the cord a good hard yank and nearly fell over the bed behind me from the flood of brightness. The view was incredible; miles of rolling hills stretched before me with cacti in various stages of regeneration. In the distance, several horses wandered over the hills; all the surroundings in dazzling sunshine. Realizing I slept through dawn, I tore myself away from the view. I took my new dark blue jumper and white blouse out of the closet, dressed, making the silence pound in my ears with the effort. I was really looking forward to not applying make-up. Going *al natural*, I was ready in no time.

I stood frozen wondering what I should do next training to hear movement; there was not one rusty hinge, or the creak of a closet opening, a drawer being pushed in, or sounds of water running, or toilets flushing anywhere. I opened the door and staggered out hoping my plain face, the real me, wouldn't scare anyone. It scared me.

With daylight lightening it, I stepped into the long, hallway thinking, *so this is what the inside of a monastery looks like.* Studying my new surroundings, I took a few tentative steps to a place I was familiar with, the chapel. I positioned myself against a shadowed wall far enough away it wouldn't be obvious I was slinking around unescorted if someone happened upon me. A stranger standing motionless in the bosom of the monastery would arouse suspicion. I could see their distrustful faces now as I fumbled to explain my presence.

On my right, a knotted rope dangled from the steeple. I had to restrain myself from giving it a good strong pull to let them know I was awake even though it would make *some* first impression. The rope was hanging in front of a large red brick window in the shape of an arch that looked out on a field in back of the monastery. Large white puffy clouds floating by made me do a double take, they were so beautiful. Suddenly realizing again where I was, I pulled my eyes away and flattened my body against the back wall hoping my blue jumper wasn't too obvious against the red bricks.

Without warning, the door in front of me opened. To my embarrassment, I was flushed into the open as out walked the sisters wearing long flowing robes like Reverend Mother the night before. They smiled shyly at me as they passed but didn't say anything.

The one on the end was Sister Esmeralda. She ushered me into her office and in a loud whisper, said, "You're awake. I'm glad you slept in. I'm Reverend Mother Esmeralda," reintroducing herself. "I hope you didn't have too much trouble finding the monastery in the dark last night? It *is* off the beaten track."

"No trouble at all in finding it again," suggesting my arrival in the middle of the night was a trivial matter to ease her mind. I had been here once before on an observership when it was the middle of summer under the full rays of a sweltering August sun. Last night, everything looked so strange and different in the dark.

"There *is* a doorbell," she continued, "but it's being rewired so it's illuminated."

I just smiled.

As she spoke, I looked closely at her face. I was surprised to see her skin looking so smooth without the aid of dermabrasion, laser surgery or face peels and assumed her unwrinkled skin was due to a stress-free life and good clean living. My face on the other hand, after one night in the dry desert air worrying, felt like it had cracked into a thousand pieces already.

I was told the robe she was wearing for warmth was a cowl for professed sisters (under solemn vows) and novices wear cloaks. A diverse visual gallery of religious clothing paraded through my mind. I'd seen the stiff wing-like veils some orders wear, the starched wimples that leave only the face exposed, the large distinctive cone-shaped cornets resembling horns on the wearer's head.

Was I was relieved seeing the modern looking white mid-length habit of the Cistercian: a black outer garment called a scapula hung from the shoulders that matched the length of the habit. A handmade leather belt held the two pieces together. It was a habit I could feel comfortable wearing. I preferred to blend in. Sister Esmeralda had large soulful brown eyes under thick brown eyebrows that were pulled back by her black veil. I took notice of her calm, unhurried manner; I didn't know much about these things but it stands to reason, as the Superior goes, so goes the community. Her peaceful nature told me she was firmly attuned to her intuition and she was listening attentively to it while running the monastery. I was convinced I had chosen the right order."It's nearly dinner time," the sister said. "We call our lunch, dinner, and have a light supper at 6:00.

The dining room is called a refectory and the oblong room next to it is the Community room." She told me the routine for meals is always the same. The one with the least seniority goes first in line for food, in keeping with the idea that the longer a person was here, the more self control she would have developed. Reverend Mother Esmeralda was always last. Starting tomorrow, I would go first until the next novice arrived. "I hope you're hungry."

She opened the door and we fell in line with the others who had taken off their cowls and cloaks and wearing habits.

We went through a narrow hallway filled with the delicious smells of cooking that more than anything else, made me feel at home. All the different food and baking odors hung in a luscious humidity in the hallway, growing stronger and stronger as we walked. Was I detecting biscuits or rolls? Maybe it was cornbread. As my first monastic meal, I was very interested seeing if nourishment fit for ascetics was something I too could live on too.

We entered a large open area. If this large room was the refectory, it didn't look like it belonged in a monastery. Hanging over the dining table was a large chandelier made from an authentic wagon wheel complete with nicks and cuts bringing to mind the image of someone having positioned a rifle against the rungs at an outlaw in the past. Lights had been connected to it and a round dimmer switch on a wall so they could be adjusted as needed. It was unique and set off the entire room with a southwestern tone and made me feel I was on a ranch, we the ranch hands.

On our right, a large case full of books took the place of a wall to make a very small library. In front of it was another small area. Light from an oblong window fell on desks that had been squeezed in to fit. Two men were seated at a small table in front in silence. Next to them, a door led outside.

Taking me to my place, Esmeralda slowed at an empty setting near the end of a hand-crafted rectangular wooden table about 15 feet long. It was a centerpiece I itself. The image of highly paid executives smoking cigars at its dark uneven surface during board meetings came to mind. The chandelier was hanging over it. Putting her hand on a chair, the Superior said, "This is your place." I stood behind my chair and stared at my cup and silverware setting like everyone else. We listened to the noontime grace Esmeralda read from a small booklet next to her place setting, turning the page to the correct date. Every blessing would be a different one, at least for a year.

When she finished, I followed the sister next to me into the kitchen where I hoped monastic food wouldn't be like cafeteria food with jello for dessert with every meal. Recalling pictures of emaciated monks and hearing stories about spiritual people surviving on only celery and sunshine, I was prepared for the worst. I was never happy to be so wrong! It wasn't at all like the tasteless gruel I imagined. Spread over the counter was fresh, steaming homemade bread, quiche with pieces of green spinach, cauliflower, cooked carrots, undoubtedly canned from the last harvest, and a large green salad with trimmings to add along with several store-bought dressings. We could help ourselves to as much as we wanted of everything, but with everybody watching, it was easy not to overindulge. In a monastery, it was up to each individual how healthfully she wanted to eat with seconds (or thirds) readily available. Then again, with the sisters sitting at the refectory table, it made the walk back to the food counter self-consciously long. Nervousness had never diminished my appetite, but I didn't want to appear gluttonous, not right away anyway.

As I ate, I realized how meals in a monastery are not for the sensual pleasure of tastes, there are no choices in what is being prepared; tastes are also subject to discipline in the mastery of the entire body. I knew this having studied monastic practices for years, learning as much as I could before entering. I was aware there could be no stuffing down feelings with food here. Anger, shame, loneliness, lack of love, or lack of sexual fulfillment could not be substituted with food. These problem behaviors have to be dealt with by getting at the core and facing them, which sometimes takes a lifetime. In this respect, the monastery can be seen as a large therapy facility, where facing one's struggles is the only way to find peace. The enclosure keeps distractions out, but it also prevents sisters from running away from their problems.

Using food to quell or pacify internal struggles could be done in oversized portions only; there was positively no food available for snacking. I knew eating double helpings and creating a noticeable weight gain could be an expression of autonomy, being able to control at least this one aspect in an environment where control had been voluntarily given over to Superiors. This visible bulking up could also be a way of consciously flaunting anger in an expression not hard to miss—even to oneself.

A little extra layer kept between others, may in essence be pushing them away, a subtle way of saying, "don't come any closer." Just because a person doesn't look *fat*, doesn't mean they don't have struggles with weight control. I, for one, was looking forward to eating more healthfully. I was glad the temptation was taken away of not being allowed into the kitchen to whip up a cheese cake or anything else I felt like eating. Gone are the days of having 10 cookies and a banana for dinner.

I looked at the others. They wouldn't know I could hardly take the blame for being pleasantly plump. When my mother was in the delivery room, after I was born, one of the nurses told her she didn't have to start me on formula; she should give me ham hocks and lima beans. It was baby fat that happily never turned into obesity. It did make me wonder. As my first impressions in life, what effect did seeing the wide-eyed horrified looks on nurses, relatives and visitors at my fleshy pink size have on me when then peered into the crib. Did it make me persona non grata at an early age? Did it make me standoffish, suspicious, fearful or distrustful? It was an inauspicious base to work from at the start of my life, in any case.

Vegetables had never appealed to me, but I forced myself to take a little of everything, settling for seconds only on a thick slice of warm bread on a table in back where I spread a generous amount of thick crunchy peanut butter over it. Vegetarians lived long lives, didn't they?

When we were all seated, our food in front of us, I wasn't surprised when the main meal of the day was accompanied by refectory reading. A novice wearing white was sitting with her ankles crossed in a school desk next to the stone fireplace reading from a book that was about half finished. Eventually I would catch on to the storyline about a hermit, but today my attention was on my table manners and took care to lightly dab the corners of my mouth with my napkin.

Following the sister sitting next to me, I too, took my mug over and filled it full of hot coffee from a thermos. It was next to bread and butter in the back of the room, as were different flavored Trappistine honeys that looked inviting; I'd be sure to taste them at some point. I walked back to my seat where I could now look at the room in detail.

The refectory was a long open spaced room with a comfortable feel. I had never been church religious and this room mirrored God with its simplicity. This unpretentious and simple room typified the plainness of monastic decor for me, and told how the people here cared more about what went on on inside rather than placing importance on outward ornate symbols.

Another eye-catcher in the room was a massive stone fireplace made from the smooth stones collected from the surrounding washes. Cabin-like and attractive in its rusticity, I could easily imagine pioneering women cooking meals in worn blackened pots hanging from metal rods before the kitchen had been modernized. Seeing me eye it, Esmeralda explained years ago the monastery had been a ranch before the sisters acquired it and built on to the original structure, one wing for the bedrooms and the other for the chapel.

There were a couple plain crosses made out of small driftwood pieces hanging on the walls that were artistic in their simplicity and suited the emptiness of the monastery. And even though the rural atmosphere made it easier to imagine Matt Dillon, Doc, and Kitty sitting around the refectory table instead of Jesus, Mary, and Joseph, one would never forget they were anywhere else but a monastery because of the peace that permeated every breath.

I never really noticed before, but it is difficult to eat quietly. I listened to the cacophony of sounds made by a group of hungry people eating in silence; it is an ugly noise to hear—silverware scraping, chewing, slurping, swallowing…times ten. I became aware there were two types of swallowers: some can swallow quietly and others were gulpers. Out of ten people, two were definitely gulpers.

It felt strange not making conversation with the people around me, but also a sense of relief at not having to make small talk with complete strangers. I picked up my spoon and quietly stirred my coffee. I didn't think it was going to take long getting used to living with a vow of silence.

I looked around. Large sliding glass doors let dramatic views of the desert in from every side. My eyes went casually from rolling brown hills of shaggy brown weeds to incredible backdrops of far off mountains, all drenched in wonderful desert stillness. From this vantage point, my vision was limitless and I stood as if in a trance, mesmerized by one indescribable scene after another. Wide empty stretches of withered weeds in natural ocher and earthly pigments on uninhabited fields surrounded the entire property in all directions, making a convincing argument for the beauty of an unencumbered soul.

Dinner was a relaxed, slow meal with the sisters taking their time enjoying their food in silence. Even so, without conversation to prolong the enjoyment of a meal it speeds up meal time considerably. With no after-dinner-mints or cigarettes to cap off the meal, or relaxing to let our food digest, everyone cleared out quickly. I sat satiated and content appreciating the generous use of onions in the quiche.

When the two men finished eating in the adjacent room, they stood and left through a door beside them. We bussed our own dishes piling plates, silverware and mugs on a kitchen counter. One sister cleared away the mens' dishes in the side room, hurriedly wiping their places in no time, while another went to work rearranging the room.

The sisters were guided by silent hand signs from Esmeralda and adjourned to the rectangular room next to us that didn't have a wall separating it from the refectory. I brought up the rear.

As I kept up with the pack, I felt a distorted twist of a smile spread across my face. It was a reaction to what was undoubtedly coming next and it scared me even more than the vegetarian diet: introductions. I groaned at the thought of standing in front of the community where I would be picked apart like a scaled fish. What would they think of my new baggy jumper instead of my usual attire, jeans? What would they think of my new short hair cut in place of my blonde straggly hair, years in the making? Would they like my new brown step-in loafers in place of usual casual flip-flops? I was prepared to make certain concessions; if my big toes never saw the light of day again, those were the breaks.

I straightened my jumper, plastered a big smile on my face, or the best one I could under the circumstances, and traipsed behind the sisters to the oblong alcove next to us, prepared for the worst.

CHAPTER

3

The desks in the Community room had been dragged into a U shape with barely enough room to squeeze between them. A tan vinyl chair in the front was waiting for Reverend Mother Esmeralda near the priest's table. A large round can had been placed on the table. While we stood at our assigned desks, I looked down at the desks. They were typical school sized desks with sloping tops for writing, and a groove for a pen; with one exception, no graffiti. I didn't see one cross cut into the wood, not one cactus, nor one Desert Rules, scratched in any of the plywood surfaces. When she was seated, we all sat. She explained how at times she holds these impromptu get-togethers to talk about pressing matters and, I assumed, making me feel welcome was her immediate concern.

She passed around the tin that full of large home made chocolate chip cookies. We each took one cookie. I watched how easily and quickly hand signs were exchanged between the sisters, like they were magicians performing sleight of hand tricks. Every so often laughter would break out making me wonder what had been signed or even if a rabbit had been pulled from a sleeve. Without speech, it gave me the feeling I was definitely missing out.

Because this (I) was a *special occasion*, Reverend Mother gave permission to the sisters to ask me questions. All questions and comments were addressed through Esmeralda as proper monastic etiquette. I answered all kinds of queries about myself, current events and world affairs—anything they wanted to know. I quickly began to feel as important as a presidential press secretary conducting a news briefing of the latest up-to-the-minute AP and UPI reports like I was an 'outside' correspondent. No one interrupted me or offered opinions. I wasn't a communications expert or orator, but like it or not I became for the moment their human wire service.

Going without a radio or television will be difficult, I realized, but at least I noticed there were a few informative magazines namely *Newsweek* and *Time*, spread across a back table. Because this monastery was in Arizona, I assumed for its useful pointers and instructional advice, *Arizona Highways*.

The sisters laughed often with an easy natural laughter. I laughed heartily along with them so they couldn't tell how nervous I was, even though I didn't know any hand signs yet.

When the thought came to me I might be the punch line, I didn't laugh as loud. The superior introduced each member of the community. Sisters Esmeralda, Gail, Lorna, Drusilla, Teresa, and Viola, the original six, had come from Massachusetts to start Cistercian life in Arizona, and were considered pillars of the community. In spite of years of discipline, the youthful appearance of each made of their length of stay hard to believe.

Guiding the sisters over this irregular route of faith was Reverend Mother Esmeralda, the monastery's spiritual leader. She knew the passageways and dead ends that occasionally led to errors, and the way proven the most passable. It was easy to trust her gentle and mild manner, and I found it reassuring knowing this experienced personal advisor was leading the way.

Sister Gail may have been the eldest, it was hard to tell. At five feet one, her welcoming and gracious countenance nevertheless gave off a strong and forceful personality dictated by a serious attitude. She was the only sister with light streaks of gray pulled beneath her veil, which added a softening affect around her face giving her a classy look. As the bookkeeper, she fit the role, and looked like she had never bounced a check in her life. If she did, she undoubtedly could prove it was the bank's fault.

The tanned face of Sister Lorna displayed the telltale laugh-lines and healthy color of the many hours she spent outdoors. She was the head gardener responsible for the majority of food put before us all year round. Experienced in canning, she knew how to preserve and stockpiled jars and milk cartons (and practically anything else that had a lid) full of vegetables that would last the vegetarian community through the winter. "Wash, size, blanch, and chill," she said with quick direction. And wagging an index finger close to my face warned, "Watch out for flat sour!"

Next in line was the Novice Director. Esmeralda explained she was to become the most important person in my life and I was to go to her whenever I needed anything or had any questions.

The Novice Director, Sister Drusilla, was a uniquely visual person. Shaking my hand in welcome, her strait black hair was pulled tightly under her veil that bespoke her no-nonsense personality and made it seem like a wayward strand of hair would never dare to fall out of line into her face. She had piercing black eyes I assumed could cut swiftly through any false-hearted statement; a good quality for a Novice Director to have, I thought. A purity shone from her unblemished skin that could not have been rubbed in, sprayed on, or smoothed over to achieve, as if the purity of her heart aided in toning her skin; the ultimate skin care secret. A piece of white tape on the bridge of her glasses holding them together gave her the impression of the classic nerd. And if body language serves as non-verbal communication, I didn't know what to make of the length of her unusually long blinks, as if she was trying to shut me out and didn't want to see me at all. Maybe she was hoping I'd be gone by the time the blink was over. I supposed I would get used to it, as long as her eyes didn't start to look around independently of each other.

Next in line was Sister Teresa who was responsible for anything that flooded, cracked, loosened, leaked, sparked, or clogged—inside or out. With years of practical maintenance experience, she was invaluable to a place where the nearest help was over an hour's drive away. competency showed in her hands from, pounding with hammers, tightening with wrenches, and turning screwdrivers all with the skillful proficiency of one who put the saddle on the right horse every time. It didn't surprise me learning she was responsible for the care and upkeep of the few horses the sisters boarded, but were not allowed to ride. These were horses I'd seen grazing on distant hillsides, too far away to see what kind of mounts they were. If Teresa hadn't chosen to be a contemplative nun, I could have easily seen her, in a prior age, being a rider for the Pony Express: leaping from horse to horse, slinging saddlebags behind saddles, riding in the blazing desert heat, doing whatever it takes to deliver the mail on time. She laughed the loudest and had a dry humor that seemed instinctive. Of the six pillars she had been the youngest to start monastic life having entered at 17! This was her calling; she never wanted to try anything else. Most monasteries ask candidates to wait until they're 21 – 35 years old, with some life experience: mature enough to make such a monumental life decision, it's not fair to the candidate or the order if the novice decides later this isn't the life for her eventually.

The last of the founders was Sister Viola, the monastery's music director. An animated purveyor of nuances that only she could hear, her exuberance brought energy and vigor to an activity that could develop into drudgery, depending on how musically talented one was. Tall and slim, this bouncy music director expected full participation in her musical gift. She had the unruly brown hair of a maestro that would work free from her veil from time to time, as if her musical vitality was forcing it out with a boing.

She had been a professional singer before entering. Seeing my surprise, I was told she wasn't the only one; Father Macintosh, the monastery's resident priest, had sung professionally as well. "We are very lucky to have him. Mass would take on whole new character if the celebrant had a hard time carrying a tune, but because his voice is so good, visitors regularly record our singing."

It surprised me how the sisters, even after living in a cloister for twenty years or more, still had their and quick wit and spontaneity. It made me feel right at home.

I was happy learning there were three other fledgling novices like myself, all wearing the white habits and the veils of novices; sisters Patty, Dorothy and Cathleen. As sister-wannabes, they were grouped in the front row with me most likely so everyone could keep their eyes on us and wouldn't step out of line.

I learned the first novice to enter was Patty, a tall hefty woman of strength, about thirty years old, who had entered twice before. Her last exit was unannounced. She strapped her guitar case across her back, walked the three miles to the paved road, and hitchhiked to Tucson on the back of a motorcycle, where she phoned Reverend Mother Esmeralda and told her she wasn't coming back. She was now on her third attempt trying to live this strict life. It was a major decision to be sure: no telephone calls, no television, limited letter writing, and no visitors (relatives visiting on approval), limited choice of food, no meat, and *no talking*. A decision of this magnitude might require three tries.

The next novice to become a member was Dorothy who after spending twenty-five years with an active order in South America related how she knew God wanted her to enter a contemplative order. While lying on her bed thinking about the decision, she felt a strong 'push' on her shoulder. This, to her, was God prompting her to go and join. She seemed the embodiment of sincerity; her speech was not clever, but candid. The other feature about her that was impossible to miss was her teeth; they were crooked, missing or blackened.

Her opposite was Cathleen, a skinny girl in her early twenties. Dorothy was the oldest novice who had been here the longest. Cathleen was the latest addition and had been here two years. Shy and retiring, she struck me as cheerful and perceptive with a thin skin to match her slight frame.

Then there was me. I had studied monasticism for years and was overjoyed when I was finally accepted. I was more than ready to start my new life; the fact that I was raised with someone who liked a bit of the bubbly now and again didn't matter. I was leaving all those vivid cocktail hours behind. As of yesterday, I was beginning to fill my tabula rasa with prayers and good works instead of can openers and corkscrews.

Pointing to her watch, I was glad Reverend Mother reminded us we had talked our way all the through to the office. As basically a shy person, I breathed a sigh of relief now that the initial part of my getting acquainted session was over. As informal as the gathering was and as nice as they all were, it was still stressful being under the watchful eyes of my new community. And they were seeing the *real* me too; for the first time in years, I wasn't wearing *any* make-up. That, in itself took guts.

Everyone rose. Without so as much as a hup two three four, they went dutifully off to the Office of None (pronounced known). Except me, I was told to wait for the Novice Director. During the ten minute wait, doubts started creeping in as I sat alone. I knew nothing about how to conduct myself around people who were so religious. With my head sinking lower, I thought how I didn't even have a theology degree. I attended Catholic school for four years but that was a long, long time ago. I didn't hold a Th.D or a Ph.D; I hadn't even contributed to a religious journal. What was I doing here with these super spiritual people? I didn't know what to expect, but told myself to do my best. If the people here were somewhat congenial, that would be half the battle.

They were probably thinking the same thing about me.

CHAPTER

4

Soon the Novice Director ~~bustled~~ (she never rushed) walked calmly toward me pointing to her office a few steps to the right in the hall. I went into a room filled with natural light from a large oblong window above her desk where she sat with the most perfect posture I'd ever seen; I didn't think I could ever get my back that straight. I scanned the uncluttered room, so neat and orderly it looked like she hadn't finished moving in.

Knowing my novitiate hinged on how well I get along with the Novice Director, I was anxious to get to know her. Was she a modern easy-going nun with progressive ideas, or did she still cling to pre-Vatican II ideas? (Aggiornamento, or bringing up to date, changed tradition by promoting renewal, like using the vernacular for Mass and having the priest face the congregation.) I sighed in relief knowing the changes didn't affect clothing. It was still up to each institute to set its own guidelines. Thank God for small favors because depending on the year the Pope was installed, I imagined the costume an elderly Pontiff might think was acceptable daily wear. A picture of a nun waddling around in a drooping, long-sleeved black habit and long train, came to mind. I quickly dismissed the image of myself bowing in a bustle.

With her hands neatly interlaced on the clean un-doodled desk blotter, she asked if I felt up to beginning instruction that day. If not, I could wait a day or two until I had become accustomed to the altitude. Flying in from sea level, I could definitely feel the difference 5,000 more feet makes. It was hard catching my breath, and when I did, the insides of my nostrils were still raw from the dry air. I had a slight headache from lack of oxygen, and/or lack of caffeine I hoped wouldn't affect my alertness. I caught myself staring dully a few times from overexertion, but other than that, I was raring to go.

"Okay," she said, probably as anxious as I was to get my novitiate underway. It was the beginning of a crash course in how to become a Cistercian in three easy lessons.

"You can sleep in tomorrow till 6:00, but if you feel up to joining us, we'll see you at Vigils. You'll hear the bells at 3:15."

I told her I couldn't wait. I had prepared so long, now that I was actually here, I was eager to see if I had what it takes to be a Cistercian.

"You should know you'll be sharing the bathroom with one other person, Sister Dorothy."

I thought back. Sister Dorothy. She was the one with the bad teeth. I told the director I noticed a toothbrush and hairbrush on the counter this morning. If she was there last night, she was so quiet I didn't hear a peep from her. I was glad there was no show of impatience from the Novice Director who was resolutely trying to bring another novice up to speed.

She said with authority,

"The search for God is the purpose of the monastic day. *Opus Dei*, Latin for *Work of* God, is reflected in the schedule. The daily monastic timetable, or horarium, varies from monastery to monastery, but it generally follows the same basic schedule: we rise at 3:15 for the non-singing Office of Vigils at 3:30 followed by quiet time of Lectio Divina at 4:15 followed by breakfast. There's Lauds, and at 9:30 we have Tierce. For a Cistercian, by 9:30 a third of the day is gone. The first work period is about 9:30 to about 11:30." Sister Drusilla continued relaying the schedule. "Midday Prayer starts promptly at 12:00 with dinner following at 12:15. Lunch is considered dinner here and is the *main* meal of the day. The Office of None is recited at 1:20 and the afternoon work period starts around 1:30 till 4:00. There's free time for personal use for showering etc. until 5:15, then we go back to the chapel for Vespers at 5:15. Supper follows. The last Office called Compline begins at 7:00; then we retire, and it's light's out by 7:30. The Grand Silence follows. NO speaking till morning," she warned. Seeing my look of amazement at the strict schedule, she added, "Don't worry; you'll catch on soon enough."

"You'll need to know enough signs to get you through the week. They take time to learn so don't be discouraged if you forget some. I just want to give you a couple. THANKS'—place your fingers to the mouth, and quickly push them away, 'WORK'—two fists hitting each other." Putting her tight fists out, she curled her two little fingers under and said, "This is the sign for 'TIME'".

I tried committing the images to memory; curling my own fingers, thumbs together with crooked pinkies, means 'TIME'; 'FORGET' is an index finger swiping across the forehead. A tug at a veil means 'SISTER'; pulling an imaginary beard stands for 'MAN'.

"Fingertips together making an A-frame building means church. 'BOOK' combined with church means 'OFFICE BOOK'", she said, and handed me a good sized loose-leaf notebook. She opened it to the first song we would sing during the next office. I grabbed it not losing the place. Flipping through, I could see it would take time to learn how to use it. I saw Psalms set to seasonal music, songs in English, some in Latin, hymns, and a variety of intonations. I rubbed my pop-eyes hard knowing there was no mascara to smear.

"There are different songs for each day, for religious feast days, holidays, and extra songs for Sundays. Try to follow along. Sister Patty next to you will help. Don't worry, it takes time learning to use it, then one day like osmosis, you'll know how. Be assured of the great deal of leeway given to all novices so don't get discouraged. We'll meet for instruction each morning the next few weeks. Plus, you'll be joining a regular ongoing class for all the novices called Repetition too, where I focus on the fundamentals. You'll learn what hesychasm, custody of the eyes and gravitas mean, among other terms."

I had only been here a few short hours but with all I had to remember, it seemed like a month. In a moment of panic I wondered, should I be writing all this information down? Was it information she expected me to remember after hearing one time? Suddenly, the question crossed my mind, was this lesson number one?

"Sister Viola, the music director, will give you music lessons. When you feel comfortable about singing, join in. Take it from me it's better to get it over with."

"The time after dinner, now, is a free period until 1:30. Many sisters choose to take 'meridian' (the highest point of the day; noon) by taking a short nap. It's up to each person how she wants to use it."

"About the enclosure, it's important for you to know Trappistine monasteries are *usually* gated communities, but because this cloister is on a plateau surrounded by hundreds of miles of deserted rolling hills without much chance of any outside contact, the 'enclosure walls' extend (I was told with pointing) are from: THAT ridge, to the second gully over THOSE hills, to the THIRD barbed wire fence. In other words—'try not to get lost'."

"Great," I said, trying to contain my excitement. "I *love* to explore."

"Almost every action has a meaningful purpose. If we pass someone in the hall, we should always smile at them, even if we don't feel like it, even if we've just had a disagreement with them five minutes before, even if… there was no excuse not to smile," Sister Drusilla warned.

"I can do that," I said, flashing my pearly whites as proof I was up to the challenge.

At one point a bell rang three times.

"Let me tell you about the *Angelus**," she said, handing me a card with the prayer printed on it. "This prayer is to be recited every morning, noon and night to commemorate the Annunciation. A bell, larger than the hand bell, rings in a series of three strokes. It reminds us to stop whatever it is we are doing, whether we are standing in a field or walking down a hall, peeling potatoes, or whatever, and silently say this prayer. Each interval is followed by a Hail Mary. Carry the card with you and you'll have it memorized before you know it."

I was slightly embarrassed by my intrusive presence into her personal prayer. I tried not to look at her, but emulated her head tilt and read the card she gave me.

I thought back to the four years I spent in Catholic and what I learned by rote; the *Annunciation*: the Angel Gabriel's announcement to the Virgin Mary of the Incarnation. The *Incarnation*: the Son of God conceived by the Holy Spirit. And even though it elementary school and tried recalling doctrine I learned by didn't take long for her to finish reciting it, by the time she was done, I could almost see my white oxford shoes, required in parochial school, dirty scuff marks, laces and all.

With the morning filled with so much mental energy, I was happy learning work periods started at 9:00 and again at 1:30 so I could stop thinking/praying and begin using my body with some kind of work."You'll learn how to meditate with practice. Go in on your own whenever you want."

Knowing meditation is the backbone of any monastery, I told her I knew how important it is. Like most people, I've tried to meditate on my own. I didn't have much success. Knowing how hard it is, I was leery. I told her I'd practice every chance I had.

"One of the first things you should know is how to bow. Your place in chapel is in the front on the left. You bow first before sitting. *Every* time you enter the chapel you bow. Bowing shows deep respect and reverence when entering the house of God, and should be done with thoughtfulness and consideration. Stand and I'll show you how to make a profound bow.

I agreed; the peace here did warrant an uncommon acknowledgment. Practicing in her office, Sister Drusilla bowed a couple of times to show me how it was done, from the waist in one sweeping motion.

"When the head is parallel to the floor, pause for a second or two, then slowly raise the head to the upright position," bowing to me again. I bowed back at her… again… and again, like in slow motion. Finally satisfied I had learned its subtleties, we bowed to each other.

I couldn't help feeling it would take a God-like determination to adhere to such a demanding schedule but knew it was intimidating before I entered. It would take more than laziness on my part to keep me from fulfilling my vocation.

"Besides attending daily classes with me and the other novices, you will of course take music sessions with the music director, Sister

Viola."Oh, yes. You noticed the two men eating at the small table on the side of the room? The tall man is our priest, Father Macintosh, and from time to time, our special guest arrives, Father Ivan Wyss leads us in retreats. Because he's a frequent visitor during the Christmas season and we know him so well, we call uncle Van. He'll join us for us tonight for supper in honor of Christmas. He's an author and uses his time here to work on his books. As a special permission, we are allowed to speak to him. He is a remarkable person. We all enjoy his company. You'll see."

I don't know which impressed me more; the fact he was an author, or how the sisters were able to speak to him. What better place could he pick to write unrecognized, unobserved and undisturbed than in a desert? A well-known author; I was intrigued.

With light in the window nearly gone, and hearing the end of work bells, the director concluded our session. It was time for Vespers, the sunset evening prayer service.

"Take your office book and start familiarizing yourself with it. Wait for me in the chapel and I'll be in soon."

I was beginning to learn one of the main attributes of a Trappistine monastery was the operative word *wait*. It was one sign I learned in a hurry: hands crossed at the wrist.

I made way to the chapel where I would be bowing for real. I hoped nobody would be inside praying to make me feel even more self-conscious and out of place than I already felt in my dark blue jumper with everyone else wearing white cowls and cloaks.

Opening the door a crack, I stuck my head inside and to my relief, it was empty. I walked to the front near the altar, looked around again and made a profound bow. I then took a few steps to the left and sat at my seat thinking. So far, I was happy with the way things turned out; the desert; the sisters; and the silence. Thank God the Novice Director seemed like a mature individual, someone I could turn to for help. My novitiate hinged on this. It felt good knowing my entering could have gone the other way. I might be sitting here with my head in my hands wondering *what have I done?*

I placed my office book on my lap.

Flipping through, it was clear it was going to take a long time before I knew how to use it, years perhaps, but I had all the time in the world. Marking my place with a red ribbon, I put it the wooden holder in front of me.

Everyone was still at work. It was the perfect time to look around. Large windows let in the views and across from me behind the windows was a narrow hallway with more windows so I could look through a window through another window into the desert. (Later I learned so many windows were a mistake. In the planning, it wasn't even considered a desert in Arizona at this altitude could be cold, snowy and blizzard-like, as well as being a hot and dry area.)

The chapel was exactly how I thought a Cistercian chapel should look; plain and devoid of clutter to lend an inner centering on God. Cistercian spirituality is a mystical that starts by emptying the self. This stark chapel appeared to be the idyllic place to begin my spiritual path. The prayerfulness here was so conducive to an inner experience of God, it felt like I entered a different reality, one filled with silent energies and voiceless vitalities so real they seem to stir the dust off the desert.

I looked at the white linen altar cloth, then admired the polished piece of driftwood holding the stained glass crucifix. Off to the side were two low-backed oak chairs for the celebrants: the abbey's priest, Mac, and the visiting priest. A tabernacle containing the consecrated body and blood of Christ was secured on a back wall. That was all. I would have been disappointed seeing distracting posters, banners and hymn numbers posted like in regular churches.

The miles of empty fields surrounding the chapel convinced me we were indeed in the middle of nowhere. I was glad the monastery was named Our Lady of the Desert after the Virgin Mary. (All Cistercian monasteries are named after the Virgin Mary.) Invoking her name during desperate and impossible situations was a good defense. Defender, Protector, Guardian; in the desert all three were needed. I heard movement outside the back door. It was followed by the steeple bells ringing signaling the start of None. Vespers. I sucked in my stomach, sat straighter, and cleared my throat. This was my first official office as a novice. As a skill, I hoped chanting wouldn't be too difficult to learn.

It wasn't long before the nuns entered one by one; bowed, and sat in their places.

I looked around surreptitiously. I could be sitting next to a member of Mensa or a high school drop out; I had no way of knowing. Getting to know someone without knowing their former occupations or educational backgrounds, made it impossible to judge by worldly standards. The lack of speech put us all on the same level, human beings equally loved by God. No one was better or worse than another. Identical clothing didn't help determining social status either, and make-up wasn't allowed. There wasn't a pair of tweezers within fifty miles. We were all firm believers in the saying—*Powder and paint makes a girl what she ain't.* Scented deodorant was our only perfume. Jewelry was considered vain and therefore unnecessary; except for the plain gold band the professed sisters wore, signifying they had tied the knot permanently with God. So in lieu of a groom, a honeymoon or shoes tied to the back of a car, slipping a ring over the vein finger thought to run straight to the heart could not be considered flamboyant excess, but a symbolic gesture of lasting love.

The bells rang again, signaling the start of Vespers. We all stood. We were four on one side, facing five on the other, with the organist in the back. I was clutching my office book that Drusilla had marked to the first hymn. For now, I'd skip the hymn and come in on the first line of the Psalm to be chanted, also marked. In a matter of moments I would try singing. My stomach lurched. At the same time, I could feel my heart start racing. A viselike sensation gripped my throat squeezing it so it felt like a straw. The strangling feeling spread down my neck to my abdomen. I didn't think I was having a heart attack, it felt more like I was choking brought on by my singing debut.

From the back of the room, I heard the organ bench creak as ample Dorothy readied herself to play. At the sound of the organ warming up, my mouth went dry. With the Novice Director's parting words still in my head from our meeting, "You can coast in choir for a few days, but it's really for your benefit to begin soon." I knew it was true; it was better to get it over and cleared my throat.

How hard could chanting be? I read the first line and cleared my throat. I was all set to sing. I could do it. I was in the choir in my elementary school for three years. Funny, I don't remember being this nervous. I cleared my throat again. In fact, I cleared it so many times they probably thought I had a tic. I told myself, relax; the first note is always the hardest in any piece.

The organist played the first note, and I forced my voice from my mouth along with the others. Nothing came out! The next Psalm was the same. I froze. This is ridiculous, I scolded myself. They're waiting to hear what kind of a voice I have, my stalling was only making things worse.

Long about the third Psalm, I pushed a word from my mouth like an expelled carrot skin. I strung two words together, then finally a whole line. What projected from my lungs was barely audible. It wasn't loud and confidant, it sounded more like I was choking. I was just happy *something* came out. It wasn't perfect but didn't think I put anybody's teeth on edge. Even if I did, it didn't matter; my singing debut was over.

I sat quickly replacing my office book in the stand. Out of the corner of my eye, I searched the faces of the others for some kind of telling review until I realized their blank stares said it all. The only thing that would have bettered my singing debut was if I had the ability to read music; not a necessity but a definite plus for anybody entering this order.

It was time to meditate. I was relieved when, following the others, we turned our chairs to face the altar.

Everyone was quiet, not only in speech, but bodily movements were in check as well. The sisters were so quiet, it was unnerving. I sat afraid to move during the hours' meditation I learned was really only 15 minutes long. Still shaking from my first public appearance as a singer, I felt it wasn't good enough just good to sit and stare at the floor. I had to try to meditate. I went through the motions: back straight, palms up and open, head erect. Ready, set, go.

I tried thinking about something spiritual, *anything* spiritual, but my nerve-racking singing debut overshadowed everything. When nothing came to me, I hoped God would understand at this point I was still an undisciplined Bohemian, rough around the edges. I directed my attention on meditating again; back straight, head erect, palms open.

I wanted to have a plain, simple meditation, not gigong or any other Eastern practice, or TM (transcendental meditation, the method for relaxation and stress reduction); I wanted just a simple meditation. Now I was seeing the Maharishi's grim beared face when I closed my eyes. I wondered if the others were having problems clearing their minds too, and narrowing my eyes, I secretly squinted my may around the room expecting to see the others in contorted meditation positions, but only one sister was sitting in a lotus pose. Most, like me, were on soft cushiony green chairs shifting through useless debris of words hoping most of them would sink to the bottom.

I straightened my back, lifted my head, and opened my hands to receive. Ready, set, go. There was movement in the back of the chapel. Someone left ahead of time. (It was the cook checking on the meal.)

I started again; ready, set, go. I cleared my mind to make room for God's voice. I wasn't used to sitting so correctly. A pain in my left side made me change position. Maybe I was rupturing my spleen. What is a spleen anyway? Doesn't it have something to do with blood?

One more time: ready set, go. This could get old real fast.

There was a knock in the back and every one stood slowly, stretching as they left their meditative states.

I jumped up quickly.

My first experience in choir, Vespers, was a frantic flipping of pages. Although I had been shown where the first song was, from then on I was lost. It was taxing because the songs didn't progress in any coherent manner; they seemed to skip from one end of the book to the other, with many stops in-between. Without really paying attention to the meanings, I managed to bungle through.

The angel of the Lord declared unto Mary.
And she conceived by the Holy Spirit.
Hail Mary...
Behold the Handmaid of the Lord.
Be it done unto me according to your word.
Hail Mary...
And the Word was made flesh,
And dwelt among us.
Hail Mary...
Pray for us, O holy Mother of God,
That we may be worthy of the promises of Christ.
Let Us Pray
Pour forth, we beseech You, O lord, Your Grace
into our hearts, that we to whom the Incarnation of
Christ, Your Son, was made known by the message of an
Angel, may by His Passion and Cross, be brought to the
glory of His Resurrection. Through the same Christ...

CHAPTER

5

In single file we courteously bowed and filed out the door. Because I was new, my place was in front so I was the last one out. Following along on the end gave me the chance to breathe easier without being under the watchful eyes of the others.

This evening when we entered the refectory for supper, the furniture had been rearranged. There were no chairs around the dining table; no place settings waiting for us to fill. The lights in the chandelier weren't shining. Bypassing the refectory, we ended in the Community room next to it behind long collapsible portable tables set lengthwise to each other. White tablecloths graced our place settings giving the roomlightness against the dark windows. Long white candles in the center of the tables flickered flames on wine glasses at each setting. I expected waiters, towels hanging from their arms pouring wine, to appear out of nowhere at any moment. By all accounts, we were in for a quite an evening.

It wasn't filet mignon with Brie cheese and Bordelaise sauce, but this evening's supper was just as delicious consisting of cauliflower and cheese quiche, a bowl full of mixed fruit cut into bite size pieces and warm homemade wheat bread made my mouth water. Wine was available for those who wanted it. The meal was topped off with cup of percolated coffee.

Fathers Wyss, or uncle Van, as an honored guest during this Christmas season, was seated at one end, with Mac not far away. I was surprised we were allowed to speak to him but special guests deserve special treatment, I learned. I was even more surprised when he opened his mouth and a beautiful Swiss accent came out adding interest and style to his speech. He singled out novices putting us on the spot a number of times, asking us many questions verbally sparring with us in friendly repartee, witty remarks and playful banter. Even if our perceptions weren't heightened by the flow of wine, the informal atmosphere let our spontaneity out with little effort.

We talked late into the night. Novices were not alone in his teasing. Toward the end of the evening, he even kidded the serious minded bookkeeper as she washed dishes by asking forcefully, "Sister Gail, a woman of your dignity washing dishes?!" Taking the remark in stride, exhibiting great self-control, she gave him a wry smile and placed the damp towel she was holding on the counter.

I took it all in; our shadows on the window, the smiling nuns, the numerous pastry shells holding food lining both sides of the table, the candle flames reflecting on wine glasses, the cozy camaraderie. If pleasant evenings like this came every so often to offset the strict schedule, I envisioned a long happy life for myself here.

Time is different in a monastery using eternity as a reference point. The evening ended by mutual agreement; when we were all talked out. The remembrance of what we talked about is blurred in my mind; only that the exchanges were all in good fun. I got up feeling like I belonged with this Cistercian family.

I was anxious to get the final office over after the long day. The community walked en mass down the hall. With darkness upon us, sitting at my place in the chapel, I thought how chanting lullabies made more sense at this time.

Compline is the last of the canonical hours recited before retiring. After donning cowls and cloaks, one by one the sisters entered, bowed, and knelt beside her place. This office marked the completion of the day. Accentuated by the grandeur of their graceful and flowing robes made me feel I was attending a medieval court and lent a dramatic atmosphere to the small chapel. I sat entranced, overcome by the solemnity of it all.

The lit chapel sent a beacon of light cascading up and down the rolling and fading hillsides on the high desert plateau. Surrounded by darkness, the small group of wearied-eyed nuns prepared themselves as they waited before chanting the days last Psalms.

There was a gentle knock from the back of the room. I got up happy, knowing there was no meditation period during this office. It was a good thing too, getting up before dawn, eating the special supper late in the day, compounded by the wine, I might start snoring. As we stood facing each other across the semi-darkness, I realized having a vocation to this austere and disciplined life takes more than mere will-power. Being called into one spirit with sisters with such deep interior lives, was not a decision one could make on one's own, it happened by choice, God's choice.

At the end of the session, I watched Sister Patty, directly across from me, walk to the front of the room, strike a match and light a thick red candle next to copper engraving of the Virgin Mary. She turned off the lights near her chair and sat still. The candle light, playing on the copper, sent a mystical, magical aura through the room that produced a perceptible feeling of connectedness. Someone handed my office book to me opened to a specific song, Salve Regina (Hail Holy Queen) and by the unsteady light of the candle, I followed in English what they sang in Latin*.

The pulsing red, yellow and golden flickers bouncing off the copper artwork as it caught the candle's flame had a mesmerizing effect as my eyes stared fixedly glazed in the direction of Mary's image. This haunting melody, sung entirely in Latin, conjured up ancient times and cavernous settings.

I imagined myself standing in a torch-lit cave among singing druids watching the torch flicker like it was pulsing blood trying to bring the talisman to life. My understanding of Latin was virtually nil other than it was beautiful, and I loved it.

There was no doubt in my mind that these sisters were like a clear and exquisite divine concert, a continual cadenza of a living prayer. They were the trilling of nine violins, sweet and pure, each sister one of God's notes, ever lessening the separations between one another. Gradually, the novices would learn the essentials from the aficionados, correct pitch and full tone, perfecting crescendos and diminuendos. We were a diverse ensemble of individuals, touched by the Master Musician, pulled together in a united charism of prayer. I was certain this is where I belonged, and nothing was going to change my mind.

A blessing was the final ritual of the day. I stood at the end of the line ready to receive mine from Sister Esmeralda. Each sister respectfully lowered her head to receive a spritz of holy water (*water blessed by a priest*) over her head and shoulders accompanied by a quick, silent prayer from her.

The concluding blessing gave extra emphasis to the mystical world we entered at night. The night is held in expectancy and readiness and is considered a special time by all Cistercians because mystical knowing usually comes with some degree of deprivation. The final blessing formally ended the day, and began the *Grand Silence* of the night. No hand signing permitted.

I was on the end if the line. I found my room, opened the door, pulled off my veil and sat on the bed. There was so much to learn. It felt like I had to know it all at once, especially the disordered arrangement of the music. I didn't feel too overwhelmed; I knew I had the rest of my life to continue learning.

I lay in bed utterly content knowing this was what God wanted me to do. I had no doubt. I was sure I had a vocation to this order, to this monastery, and with these people. I wanted to follow Merton's footsteps into the dark night in front of me; both of us trying to catch up with Saint John of the Cross. I knew they had set a fast pace and wouldn't slow down, turn around and wait for me, like I was a trailing little sister.

With the covers pulled up against my chin, I heard the lone bell ringer slowly walking in the hallway swinging the hand bell. I fell asleep listening to the howling of a pack of wild coyotes on the trail of some unprotected game. I was glad I was safe.

*Salve! Regina,
Hail! Holy Queen
Mater Misericordiae:
Mother of Mercy,
Vita, dulcedo, et spes nostra, salve.
our life, our sweetness and our hope.
Ad te clamamus, exules, filii Hevae.
To you do we cry, poor banished children of Eve.
Ad te suspiramus, gementes et flentes,
To you do we send up our sighs, mourning and weeping
In hac lacrimarum valle.
in this valley of tears.
Eia ergo, Advocata nostra,
Turn then, O most gracious advocate,
Illos tuos misericordes oculos ad nos converte.
Your eyes of mercy towards us:
Et Jesum, benedictum fructum ventris tui,
Show unto us the blessed fruit of your womb, Jesus
Nobis post hoc exsilium ostende.
And after this our exile,
O clemems, O pia, O dulcis, Virgo Maria.
O clement! O loving! O sweet Virgin Mary!

CHAPTER

6

Clang, clang... clang, clang... clang, clang... The unrelenting jangle of the hand bells for Vigils gnawed through my sleep like a coyote through a bone announcing the start of my first *full* day.

I didn't know how vigilant I would be at 3:15 in the morning. When I went to bed a part of me was actually looking forward to getting up in the middle of the night to pray the Office of Vigils with all the other Cistercian monastics the world over; a traditional monastic observance. Besides, it was hard to imagine an activity more mysterious and out of the ordinary than this. Lay people pray too, but not in the middle of the night and not surrounded by the growling and howling of wild animals.

I peered through the darkness in my room groaning, so this is what 3:15 in the morning looks like, certain I had just gone to bed. I rolled over and thought about the coming day; I would be starting three new activities beginning with Vigils, Lectio and Repetition but knowing this didn't make me want to jump to my feet like my neighbor who was already running water in the bathroom brushing her teeth. I didn't mind having to share a bathroom but it was beyond me how after hearing the wake-bells she was in the bathroom busy with her morning's ablutions at a moments' notice. I thought it abnormal for her to vault from the warmth of her bed like this without taking time for a relaxing stretch or two. It made me grateful *I* didn't have her neurotic need to be first in chapel.

At this hour all my good intentions came to a screeching halt, my stoicism evaporating like over zealous intention it was. Instead, muttering to myself, I felt like a groundhog carefully poking its head from a warm hovel, cringing from its own shadow and deciding another six weeks of sleep would be just what I needed.

Grumbling and complaining, I was aware I did not have the luxury of a groundhog's decision. All my muttering came to a grinding halt though, as I slid the bathroom window open to look over the desert in the darkness. Millions of stars, without competition from city lights, painted a celestial boundary into the most dazzling of ceilings. One look up and I felt ashamed at having balked at this gifted opportunity to share this private moment with God. One look up was all it took to instill amazement that I was living under this canopy of brilliance.

Undeniably, the best part of this window watching was the first breath of the sweetest, cleanest (and in the wintertime, the coldest) desert air imaginable. I would hold my breath as I walked to the bathroom so I could take the longest and deepest intake of air I could manage, filling my lungs with the luscious bouquet of the sweet moist desert sage. It was addictive. By the time I reached the chapel I was close to hyperventilating but it made getting up worth it.

This was my first Vigils, no more sleeping in till 6:00 like a beginner. This office differed from the others in that at the early hour, there is no chanting. I was in my usual seat in front listening as one side of the choir recited one stanza of a Psalm, and the other side recited the next; back and forth we read from a sitting position.

After several Psalms were completed there was time to reflect on what we just recited. I was happy learning there was no meditating during Vigils.

Stifling yawns is difficult anytime, but at this early hour, it's impossible. In vain, feeling a yawn coming on, I forced myself to swallow instead. It was no use if a yawn is considered a silent shout, because I was yawning so often, the others must have thought I was screaming. Being half asleep made time fly by. Soon, a knock from the back of the room seemed to wake me. Realizing where I was, I straightened my slouching body and tagged along everyone who were dragging themselves out the chapel door too.

The fast pace of the schedule didn't surprise me because Thomas Merton, the Cistercian writer, wrote about it. We seemed to be always scrambling from one activity to another. With Drusilla leading the way, I was directed to go with the other three novices into a small room called the novitiate for meditative study and reading known as *Lectio Divina*. Even the professed sisters were obligated to do this but in a room that was off limits to us wet-behind-the-ears-novices.

The novitiate was a very small room, bigger than a phone booth, but not much. The room was plain and simple, in keeping with the rest of the monastery. It didn't have a chalk board, a globe or even a desk for the teacher. Patty, Cathleen, Dorothy and I sat at school desks wedged together in a two-by-two formation that filled the entire room. We sat directly behind a large sliding glass window that was pitch black this time of night. With the dawn, we looked out over a vast expanse of desert, facing south in the direction of Mexico. Drusilla took her place at the front of the room.

"Nourishing the heart is an important part of the monastic day," she said. "You have two hours for Lectio; but usually 30 minutes is long enough. Lectio is one part of a four part phrase all emphasizing reflective experiences: *Lectio, meditatio, oratio* and *contemplatio.*"

Their Latin names made them special to me, practices containing knowledge of a supernatural nature thousands of years old. I felt privileged being allowed to personally participate in each one. "Remember, time spent in Lectio has many aspects that are similar to meditation. It is a reflective experience that should be approached with a calm and tranquil mind."

I settled in my hard wooden seat and tried to remain alert. I told myself no matter what, I would try and keep this time reflective and peaceful repeating to myself what the Novice Director said, 'reflective: characterized by or given to meditation or contemplation.' Yes, I will make myself be reflective, ordering myself to bring the peace in the desert landscape into the Lectio room.

Up to two hours after Vigils may be spent in reading, the novice director said.

"It's not straight reading though. This is the type of reading more like prayer. If a line or a passage spoke a personal message, this distinction should be penetrated by going beyond what can be taught or understood with ordinary levels of understanding. This subjective intuiting is done not by forcing a meaning to surface, but by reviewing a passage. This allows an undercurrent of meaning to be known and this listening with the heart leads to an absorption in God, the aim of the entire day."

She left us to our reading.

I've never read the Old Testament in its entirety starting from page one. With my head propped on my hand it didn't take long before I was engrossed in my reading. The context was in perfect concert with what I was looking at, an uninhabited wilderness devoid of life, desolate and empty, prompting a night mirage of Moses materializing, staff in hand, leading his people through scattered places to the land of milk and honey and better times.

I looked up from the Bible at the lightening desert bringing the landscape to life before our eyes, I could almost see a mass migration moving up hills and down canyons, treading over deep gorges and scaling up and over rocky ravines. I traced Moses' steps with my eyes to his first encounter with God, seeing him receiving his revelation and his mission just as dawn flooded the desert with streams of golden light.

While I was pre-occupied with the emerging desert scene, there was a commotion in the room. As luck would have it, Drusilla in the flesh had entered the room and Cathleen was caught red-handed making signs to me. I was guilty by association, my first visible infraction. The novice was answering a question I asked. It was a harmless enough question or so I thought, but making signs in the novitiate is a no-no. The novice should have known by now there was no signing in the novitiate and raced through her illegal use of hands, like a fireman with a hose to flames, instead of using the slower bucket by bucket method.

Sister Drusilla wasn't happy; a Japanese geisha girl had more color in her face than Drusilla had at that moment. I hoped I wouldn't be held too accountable, and wondered just how much slack I would be given; a jump rope or a full clothesline. All the Director said to me was, *A rule is a rule.* I was surprised; from the way she was acting I was asking when did this become a mortal sin? As I watched a flurry of Drusilla's signs going off like canons directed at Sister Cathleen, I felt terrible. She should have known this procedure by this time. She should have known better. If there is a worse feeling than being responsible for someone else being reprimanded, I was hard-pressed to think what it could be.

The occasional long yelping of coyotes added sound effects to my night vision, and with the dawn, streams of cold air blew in through the uneven glass sliders reminding me the desert was synonymous with survival.

It made me think about the last time I heard the statement, 'a rule is a rule'. I was in the company of Popeye and Olive Oil, only there was nothing comical about the situation. I was four years old when blood splattered over the comics in the Sunday paper. Because I was the chaser who ignored the "No running in the house rule, I was made to watch the gathered evidence that proved I needed stricter controls, the combing of thick, matted, blood-soaked hair. When I came to, I was slumped in a chair being served spoonfuls of whipped cream like it was a sugared coagulant. I was positive Popeye and Olive Oil would have handled the situation differently.

All this came back to me listening to Drusilla's voice scolding Cathleen. Sitting in the novitiate trying to look invisible, I thought it was strange I should think of this incident from my past *now* when I haven't thought about it in years. It had nothing whatever to do with the present.

In an instant, I realized it had everything to do with the present. After the chasing incident, not only couldn't I eat whip cream for years, I had changed into a thin-skinned individual, overly sensitive to criticism. The Novice Director didn't have a chance in hell of me trusting her, let alone taking her into my confidence. Discussing personal problems with her was out of the question when just seeing her made me feel upset, judgmental, and retalitory. My major objective in the abbey had turned into protecting myself from Drusilla. I knew this was not her fault. I came in damaged. But after years of acting out these defensive behaviors, it was hard to change overnight.

From then on, whenever I saw Drusilla walking in the hall; singing in choir, eating meals, or even giving her the sign of peace during Mass, I had to fight the urge to pull my top lip upward in an involuntary sneer of disproval, like it had been hooked by a fish. It was immature to be sure, and totally at odds with the life I wanted to live but I was unable to fight the spontaneous result of my former emotional bruise. I did the next best thing. I never once let her see my childish behavior.

It was unfortunate I saw her scolding Cathleen on the very first week I was here because I set the tone for the rest of my novitiate. But how could I overcome this monumental obstruction when it was all I could do to be civil to her? My time here had turned into 'avoiding Drusilla', the only person I was allowed to speak to. I knew this and worried how it would impede my vocation. Mainly, I'd have to find a substitute willing to listen to my problems. In a monastery where there is supposed to be no speaking, this probably wouldn't happen. I'd be forced to come up with solutions to difficult situations on my own. It was no way to start a novitiate.

Looking down at my Bible, I commanded myself to realize 'the comic paper' incident was a long time ago. That was *then* and this is *now*; I need to keep my focus on my reading. There was no way I could concentrate on God after witnessing such unfounded hostility. Cathleen was making signs where she wasn't supposed to; she wasn't sticking pins in a voodoo doll. By association, I felt I was now on the Director's bad side too just seeing her made me feel upset, judgmental, and retalitory. Now one of my main objectives in the abbey had turned into protecting myself from her.

With the sun adding light to the room, I watched a dejected Cathleen pick up her belongings and leave. Avoiding her eyes I thought, so much for a reflective and tranquil mind. Disheartened in the wintry morning, I thought again of the Director's cool attitude but wasn't going to let her spoil my chance for a new life and I reaffirmed my decision about entering. Examples of desert survival were just outside the floor-length sliders in the wilderness beyond. Thorns in a cactus were a haven for some small animals and birds to build nests. But their main purpose was to serve as protection from unwanted contact. People cannot grow bark to cover their skin, sprout leaves to help with camouflage, or burgeon thorns to ward off predacious animals. Our spines are grown on the inside, budding defense mechanisms as protective solutions for ways of surviving in the world. That's when it hit me; *Lectio Divina* was going to be harder than I thought.

Dawdling like I was, I was the last one to leave. I stowed my brand new Bible in the desk and walked toward the smell of food and breakfast. Even with all the windows, the refectory was warm from the gas stove and heater. I didn't have to guess how cold it must be outside; I remembered. One sister was in the kitchen stirring a pot. I took my seat at the table wondering what was for breakfast. I wanted to ask, but held my tongue.

I didn't overlook the fact I had gone through Vigils and Lectio Divina without so much as the whiff of caffeine, so a cup or two of coffee would do just fine. Following the others, I took my mug to a the small table in back and dumped in a big teaspoon of instant coffee, powdered creamer and sugar and tried stirring the goopy wad of floating substances together. Sipping, I waited for the caffeine to kick in, so I could remember why I joined the monastery in the first place.

Periodically sisters came in from the hall, most still wearing long robes. If I caught someone's eye, they made a point to smile at me but without having coffee, I wouldn't blame them if they scowled. This was one meal where the Superior didn't read grace from a booklet. Nor did we line up for food. This was a come-and-get-it when you want it, serve yourself, meal. I waited till the line to the pot lessened before joining the line in the kitchen. There were stacks of toast next to butter dishes on the counter. Taking the top piece of toast I coated it with about an inch of light-colored *real* butter. The pot on the stove contained oatmeal. No big surprise, although my mouth was all set for sausage links.

I took a bowl off the pile, ladled in a scoop, walked back to my seat and followed the others who stopped momentarily at their place to silently pray, I was sure, the longer prayer of thanks before eating: *Bless us O' Lord in these thy gifts which we are about to receive from thy bounty...through Christ our Lord. Amen.*

Being here a little over 24 hours, I hoped God accepted my abridged version—*"Thanks for the gruel, God."*

I ate quickly and wandered into the chapel way ahead of time so I could look through my thick office book.

Time went by quickly as it always does in the morning and soon the bell rang for the Office of Lauds, Lauds combined with Mass. Entering from the sacristy (room where the sacred vessels, chalices and vestments are stored) walked a tall, nice looking gray-templed man about sixty, one of the two men who had been sitting at the small table in back of the Community room. He wore the black and white Cistercian garb over black dress slacks with a hand-made leather belt around his black scapula. As he crossed to his seat he gave me a wide smile, and with a wink told me his friends called him 'Mac'. Sister Viola had a lovely flowing voice, but when it blended with the strong deep voice of the Priest, their symmetry was one telltale of years of training and practice. Mass was a concert.

There were no surprises during my first Mass, other than Uncle Van not showing up. Typically, another priest is a co-celebrant in the sanctuary with the celebrant reciting the words of the consecration along with him. This is a normal procedure so I thought his absence unusual.

I didn't ask, of course. I went to my bedroom, opened the blinds, sat on the bed and stared out the window. Blundering through the morning like I did, it felt good to regroup. It wasn't long before I saw myself dashing over the hills, loping casually around cacti, scampering over red sandstone. As of yet, I hadn't had time to investigate the surroundings. I couldn't wait.

It was mid-morning. Time for me to attend the class called Repetition with the three other novices. I was on the edge of my seat looking forward to learning obscure old theories, hidden principles, and secrets of Cistercian life.

But when Drusilla went to the front of the class, the left side of my upper lip involuntarily went into sneer mode. How could I learn *anything* from someone who treated Cathleen so unfairly? I had inadvertently put Drusilla in the position of having to prove herself to me. In any case, I thought I was in for a challenging novitiate.

As she read the list of theological subjects she would discuss from a syllabus, I felt my belligerence lessen and my lip relax. Over the next hour and a half, the novices and I sat in the novitiate listening to the dedicated Novice Director deliver her spiritual acumen in a fresh and absorbing way; one that would belie the innumerable times she probably delivered the same topic.

If a Yeshiva is a Jewish school for the study of the Talmud I assumed Repetition, the daily monastic class for the study of the Bible, had similarities to its Jewish counterpart with the study of religion and culture. I looked forward to the class that was based on the assumption students need to hear something four to six times before they were able to retain information and not because they previously failed; memorization by rote.

Everything was new and challenging to me and I was thrilled to be finally starting to advance in the interior life with the examples of the sisters around me who had spent years in contemplation. I would be learning the same things Merton learned but now I would be able to put what I learned into practice. I was confident my soul would be expediently stretched as effortlessly as I breathed and I was ready; before I entered I made sure I read everything considered to be classics in mystical theology. I knew about the nature of the *call* in the readings of Saint Aelred and his three ways: exterior admonition, example, and secret inspiration but I had gone as far as I could by myself.

"Throughout the coming year marked by the calendar of saints, we will study monastic observances, customs, a few regulations, and cover the history of the Cistercian Order with an in-depth study of Saint Benedict's *Rule* he composed for his own monks at Monte Cassino, Italy. It is the basis for practically every monastic community.

"I intend discussing the vows of poverty and chastity, together with a long list of terms that will scare the unmotivated away." Sounding like a strict schoolmarm, she said, "Manual labor, celibacy, purgation, poverty, fasting, asceticism, self-renunciation, and hesychasm," like she was giving us advanced warning. "Small portions of Saint Benedict's *Rule* are read daily in choir outlining a cenobitic way of life *(life in a convent or other religious living in a community)*, stressing commitment to principles of obedience, charity and humility. She pushed her glasses back to the bridge of her nose looking at us like she expected one of us to jump up and run. Satisfied we weren't going anywhere, she continued with her lecture, "Arnauld de Rance, the Abbot of La Grande Trappe, reestablished monastic observances to a high degree for his monks: manual labor, prayer and silence. Trappists and Trappistines, monks of the Order of Cistercians of Strict Observance or O.C.S.O., intend on living and dying in the monastery where they made their 'stability,'" she stated matter-of-factly, peering intently at us from one to the other. "It is entirely possible you will never see the inside of another monastery."

The threat of staying here didn't bother me, stability had the opposite effect on me, *not* moving was a big part of my attraction to this order. In my former secular life, I had moved so many times in childhood having a permanent address seemed like a novel idea.

Sidetracked for the moment, as Drusilla was going on and on about something, an incident came to me in large purple flowers. Growing up with a father who enjoyed a bit of the bubbly more than he should, when his drinking ended in the loss of his job it also meant moving and changing schools. This happened so frequently a classmate once asked if our family was with the circus. This is where the bougainvillea came in. Growing up in the earthquake state of California, almost every ceiling had cracks. Once, in an effort to thwart realtors from selling the house we were renting that had a very large and beautiful purple bougainvillea plant growing on the roof, I took a piece of the vine and stuck it in a crack in the living room making it look like the vine was growing through the roof, the attic and the ceiling. When look-i-loos wandered through, I found it so hilarious I'd have to hide in another room so they wouldn't see me doubled over with laughter. Needless to say, it was one rental property considered to be a *slow mover*. Even now, listening to Drusilla, thinking about the vine, I was stifling giggles in my sleeve, hoping my smothered laughter wasn't disturbing the others.

I went back to the business at hand, being one of four novices sitting in the novitiate learning the Director's tried and true methods to enter eternal life. Remembering it was the Novice Director's duty to weed out lukewarm vocations, as she walked down the aisle passed me, I sat straighter.

Looking at the three other novices, I imagined their reasons entering such an unconventional lifestyle, one that was more suited to the Middle Ages. Soon Drusilla's voice was background noise to my all *important* thoughts.

Each of us had our own private retrospective; and certainly we all had searched for meaning in our lives; but there must have been a deciding factor. Living with someone who drinks too much, my life had not been a stroll in the park; it was more like a walk on the wild side. If it takes a life of struggling to make someone consider this life, my God, what kind of hells had they been through? I could only imagine.

Sister Dorothy in the front row was paying close attention to the lecture; her stalwart body seemed the epitome of health, all but her missing teeth. An unsuspecting Novice Director wouldn't know what kind of problems she was bringing in with her. Regarding her more closely, I remembered she had already spent 25 years on a mission in South America with a missionary order; is it possible for malaria and yellow fever to lay dormant for years? If I experience chills, fever and sweating, I won't blame the vegetarian diet.

In the brief time I knew Sister Patty, she seemed aloof and uneasy. After three attempts, her time as a novice was undoubtedly spent deciding whether she had a vocation at all. Even now, as she was looking intently out the window, was she planning to scale the walls to freedom. What was she running from? Were thugs hot on her trail? Looking at her with suspicion, I checked her forearms for tattoos suggesting a criminal past.

Young and innocent, the third novice Cathleen looked the studious type. She was skinny and frail with the constitution of a bookworm. Her tortoiseshell shyness made me think this was the first time she was away from her family. She had a friendly disposition and even though we were under orders to smile all the time, I felt her friendly nods would have been there anyway.

And then there was me. I saw the monastery as a place where I could to learn to listen with my heart, a place to get a head start on the intense silence of heaven exemplified in the saying, *Still waters run deep* that sums up my reasons for entering. I was convinced monastic life was an easy way of learning to live in the spirit, which could not be done if I was talking all the time, not paying attention to my inner self. It's why I find it hard being around talkative people; gabby people brimming with ego, constantly needing attention, wouldn't last an hour in a monastery. When I pass from this world, all words will stop too, I won't be able to 'persuade' God why I should be admitted into heaven. Healthy communication satisfies a need in all in of us, but if I want to be ready for the absolute quiet of heaven, it makes sense to start practicing **now**. What a relief it will be in heaven not making small talk. Like the Psalm advises, *Be still and know that I am God.* To me, it's that simple.

I kept my eye on the Novice Director pacing in front of the class spinning her spiritual wheels as I thought. My entering wasn't a mystery to me by any means. My choice was based on something I've always known; God is bigger than family. The Greeks said it best: "Know thyself." Or as Socrates stated, *the unexamined life is not worth living.* Doesn't everyone take a couple years to find out who they are, why they're here, what life is all about? People without this spiritual curiosity I find are boring, one-dimensional people with no depth.

I slumped lower at my desk. As the second of six children with a father who enjoyed drinking more than he should, I felt it was my duty to explore questions like these. I was lucky, he wasn't a wino drinking from a paper sack; he was just an ordinary guy who liked to soak in it every so often. And other than uttering colorful profanity when he hit his thumb with a hammer, he wasn't abusive in any way. I can safely say I didn't have any detrimental effects living in a family catering to a parent who likes to drink.

I watched my index finger imperceptibly scrape the varnish off the top of the wooden desk.

I had seen the loss of his jobs and having to relocate time after time as *'adventures in moving,'* which my mother was always quick to point out. Making new friends, meeting strange new neighbors, being challenged to find the way home from every new school *was* adventurous; my mother was right. We moved so many times, a classmate asked me once if our family was with the circus. That was embarrassing. I was glad when we moved. Knowing it was only a matter of time before we'd move again, I stopped unpacking *every* single box. I put them in a pile in the back of each new bedroom closet. It saved time and energy.

The smooth finish on the desktop now displayed a deep scratch. I glanced at the director making sure her attention was still on what she was saying.

Feeling a spasm of laughter coming one as I remembered one of my sneaky tactics, I put my mouth on my sleeve again. As payback for being moved so often, I'd tuck an alarm clock under my arm and pretend to go to school. Instead, I would slip into the garage and crawl under my grandmother's stored furnishings, where room by room her past existence had been stacked like a monument to her life. Huddled in a dark garage, concealed by large wooden dressers, paintings of French noblewomen and fancy mirrors, I would sit cross-legged under my grandmother's aesthetic comforts until it was time to walk in the front door and announce, "I'm home." I got a kick knowing I pulled something over on those in charge, teacher and parents alike. Time after time, I would sit in the quiet, absent to the world, under my grandmother's forgotten furniture, thinking. I would do this for two or three days and pretend to be sick the next so my mother's vague excuse would excuse all my absenteeism. The combined odor of dust and car oil became like salve I could apply whenever I didn't want to face another new set of classmates.

I don't know where my consciousness went during these six hour stints. I considered these timeless periods in my childhood helpful by introducing me to conditions that are vital to a contemplative way of life. In this respect, I was way ahead of the other novices. What a lucky break!

I realize now they were an introduction to contemplation. In yoga, breath is known as prana or universal energy. By controlling my breathing, I learned to control my life energy. By learning not to be caught, I learned the *physiology of breathing*, the rhythmic process of expansion and contraction of my body, and ultimately my spirit... along with my blood pressure, heart rate, circulation, digestion and other systems. By doing deep abdominal breathing, I experienced an overall sense of well-being.

A ripple of numbness went through me when I realized wives with husbands who drink too much have their own problems. I counted on my mother not to disturb our happy home by asking leading questions; I might have to own up to what doing. I was grateful she looked the other way. The combined odor of dust and car oil became like salve to me I could apply whenever I didn't want to face another new set of classmates.

Instead of feeling sorry for myself, I didn't feel that way at all. On the contrary, because playing hooky was *so* easy, I thought I was clever and my parents were the stupidest people on the planet. Thinking back, I realize this may have been the start of my underlying hubris.

I followed the now deep groove in the wood with my finger as I thought. If I hadn't spent time alone avoiding my fears, I never would have never realized how much I was like my parents: my father lying to himself believing he could stop drinking without help, my mother lying to herself believing her husband would stop drinking. I was a chip off the ol' block, all right.

Confident those kind of problems were all behind me now, I gave an imaginary toast to honor us all, I almost said out loud, "Oi vay; here's to gutless living," but caught myself in time.

As Drusilla was wrapping up today's lesson about this and that, I felt angry with myself I had wasted the entire hour of Repetition daydreaming. It was becoming increasingly clear I couldn't keep my mind on one thing. If I could fix this one problem area, there was no doubt I would sail through the rest of my vocation trouble free.

Inconspicuously, I pushed the results of my thinking in the form of a little pile of shavings off the edge of the desk, leaving it for the housekeeper to clean, probably some lowly novice. When it occurred to me, *Wait a minute, that's me!* I stopped scraping. On the other hand, if I did own a housekeeping business, I'd call it—Spitshine Housekeeping with the motto: 'we never overcharge' I began to laugh. I laughed so much I knew it was nervous laughter, the kind that comes from the throat and not the belly. I t was a physical reaction to the stress and tension I felt just *thinking* about moving.

From this point on, I saw the monastery as an extended therapy session. This didn't surprise me. To reach perfection, problems surface for our good and need to be addressed; problems involving patience, tolerance, kindness, understanding, forgiveness...

Getting up to leave, I wondered if the Novice Director felt this way too. I could only hope.

CHAPTER

7

True to my word to Drusilla, finding the chapel empty, I edged way to my seat to practice meditating. It seems childishly simple: stretch to relax the body, start breathing deeply and focus the mind on God; simple. It won't be hard at all.

Light from a window flickered on the red canister holding a devotional candle under the copper intaglio of the Virgin Mary, caught my eye. I stared at the candle inside.

Despite my efforts to center myself, I was watching the glowing red embers of my father's cigarette on the end of one long ash. I could see the slender gray ash clearly as it toppled off the tray onto his favorite maple table, marring the finish like so many cinders before.

The pleasant scent of incense was sweet and fragrant as it tangled with the stale smell of nicotine, making clothes, furniture and my father, smell with its distinctive odor. As I rubbed my eyes to clear the irritating smoke, I saw numerous burn marks seared in the table around the ashtray, wedge-shaped and foreign-looking, like characters from another age. Once again I felt lucky he never set fire to any of our houses, with us in them since he was in the habit of dozing in his recliner at night.

I opened my eyes and looked at the altar waiting for the next service, at the clean white cloth, at the stained glass crucifix sending colors throughout the church, at the shiny driftwood, and at the wooden podium waiting for a conductor of words.

With the pew hard against my back, after 15 minutes of useless trying, it felt like I was only playing at meditation and gave up trying. Instead, I finished my meditation remembering how I had put the scorched letters burned in mind together in a meaningful way, a fitting epitaph on his future grave: I finally quit smoking.

CHAPTER

8

It was time for my first music lesson and I couldn't help feeling apprehensive because I couldn't read music. I never had any formal instruction playing a musical instrument or vocal lessons for that matter, where teachers show students how to sit, how to breathe, how to position the head, chest, and mouth for good vocal tone.

I met Sister Viola in the refectory and she walked me to the music room, an oblong room off the dining area where I stood blaming my parents unfairly for not making me take piano lessons as a child. It was too late for blame now.

Viola switched on a light attached to the wall letting me see how the music room was a converted bathroom complete with plumbing: a sink and a toilet, and a bathtub that was partially hidden by an off-white shower curtain. At the end of the room was a floor-to-ceiling window with bumpy yellow glass directly behind the bathtub at the far end of the room that let in a glare of light. The shag rug had startling colors: orange, red, and yellow and dominant splashes of black all swirled together like scribbling. Worn and foreign looking, this could have been the original flying carpet like in Aladdin's day; I quickly glanced around for a magic lamp. Seeing none, I was disappointed and thought, too bad, now I'll have to learn how to chant the old fashioned way.

A large crucifix, too big for the small room hung against a background of knotty pine paneling.

There was a small free-standing electric organ off to the right; a wooden stand stood next to it. The stand was stuffed with sheet music and music books to qualify this room as the music room. Noticing me looking at the titles of the old fashioned songs such as *I'm In the Mood for Love, Long, Long Ago, Silver Threads among the Gold*, Viola told me, "When we change the words, we use the melodies at times for feast-days and special occasions."

She reached over and showed me where to turn on the organ. I heard the musical instrument gradually grow louder as pressurized air caused it to vibrate. It didn't have pipes on the back producing sound at a specific pitch, but the note she struck did have a nice tone.

The small room looked and felt dusty due to the yellow glare from the window. When Viola's back was turned, I was tempted to trace a message on the top of the organ like: *"Desenex; kills athlete's foot on contact"*, for a joke. Instead, when she wasn't looking I doodled on an abstract looking clef to match the loud carpet.

"Gregorian chant," the music director went on, "was standardized by the *Schola Cantortum*, a school of music established by Pope Gregory in Rome. It was the chief form of music in the 11th century. Secular music such as madrigals and folksongs became popular. By the 16th century it not used at all. It was Pope Pius the X who decreed the Church use Gregorian chant." I was surprised how knowledgeable she was proving to me again, if you like what you do, you'll be good at it.

"The simplicity of the chant," she began again, tucking a wavy lock of brown hair back under her black veil, "reflects the monk's inner nature of peace and harmony. Our lifestyle: forbidding personal conversations, using sign language, writing and receiving just one letter a year, are all part of the marginal existence chant embodies." These were familiar reasons I considered before entering, but they held more importance coming from someone who was actually living them.

"The office is also known as the Liturgy of the Hours. It's based on the cyclical chanting of the Psalms." She paused before rapidly naming the seven offices from morning to night in one breath: "Vigils, Lauds, Tierce, Midday prayer, None, Vespers, and Compline." Hearing the list again I realized my carefree days were over.

"Liturgical seasons change and Psalm substitutions occur, but basically, chanting the office *could* seem like one long endless performance if the main concerns are knowing stage directions like when to turn, when to bow, when to intone, when to read, when to kneel, when to stand. Chant has to move from devotion to love."

"I get it," I said with conviction, confident this 'being moved by love' would happen to me too.

We walked to the tub. Like it would help clarify her explanation, she pulled open the shower curtain to let in more light. "Learning about the monastery is learning all about chant which is based on the Gregorian calendar, named after Pope Gregory XIII. Seven times a day we gather for communally chanted prayer, but this will all be explained in greater detail by the Novice Director."

"By practicing, you'll learn to identify the different modes and scales peculiar to chant," she encouraged.

I could tell Sister Viola was the linchpin of the choir, the person responsible for holding the choir together, making it run smoothly. I could tell liked what she did. Having to train every new voice that comes along, like mine, wasn't a difficult job to her. In fact, she acted like she enjoyed it. She knew how to handle novices who were constantly hitting sour notes. It was a blessing knowing she wasn't going to walk around the room covering her ears in disgust at every off-note, exclaiming, "Why me, why me?"

"The music room doesn't have the sound quality of a Carnegie Hall," Sister Viola admitted, "and it doesn't have the echo effects of most bathrooms because of the carpeting, and it's not even soundproof, but it's better than practicing in the chapel like we used to when we first arrived."

"At least it's private," I said, noticing she'd left out this most important point.

She said, "Music is the art that employs organized sound as its medium; the sensation of sound is produced in the human ear by vibrations in the air. The key or tonality of a scale is its main tone, or tonic, to which all the other tones are related. In Gregorian chant other tones than the lowest are often used."

I managed to keep an even smile on my face as if I knew what she was talking about.

"Each office has its own set of Psalms. They differ from office to office and are set with their own Gregorian modes used for 'chanting'. Gregorian chant which sounds so effortless is not so easy, you'll find."

It felt like she was letting me in on a trade secret.

"Chant combines any number of certain fixed arrangements of the diatonic tones of an octave. Modes are tones of a standard scale without deviation, hence the monotonous level Gregorian chant possesses. Antiphons are short simple melodies in which words are intoned to the same sound of the liturgical text and are sung responsively preceding or following a Psalm.

Seeing the bewildered look on my face, I was happy it caused her to dumb it down for my benefit. Giving me an abridged definition, she said, "There are no *techniques* involved. Chant is uniquely simple. Think of it as refined rhythm."

"Yes, of course," I replied, knowing *this* was a definition I could remember.

She touched briefly on vocal resonation, vibratory patterns, registration and range. I was glad she stopped before pulling out flip charts showing anatomical diagrams of the epiglottis and trachea she mentioned in passing. Instead, I was taught about pitch, volume and timbre, common terms associated with a Music 1-A class.

"The important thing is, singing chant well depends on your perseverance in practice. The Psalmist uses experiences shared by everyone. In time, the words begin to take on a depth like they're coming from your heart. The Psalms we sing are the very ones the monks of old sang. But as Thomas Merton wrote, we don't "offer large amounts of prayers to God and then look into the world to count the good works that result. Monastic life is not "quantitative." It's not the number of Psalms you say, the number of Psalms we sing, or how many good works you perform or even the multitude and variety of ascetic practices you accomplish. What counts is how genuine you are. The Latin *precari* means to speak, so it's a matter of simply learning to pray with your heart. Come in and practice on your own whenever the room's free," she ended, and turned off the organ.

Looking over the organ at her, I told her I'd try, but not before giving a quick glance at the doorknob to see if it had a lock; it did. I knew I would feel much better knowing I could keep an audience of novices out while hitting my sour notes in private.

Filled with beginner's resolve, I planned to come in daily to practice. There was no doubt in my mind I could learn how to sing chant. My love of this rich music outweighed any difficulties its instruction might hold.

Learning to sing chant was all the incentive I needed. I could hardly wait to come into this converted bathroom, close the door, and once I was alone, sing.

CHAPTER

9

It was bound to happen sooner or later; I had to turn in my street clothes. I stood in Novice Director's office as a chilling sense of personal loss enveloped me.

Since a daily work schedule had not been assigned to me yet, Sister Drusilla wanted me to attend to practical needs, such as being fitted for a habit; the same style jumper all the novices wore: white, complete with a white scapula and veil.

I was told to meet with Sister Lorna, the Cellarer, the sister responsible for maintaining the supplies and is chiefly responsible for the abbey's provisions. From my studies before entering, I knew the Cellarer made sure any leftover food was set aside for the portress (doorkeeper) to be distributed as alms to the poor. I learned on Maundy Thursday (Thursday before Easter commemorating the Last Supper) when the abbess ceremoniously washes the community's feet in imitation of Christ, the Cellarer brings her warm water and towels. I knew the Cellarer plays an important role in the monastery. Wearing many hats, Sister Lorna was also one of the main cooks, the head gardener and seamstress for the entire community.

I knocked on her workroom door and my first impression was she had cleaned out the monastery's attic. The room looked it was stored with 'better hang on to this, we might need it' items from each sister's occupation, one trade mixing with another. Once put down and now forgotten, were bits and pieces of different materials: moccasins, fans, candlesticks, clocks, a weather vane, mending, embroidered fabric, blankets and quilts. There were bowls, measuring cups, scales, yellowed hand-written recipes and magazine articles, boxes of canning jars, sacks of flour and stacks of plastic glasses.. I saw parts of pipe-fittings, bundles of rope, sprinklers, and hoses that needed to be patched, work gloves for every size hand, vases for all occasions, and envelopes of seeds stored in old cigar boxes.

As I walked by the long narrow tables of miscellaneous articles, I had the feeling the storeroom was Sister Lorna's private rummage sale. It was full of reusable items that had been picked over and handled in numerous transactions. Nothing was indispensable. Which sister received what, was determined simply by need. The household items sloped against every wall, half on, but mostly falling off the crowded tables in an endless shuffling for more space.

Sister Lorna walked to a mound and whipped off the sheet covering a sewing machine and said, "Step carefully around the ironing board, I'm pressing flowers under the iron." It was obvious that in all this pandemonium, she knew exactly where everything was. As I walked by the iron, in addition to flowers, stems and leaves were hanging out from under the iron too. My guess was seedpods, pine cones, grass (the kind growing on lawns) and berries were stashed away somewhere in the room too.

In all this, my ~~dress~~ habit making session began. I was measured, fit and my posture assessed. We were standing on the other side of the room away from the makeshift dried flower press in Lorna's most unique dressmaking work room/reservatory. I soon learned her speech was perfectly suited to the room in the very unusual way she had of pronouncing her words. From the eastern part of the country, she had a distinctly different accent. I quickly learned she didn't know that the letter 'r' in words was there for a reason. Otherwise, asking for a fork could mean something obscenely different. It took some getting used to.

I could tell she was the gardener from the look of her hands. They were rough and weather-worn with deep lines and calluses. They looked out of place holding a piece of clean white material. It was much easier imagining them holding a hoe threading a rivulet of water through a bean patch, than threading a piece of white thread through a needle. She was an easy-going person and smiled often, but shyly. There was one other noticeable feature about her besides her accent that couldn't be missed; every time she took a step one of her ankles gave a good loud C R A C K.

The Novice Director told me talking was permitted only during work periods, and about work related subjects. After spending five minutes listening to her eastern accent though, I learned how to turn any question into a work related question: "Where did you learn how to make a veil?" "What was *that* monastery like?" "Was the weather much different from Arizona?" She went about her work with pins and yellow measuring tape hanging from her mouth didn't help me understand what she was saying.

It dawned on me; I had found a willing replacement for Drusilla.

Adjusting my habit with all the precision of an Italian seamstress, she put the finishing touches on my one-size-fits-all habit.

Pinning here, and stitching there was all part of her speedy alteration service. Mumbling through straight pins her lips were holding, she said "Don't worry though, I'll store what you wore in, just in case you decide to leave."

"Oh, no need to do that," I said, certain nothing would make me change my mind. "I've waited so long to enter, I'm not backing out now." My entering held great personal satisfaction for me. All my preparations were being realized; I was finally doing what I wanted. Her statement made me wonder though, how many novices, after seeing the shocking transformation in their appearance, became distressed, threw the habit off and beat it back to secular life.

Loud bells sounded the end of work. There was a forty-five minute interval for showering before the office of Vespers. With my dimensions in her hand, I left her to make the final alterations and finish my habit. "Make sure to close the door on your way out," she said as an afterthought. 'Out of sight, out of mind,' must have been her thinking, in case someone would take it upon themselves to remind her that cleanliness is next to Godliness. I was sure it would take a month of doing nothing more than sorting through her treasures to clean her jam-packed clothier chamber. Better yet, she could hold a garage sale where 'early birds'searching for deals on used clothes, toys, best–selling books, ornamental items, knickknacks, lawn and garden tools, sports equipment or board games would be sorely disapointed.

I thanked her for her talented efforts as a seamstress before walking to my room glad this big hurdle was over. I flopped on the bed still not believing I had entered a Cistercian Monastery of Strict Observance.

Alone in my strange new room, I thought about my new life and was filled with happiness and gratitude. I didn't know which I was more grateful for, my new life, or being able to leave my old one. As I lay in my street clothes, for the umpteenth time, I went over the circumstances that helped introduce a spiritual vision that led me here. Being kicked out to the house, I wondered if my father realized he had drop kicked me all the way to Arizona.

Sitting on the bed, I observed my life with a critical eye. I was confident by entering, I wasn't running away. I wasn't leaving name calling; no one in my family called me fat, stupid, or worthless; there was no violence or sexual abuse; no neglect. I never worried about having to respond in the right way, having a place to sleep or where my next meal was coming from, in fact, I always felt welcome. There was however, the continual running debate about what should be done about my father's drinking that took a great many discussions and heated arguments. We ended doing nothing at all.

A half hour later, I heard a knock on the door. It was Sister Lorna dropping off my new one-size-fits-all habit, serge (long under-slip), cowl, and veil. Before she left, I asked, "What's this number 11 on the hem for? I'm the ninth person here, so if any number should be sewn into my clothes it should be a 9."

I learned because the number zero is difficult to make on a sewing machine, it was decided to skip to the next straight number—11. I could understand the reasoning behind it, but there was something unsettling about being annihilated before I even started, removed from the abbey without a trace; I was the non-existent novice and now I had every piece of clothing I owned to remind me I had been voided. Fingering the numbers on my habit, I hoped it wasn't a foreshadowing of things to come.

I laid everything carefully on the bed. I was anxious to slip into my new outfit. Excited, proud and scared all at the same time, I knew what this symbolic change of clothes meant. I was taking off my old way of life, and exchanging it for the opportunity of living for God. I was now going to walk the mystical road; one hidden under a sedate life of routine and discipline. *This* was the exciting way to live, I knew.

The dramatic moment had arrived!

Feeling the coarse material, I was careful not to crease its freshly ironed look trying it on. No need to worry about misdirecting the nap of this sturdy white material, I laughed, it was rough as pup tent. Straightening the serge, I pulled the habit over my head. Easing into the habit next that lined up in the right places, even the pockets. With a great deal of relief I realized, from this point on, I wouldn't have to worry about what I was going to wear everyday. I had two choices, the jumper or work jeans, with no in-between decisions. Not having to come up with little outfits every day would definitely be a plus. It was a reason to join in itself.

For one last moment, my thoughts trailed back to that night in the garage. If the circumstances had been any different, if the box of books hadn't been left unattended gathering dust in the garage; would I be here—grateful and optimistic, a link in a long line of spiritual seekers—novice #9?

My Cistercian look was almost complete, all but the veil. Little tabs of Velcro on each side of the strap across the back of my neck held the veil in place. Standing in front of the 8 by 12 inch mirror in the bathroom, I tried it on several different ways hoping to find the best look, but gave up and decided there wasn't one. No matter how I placed it, I felt silly. The last headgear I remember wearing was a beanie in the Girl Scouts. One thing was sure, I didn't feel like a lay person any longer, and that was important.

Grateful for her skilled and capable work as a seamstress, I fairly flew through the hall to thank her for the quick alterations. Using one of the few signs I knew—*thanks,* I hoped she understood I was thanking her and I wasn't just smacking my mouth for fun. She nodded and waved as I left the room, pleased with the way it turned out.

I kept fidgeting with the cloth belt, snapping and unsnapping the fastener, readjusting the veil towards the front, then to the back. Stepping into the hall took courage. As I walked along, I felt as conspicuous as if my new habit had been made of purple polka dots. I resigned myself to the fact that I looked exactly like the other novices. Passing darkened night lights, I was ready to wave to anyone who happened to pass me like I was in a parade.

I made myself take on a 'like it or not, here I am' attitude, and opened the door to the chapel for Tierce, the third canonical hour. It was empty. Now instead of feeling out of place and conspicuous during an office, I fit right in. Come to think of it, the habit wasn't so bad; it had deep pockets on the sides. Without a bathroom scale, the belt will monitor the size of my belly. I stood in back in my white habit, white veil, black tights and sandals. I knew I had been given a rare opportunity. Bowing a full bow, I felt genuinely happy. I took a couple steps to my left and sat at my place.

Tierce, Midday Prayer and None are called *Little Offices* because of their brevity. Tierce was so short I didn't have time to become distracted. There was no meditating. When the sisters began entering for the start of the office, I was grateful they acted like they didn't see me kneeling at my place outfitted in my new garb. I did my part. I sat still, praying I was invisible.

CHAPTER

10

When Tierce was over, I went to Drusilla's office to see what the Director wanted me to do next. Hesitantly, I knocked on her office door and sat across from her at her desk. She never moved. The window behind gave her a shiny backdrop, as though patience was radiating from her.

All of a sudden, she blurted out, *"Idle hands are the devils workshop."*

I knew what was coming and was overjoyed the subject was finally here: *work*.

My distrust of her now brought up a number of jobs she could stick me with: schlepping out the music room by shampooing the wild carpet, cleaning the toilet, tub and sink. Cleaning the kitchen, scraping burned food off the racks in the oven, scrubbing the floor on my hands and knees with a toothbrush. Or washing and waxing the truck and car at high noon.

She put her hand to her chin and looked at me over her glasses. To my surprise, and relief, she did the opposite. Eyeing me closely, she asked, "How would you like to work in the garden?"

"Would I like to work in the garden?" I repeated, unable to believe my luck. I told her I would rather work outside any time rather than in a confining office. Hearing my own voice sounding higher than normal, I squeaked, "When do I start?"

"Today, if you're certain you're up to it."

Not believing anyone would prefer to work in dirt, she eyed me curiously and said, "Work assignments last a full year so it helps if you like what you do. If you're assigned something you don't find personally rewarding, growing with the challenge is a possibility by working against likes and preferences. If the assigned work turns out to be something personally repulsive, just think how the year's sacrificing will open you and help you grow."

Just think, I thought sarcastically, hoping it would never happen to me.

"I would rather look at a mountain than up at a clock on a wall any day," I told her, adding that I preferred calluses to paper cuts anytime.

Sister Drusilla gave me a short spiel on the value of work and how traditional manual labor was viewed as exceedingly important to Cistercian life. "Ora et Labora; work and prayer," she said, sounding like a commercial for Cistercian life. "Not worrying about visible success or being preoccupied with the fear of failure, work is a spiritual discipline used for the growth of virtue." Making her point clear she added, "Theoretically, if the work is kept simple enough, it will be combined with interior prayer, or prayer of the heart. This is known as active contemplation." She dispensed important principles of the Trappistine trade as easily as cherry Pez.

"I'm ready," I said, getting up. Having waited for years to enter, I thought, *more than ready.*

Today was my first day of work and I couldn't have been more elated. Racing along the hall to my bedroom in an orderly way, I threw off my jumper and pulled on my jeans, putting on the cowboy hat on my head instead of a veil, and edged my way down a path that had been carved out of a steep slope. It wound down sharply, causing me to hold onto rocks and clumps of bushy weeds for support along the way.

Halfway down, I spied Sister Lorna waving a white handkerchief at me in greeting. It may have been a flag of surrender, I wasn't sure. Withered stalks of corn were standing limply ready for the compost pile. Various leftover vines were crawling conspicuously throughout the plants, and weeds were growing over everything even in the surrounding wire fences, making it look like they were holding the rotting wooden posts upright. Other than a thriving oak tree on the east side, a grateful recipient from the daily watering of vegetables beside it, this garden needed help.

I pushed a heavy wooden garden gate open scraping the ground with a wobbly creak like the earliest of wheeled carts. It wasn't a familiar city noise. It matched Sister Lorna's outfit of mud-caked work boots and baggy tan pants with patches of denim on the knees. She had dirt smudges on her neck where her fingers had retied a faded blue paisley cotton scarf in place of a veil.

It was permitted for Lorna to break the silence and talk to discuss work duties with me until I knew Cistercian sign language. Cistercian signing is very different, if not completely different, from the sign language most deaf people use to communicate. Trappist signing does not use finger spelling at all, although out of exasperation at times, when the meanings could not be understood, letters were traced in the air like a giant invisible chalkboard. Most of the signs are not precise, and many had more than one meaning; the word 'finish' could also mean 'past,' but in either case, both meanings precisely described the state of this garden. I followed her to a shed that was the size of an outhouse and had a half-moon on the door; somebody's idea of a joke probably. It made me laugh. The shed had an overwhelming smell of cedar from wood donated by a local resident and I loved the wood smell. I was handed a pair of work gloves.

"A monk must never remain idle," was the first thing she said to me, while handing me a pair of heavy gloves.

So much for sign language, I thought, but was happy she spoke. So far, she was the most likely candidate to replace Sister Drusilla as my new confidante.

"A monk works with his hands," she said in complete agreement with the concept, "not only to earn a living, but for the good of his soul. That's Saint Jerome."

I never thought I'd be receiving spiritual guidance in the cabbage patch.

"And if we remain constantly in the Presence of God, He will be found in ordinary everyday events," she said, pointing to clumps of weeds growing out of control over the round heads.

I wondered if this was Sister Lorna's opening motivational statement for every new novice they sent to work for her. I picked up a hoe because there was nothing more ordinary than pulling weeds.

It felt good to be working with my hands doing physical activity. Learning how to plant, cultivate, and harvest different vegetables would definitely be a bonus. I had always been active and athletic, and garden work felt good. I would be digging shoveling, watering and weeding. My body would enjoy kneeling, bending while doing these useful aerobics.

Stretching my body to its limit was something I was good at, and I enjoyed the feeling of relying on my stamina to get the job done. My competitive feeling bordered on pride as I made it a point to be the first one to the top of a mountain, the first one over the finish line, the longest one to stay under; I could outlast any veteran sunbather and always had the deepest tan to prove it. I flaunted my endurance level thinking others weak when they came up short. If they couldn't keep up, hold out, or withstand pressure, I saw it as a sign of weakness, a character flaw. Everything was a competition to me.

Working hard pulling weeds made time go be quickly and before I knew it, I heard the sound of bells ringing from the steeple on the top of the hill signaling that work was over. Time had gone by *too* quickly, I barely started. I looked at the cabbages proudly with no weeds covering the area and thought, "Not bad for a first day's work; let's see the other novices can top that."

Sister Lorna tried to keep all her speaking to matters pertaining to garden work but a little normal conversation slipped out now and then. I knew this from our dress making session. We rinsed the mud off our hoes, put them in the wooden tool shed, and scrambled our way back up the steep worn-in path.

There was time for a shower before the Office of Midday prayer, where I would be turning pages with a blister on my right thumb. When it was over, I followed everyone through the smell of food wafting in the hall. We stood behind our seats at the long table in the dining room.

While we listened to Esmeralda read grace for the day, I tried to recognize the food odors coming from the kitchen a few feet away. My hopes were dashed though, when with a quick glance I saw the food on the counter: stuffed green peppers, spinach salad and carrot cake, a vegetarian's delight; I would be healthy whether I liked it or not.

Life in the monastery *was* busy. Gardening was my assigned work for the mornings, and my afternoons were to be spent learning the art of stained glass.

I looked at my watch: 2:00; time for afternoon work. I walked across the field in back of the monastery to a two-room brick building. I opened the door and saw colorful confetti on the cement floor: bits of glass, shavings from black plastic insulation, pieces of copper wire, and bark scrapings. I was struck immediately by three things: the warm heavy odor of burning solder, the tap—tap—tapping from two novices trying to break their glass, and the occasional yell of 'Whoops!' blasting the quiet from someone whose glass had broken in the wrong direction. And like all the others buildings; no air-conditioning.

The large studio had one room for making ceramics complete with kiln, and one for cutting and soldering stained glass. I was met by the art director, Sister Gail, who was wearing a white work apron caked with splotches of dried plaster and different colored paint. It was tied in the middle to protect her black scapula. A black veil held her in place. As the abbey's bookkeeper too, she went from fitting dull numbers together to piecing vibrant colored glass in designs at the ringing of bells.

After hearing a couple loud 'Whoops' from the workers, Sister Gail explained, "All tools are to be handled with respect because they are God's creation too so be careful to *place* them down, not throw or drop them." It made me wonder who had thrown what after having their glass break erratically. Other than that, there was no pop music to work by, no informal talk and no heated disputes between artisans.

Sister Gail explained how each Trappist and Trappistine community was challenged to be self-supporting, and that sales from crafts were an important source of income for the monastery. The stained glass and ceramics formed a long line of artistic items sold in the gift shop next to the chapel. Another practical means of financial support, Sister Gail said, was the guest house and pointed to a good sized building about an acre away built to accommodate the few retreatants who ventured to the monastery.

She showed me to a work station, and the technique for holding a glass cutter, letting me 'score' a few pieces for practice. I finished the work period pleased I was making progress. Because my fingers were strong, I thought I could catch on quickly. After proving myself, maybe I'd be allowed to make a stained glass lamp shade. It was something to aim for.

When work was finished, I used the free time before Vespers to take my first long hike out the back door.

CHAPTER

11

I felt a tinge of excitement at the prospect of exploring on my own. Work for today was over. I was glad I was already wearing my jeans as I looked at the honey colored shading of the sky. There was not a moment to lose; it would be dusk soon. Slinging my coat over my shoulders I briskly started walking. My route was a tractor path I had been eyeing from the top of our hill that looked like it hadn't been used in a while. It was plotted with weeds, but clear enough to follow and easy to walk on.

After crawling over a wire fence, I stopped and surveyed the terrain; fields of tall, dry grass spread out unevenly like high carpeting for miles. Beautifully formed seed flowers on ordinary winter weeds grew in unrestrained profusion through the gravel and rocks. Even the weeds were exotic looking in their unfamiliarity. Large puffs like dandelions easily disintegrated when brushed. These hearty plants practically lived on air and sunshine. Tormented occasionally by uncaring cows and the unremorseful boot, they survived despite their abusers.

Looming in the background and taking up half the sky was Mount Enright shadowed in mountain cold, humbling the entire land gradation. Viewed from a distance it was tame, gentle, and without force. But up close, it was colossally vulgar in its immensity. Those finding themselves near it were surprised at its enormity and turned away, not trusting anything that size.

The tractor path went straight without interruption offering a good long hike. Keeping a good pace, I came upon the top half of a windmill standing motionlessly erect ahead and moved in for a closer look. Cast in rusty metal and aged by wreath-like winds, this undefeated mechanical guard stood with an idle beat waiting for a swoosh of air to power it back into action.

At the top of the gradual incline I could see I could see the bottom half was secured to the lowest point of a gulch. I was excited about my new discovery and couldn't wait to investigate more closely. Before I did, I turned around and looked back. The tiny white brick monastery, minuscule against the tawny sky, looked like a plastic toy building from a child's train set. From this distant perspective, it was hard to perceive any difficulties occurring within its model community. With acres of space between us, I could regard it honestly seeing it as peaceful but exhausting, challenging but threatening, frightening but God-like. I stepped back in fear.

Taking short quick breaths because of the altitude, I circled down to the collected water at the bottom. I wouldn't think of submerging myself in the pond this time of year, not with crusty snow on the mountain tops surrounding me; I'd keep this activity in mind for the summer when it was 110°. Plunging in the secluded watering hole might be just the attitude adjustment I'd need.

Droppings marked the passage of many thirsty animals that were hard and dry on top of the small hill, wet and mushy at the banks' edges. During hot dry summer months, this one windmill situated on a plain of rolling hills behind the monastery, dribbled life-sustaining fresh water into a collection of standing water at the bottom of the gulch. It was a life saving necessity for cattle quenching their thirst.

The long, thin cries of hawks gliding effortlessly in the cloudless sky beckoned me to leave so they could swoop down and drink in safety. Clearing a spot with my foot, I took off my coat after the fact walk, placed it on a few weeds, and sat at the waters' edge instead.

Gazing steadily at the still pond, I let myself become mesmerized by the glassy coruscations floating in front of me. It felt relieved being *away* from the routine. Plus, it was a place where I didn't have to worry about running into the Novice Director.

I was lost in thought for some time. Suddenly the cabby's words of caution came to me disturbing my peaceful interlude. From then on I kept a keen eye on the perimeter of the gulch; cows and bulls were large and I wouldn't miss seeing approach, but if a boar was the size of a dog, softly pawing the ground, I might miss sneaking up to attack. Not to mention all the other kinds of creatures, drawn in by the smell of water.

My actions gave insight into my own behavior. They reminded me how I used to scour my parents' house before entering too. I know nothing about wild hogs, but living with someone who drinks too much is, at times, about as unpredictable as living with a wild boar; never knowing when it will act savagely and turn; always watching your step; never feeling relaxed; knowing a wild animal was loose somewhere in the house.

I glanced up at the trail leading to the edge of the pond again. It was empty except for two orange crowned warblers scratching the dirt. I was alone and safe for the moment. With time to reflect, I wondered if there were drawbacks living in prolonged stress, otherwise known as my childhood learning the art of mollycoddling, except headaches, anxiety and depression, that is. Probably not.

Any remnant of peace now gone, I gazed at the water imagining a hot summer day, I pictured myself diving headfirst into cool water, splashing it on the banks dousing the surrounding weeds. I could feel drips of water running down my face as thoughts of time schedules, singing, sign language and meditation floated effortlessly away on a quiet world of wet absorption. I imagined the water affectionately caressing my face with gentle touches of fluid fingers, the pleasurable feel of the water flowing across my body, bubbles surrounding my spirit with a liquid embrace.

I saw myself at the bottom wrestling in the darkness, deeper than I've ever been, swimming beyond feelings, affections and desires. In this aquatic solitude, I had gone beyond words and into a clearer understanding. With my body held under gallons of pressure, I let it relax in the tranquil motion of the water in a dead man's float, drifting,

drifting, floating endlessly upward to the light of the sky. Then suddenly surfacing in **ENLIGHTENMENT!**

It was an incredibly peaceful interlude. I tossed in pebbles and watched the back and forth motion of the water lapping on the bank as it tried to still itself. And when at last it finally rested, glassy and calm, my reflection surprised me. The face I saw looking back seemed changed. It was a face full of confidence and strength; power shone from its eyes. I stared at myself settled in a countenance of light and love and knew this was the face of my inner spirit. I smiled knowing *this* was the face that lasts forever.

Far in the distance, I heard the faint ringing of bells. Being lost in thought for so long, I glanced around to again become aware of my surroundings: the windmill was still motionless, sparkles were still floating by and hawks were still circling overhead; I was safe. I scanned the perimeter of the pond one last time before getting up; a clumsy cow I was sure to hear, but a little grey boar nibbling on roots, I might miss. A gentle but cool breeze greeted me when I stood.

I stepped on the weedy uphill path with every sense alert. The only sound was the flapping wings of a black crow as it raced to its nest in the faltering daylight.

The bells reminded me I had fifteen minutes to walk all the way back, change into my jumper, and quiet myself for Vespers. I slipped my arms back in my coat, fastened the buttons and started walking. I knew I could do it.

Sizzling hot, I hoped no one noticed I was panting like a dog to cool off as I sat at my place. Reason told me the chapel must have been chilly, but it felt stifling hot inside to me. I was in time for the start of Vespers, and was glad to be able to settle into the soft green cushion of my chair to catch my breath after the long hike.

All the novices were expected to be waiting, prepared and quieted, at least three minutes before each office. Whatever we were doing when we heard the three minute warning bell, we were to stop, put whatever we holding away, and wait in the chapel for the start of the office. This rule could be a real irritant, like being on the verge of going out in a game of solitaire and suddenly having to put the cards back in the box, *if* we were allowed to play cards. It was not an easy rule to follow. It was a small thing, but as a lesser obedience I knew it was an expression of a higher obedience. It's a constant 'turning' to again regard the acceptance of this calling. This is a universal obedience shared by the whole community, novices and professed alike.

We started with a song, followed by a series of Psalms which were chanted. This was the routine for most of the offices. I was finally learning to turn and bow in unison at the closing of each Psalm, while singing, *"In the name of the Father and of the Son and of the Holy Spirit, is now, and ever shall be, world without end. Amen."*

As the evening prayer and the winding down of the day, it was hard for me not to yawn after the input of all the oxygen on my walk, or at least try not to be conspicuous while stifling one. I knew the altitude was fatiguing, but learning the basics of the office while constantly holding a spiritual eye open was adding to my tiredness. The day had been a good indication of the level of concentration I would need to sustain a vocation here. I knew at some point I would have to take my turn intoning, by singing the first line alone like everyone else, but for right now I was happy I didn't have anything more to do than listen. I thought it expeditious Sister Viola was leading us now. As the music director, she knew which songs to use during regular days, holidays, feast days and Saints' days, not to mention knowing which antiphons, responsorials and canticles to use at a glance. I was glad I didn't enter during the Easter season when extra loooong Alleluias were sure to be in the mix.

Vespers contained selected Psalms, and two Scripture readings, followed by a fifteen minute meditation period. Theoretically, one is supposed to meditate on what is read during the readings. Sitting in the unfamiliar position not slouching, made my spine it feel like it was made out of worn out cobblestone. It forced me to hone in on the way I was positioning my body only. Posture is not an obvious pressure, but it's in the top two. Because of my constant disruptive realigning, by the time Vespers was over, there was not an ounce of rapt attention left in me. When the knock from the back finally sounded, I stood stretching my aching back, thanking God it was over.

I was at the end of the line where bent over, I followed everyone into the hall to the refectory. I spooned out a small amount of corn casserole, and had a salad of fresh dark green romaine leaves, scattered with pieces of peppers, tomatoes, onions and cucumbers, topped with a choice of dressings.

As filler, I headed back to the peanut butter and bread, poured a cup of hot water from a thermos for instant coffee, spooned in some sugar and powered creamer, and then I was full. Listening to the consuming racket of a group of hungry nuns, I settled back contentedly cradling my hot coffee, sipping in silence under the large wagon wheel.

After the meal, there was a short interval of free time before the Compline. Everyone parted and went their separate ways. After bussing my dishes, I made my way to the magazine table in back. In the dusk I could barely make out the horses on a field through a large square window in front of the table; their shadowy forms moving slowly in the winter cold. I knew how they felt. They were shivering like I had done my first night.

I pulled my sweater tighter to me. I relaxed remembering I could exchange it left for my new cloak the seamstress had left on my bed. Now I would be able to huddle concealed under the large outer garment. I walked to my room to put on my new cloak and went to the chapel way ahead of time to hunker down.

The 'Salve', so far, was my favorite hymn. It had a touching melody, together with lyrics containing words like sighing, mourning and weeping, that struck a chord in me. Because we sang it by the quivering light of a candle, the mystical overtones were heightened. This final prayer of the day made me feel like I had entered a different state of mind, a deeper level of prayer, an eternal place.

The last hymn of the day signaled the beginning of the mystical journey into the grand silence of the night, a mysterious high desert adventure we took every night on the lookout for deeper levels of prayer. This was a silence without words that beckons from the inside and lets God be felt as easily as the thin desert air on my face. This inner quiet let me see the overuse of words was like being in thick, thorny gossamer, thistledown, sticky and entangling.

Walking to my bedroom, I was prepared. I had a good understanding that the *grand silence* meant much more than just not talking from reading Thomas Merton. Monks have always known that silence can not be learned, only experienced, that it was the stillness of the mouth that stilled the heart. The grand silence is a time when a speechless hush gives way to deep interior quiet, the entire monastery bears a tremendous quickening of stillness in a spiritual ablution from words.

It was easy to become accustomed to this feeling of interior quiet during the Office of Compline. Cistercian superiors of old intentionally selected Psalms for Compline that had lines reflective to the night's mood such as, 'I close my eyes and sleep comes at once,' inviting the mind to respond in kind. 'You shall not be afraid of the terror of the night, nor of the arrow that flies by day,' encouraging a secure and restful sleep; or 'Keep me as the apple of your eyes; hide me in the shadow of your wings,' instilling contentment and assenting to a satisfied and protected sleep. All of which were instrumental during the grand silence of the night.

As I walked, my thoughts trailed off to early Christendom; to some of the memorable ways monks kept themselves from speaking that were etched in my mind. Extreme ends called for extreme measures and what was more extreme than eternal glory or eternal damnation? One early Christian monk, Abba Agathon, kept a pebble in his mouth for three years until he learned to hold his tongue, remembering the maxim: 'He who speaks does not know, and he who knows does not speak.'

There is a different version in the monastery with our sign language, but the premise was the same; 'She who signs does not know, and 'she who knows does not sign.'

Floating along in my new cloak, I glanced at the nightlights; only five more to go. My mood deepened as I remembered Saint Simeon Stylites, the Pillar Saint, and the steps he took to keep people away. A Christian ascetic, he lived on top of poles making it incapable for visitors to contact him. His first pole was only a six footer, but he ended up extended to a height of fifty feet; Saint Simeon lived this way on platforms on top of poles for thirty-five years.

The monastery's location was chosen for the same purpose; set on top a hilly plateau over five thousand feet high, in the middle of a desert unlikely of being reached by pedestrians out on leisurely walks or by through-traffic; thereby avoiding all unnecessary conversations, distractions, and near occasions of sin.

I thought of the example written by a Jewish Rabbi Abraham Cohen concerning the strict controls of the tongue I'd read in *Everyman's Talmud*: "All the limbs of man are erect but you are horizontal; they are all outside the body but you are inside. More than that, I have surrounded you with two walls, one of bone and the other of flesh."

Here, although we voluntarily decided in silence we would find God, and were convinced that a lifetime of silence brought atonement for our sins, even with the tongue in a fleshy penitentiary to help regulate our words—if a person wants to talk, a way of breaking the silence will be found, in signs, or not.

I made my way to my bedroom. Yellowed nightlights posted like road reflectors along the brick walls guided my feet forward in the chilly passageway. I shivered as I hit a cold draft. For a fleeting moment the thought crossed my mind that sometimes a road that is normally safe can be dangerous, and stiffening, I dug my hands deeper into the pockets of my habit as I moved on. I passed a series of bedroom doors like they were empty billboards, each one reaffirming the necessity of controlling my words.

I looked down the hallway through the half-light. I knew I didn't have far to go. I knew I was to continue in this direction on this private road usually concealed with noisy activity. Knowing the right effort involves doing very little, I stepped out of my way and coasted the last few feet crashing through the barricade of words.

My bedroom didn't have large fluffy pillows or a down comforter. It didn't have a white shag rug, a television, or a phone by the bed. But I knew what it housed was far more important than comfort. I placed my hand on the doorknob and pushed the door open a little. I could see through the opening a dark deep place waiting for me. This was the end destination merging every road from every direction and from any distance. This was the exit that could not be reached with words. I closed the door and stepped into the silence.

CHAPTER

12

Meditation; even the word made me cringe. If I was thinking of living here a lifetime, I didn't want to just go through the motions. I had to learn. Fast.

It was the next day and the start of another Lauds that brought the same dread of meditating. The sisters entered, and back and forth, we chanted. It came to me how in the closeness of a small choir of ten people, mistakes pulled us to the side like traffic accidents ranging from minor to serious and it was easy to detect who sang off-key. A simple mistake, I considered a fender-bender, those who skipped a whole stanza felt like head-on collisions, and someone who turned to the wrong page needed to be towed back in position. The organist was there to police us and keep the chant flowing smoothly, because if one person chanted too slowly, it caused a major backup and if one person chanted too quickly, it sent the rest of us recklessly heading for the exits. Both were hazardous conditions, like both sides of the choir merging into one narrow lane.

Then it was time for a short reading. Sister Gail, the appointed reader for this week, stood and read a piece she had singled out from among the hundreds of previously screened writings collected especially for the offices. The readings were by many different writers, predominantly Cistercian. Gail, as a long time professed with years of reading experience, was a good reader with clear enunciation and fluent delivery, which made listening to her as easy as listening to my own thoughts.

It was time for a reflection/meditation period. I was relieved when, following the others, we turned our chairs to face the altar. I told myself, 15 minutes is not so long and settled in. Back straight, head erect, hands open to receive. Ready, set, go.

It turns out trying to *remember* what was read is as hard as meditating. I sat poised, sitting straight, for the meditation where I hoped I wasn't doing irreparable damage to my spine. I was struck by the thought; what do I really know about meditating? It has always been easy for me to sit still, but it was always been hard to sit in a lotus position, legs crossed, close to the body. I sat poised and ready in my soft seat thinking how I *could* have joined a cenobitic order striving for aloneness reflected in the words of Simeon the New Theologian:

Leave me alone, sheltered in my cell.
Let me be with God, who alone is good.
Stay away from me—even further away.
Let me die alone before my God who has created me.
No one should knock at my door; none should raise their voice.
No one should visit me, neither friend nor relative
No one should draw my spirit away from meditation.
Why should I move out of my cell?
Back to that which I left? Let me be.
I want to cry and mourn over the days and nights.
   (949-1022)

While I can appreciate the sentiment of living like a hermit and not having to meditate if I didn't feel like it, I felt the combination of solitude *and* community of the Cistercians was right for me.

It wasn't until the words came to me from her selection by Thomas Merton: "Meditation is one of the ways in which the spiritual man keeps himself awake," and went on to finish the piece by him from *Thoughts in Solitude*, "It is not really a paradox that it is precisely in meditation that most aspirants for religious perfection grow dull and fall asleep. Meditative prayer is a stern discipline, and one that cannot be learned by violence. It requires unending courage and perseverance, and those who are not willing to work at it will finally end in compromise. Here, as elsewhere, compromise is only another name for failure."

I didn't yawn once after that; spiritual peer pressure.

Faced with my own meditations, I found it peculiar how my thoughts meandered down the strangest paths. Disrupted circadian rhythms certainly could have had something to do with my inability to hold my concentration on a specific idea. Being half asleep did give free reign to my subconscious, inducing ideas to surface that normally don't. I would gently restore the original scriptural character of my thoughts, only to have them again run wildly in all directions, as if an order had been given to *release the hounds!* But like trying to entice a pack of untrained dogs, enjoying the freedom of open countryside to come home, giving active consideration to every thought that passed through my mind, was pointless too.

Thinking back, the only preparation I had on meditation before entering was the four major works of Saint John of the Cross describing in detail the way to mystical union with God; but his books didn't describe meditation practices or positions at all. It helped knowing one of the most important aspects of meditation is the active effort of trying. Armed with that, and the saint's example of *holy hatred* to serve as my guide, I persevered doggedly trying not to pay attention to distractions: *'who's clicking her nails?'* or *'who keeps clearing her throat? Why doesn't she cough and get it over with?'* The list of distractions is endless.

Trying to think of something from the reading, out of desperation I thought a handy insert would help first time meditators like me. I looked around the chapel to make sure no one was watching me, as if I was telegraphing my thoughts. They looked like they were all deeply absorbed in whole brain meditations. With my mind lost in this advantageous diversion, there was no holding back now.

My ~~Meditation for Dummies, Meditation Made Easy~~ Beginners Guide to Meditation should start with a quote from a source taken from the Bible and Church tradition: the *Catechism*. "Above all meditation is a quest. The mind seeks to understand the why and how of the Christian life, in order to adhere and respond to what the lord is asking"

The guide should include a flattering illustration of an attentive sister meditating in the correct posture and be self-explanatory at a glance. I would place it conspicuously at the front of every novice's office book and stress the fundamentals: the simpler, the better and refrain from using examples from *The Spiritual Exercises* of Saint Ignatius of Loyola until much, *much* later.

I was far off course in my meditation now but knowing there were vocations in the balance, I couldn't stop.

The insert should include several definitions; some by Catholic authors, others who weren't Catholic, and still others considered unorthodox, other than sleeping on a bed of nails, that is.

I would list Catholic definitions first, starting with Merton's *Thoughts in Solitude*: "In meditative prayer, one thinks and speaks not only with his whole mind and lips, but in a certain sense with his whole being. Prayer is then not just a formula of words, or a series of desires springing up in the heart—it is the orientation of our whole body, mind and spirit to God in silence, attention and adoration. All good meditative prayer is a *conversion of the entire self to God.*"

I would cite an explanation by Saint John of the Cross:

"We must therefore not apply the understanding to that which is being supernaturally communicated to it, but simply and sincerely apply the will to God with love, for it is through love that these good things are communicated and through love they will be communicated in greater abundance than before."

I'd add a definition from objective sources like *The Encyclopedia of Religion*, "Meditation involves the narrowing of the focus of consciousness to a single theme, yet it remains cognitive and intellectual." It was right to the point. Any proper guide wouldn't be complete without the definition, "Meditation investigates, contemplation wonders," by Richard of Saint-Victor. It was short and one easily remembered.

I'd *have* to put in a quote from the secular researcher Edgar Cayce to be fair: *"Whereas prayer is 'man talking to God,' meditation is 'man listening for God's voice'."* A more succinct description than any Trappistine might give.

As I sat, I was aware of the power struggle going on in my mind. I didn't want to, but I allowed a parade of thoughts to march in full of distracting regalia starting with the imagined insert. The distractions didn't stop there. There were so many, it was overwhelming. As soon as I rid myself of one, another distracting thought popped up to replace it. I had my very own hidden saboteur, which in a monastery some might call the machinations of the devil. In other words, I was full of myself. Keeping my mind on God, I was learning, wasn't easy and left me dispirited.

Taking back control of myself, I sat straighter and took three cleansing breaths, resolved to ignore the relentless distractions. Having developed my second wind, my energy was restored. I was now I was now ready to make a good meditation.

There was a familiar knock at the back of the room. The meditation period was over. We all stood. Dipping my fingers in the holy water fount, I promised to do better next time and quickly followed the others out the door toward the smell of supper.

CHAPTER

13

That evening when the bells chimed announcing the start of Vespers, a fretful new disturbance made itself known. It was as if someone had flagged the start of a race because everything happened at once; the organist began playing; the other side of the choir started chanting and another unfamiliar sound broke out as well. Someone on the other side of the choir began to sob. And even though the crying sent an uneasy feeling through me, I had to marvel at her I incredible timing, just as we were about to sing.

I glanced around the room for reactions; the organist continued to play, the sisters continued to sing, eyes remained focused on office books. No one did anything, as if they were all used to it. I learned during a Repetition class the meaning of *Custody of the eyes* was the practice of keeping ones' eyes to oneself to help promote a calmer, more peaceful heart. It means not looking with curiosity at another person or situation that is none of your business. It sounds easy but it's harder to put into practice especially when someone on the other side of the choir is unabashedly crying out of control.

I tried to ignore it, doing my best to think of other things—the funny shaped zucchini I brought from the garden for the cook, the bent beak I fashioned on a road runner in the glass shop, or the sour notes I hit during music practice: all to no avail. As an attention getter, weeping had to be a big alert every time. Like a loud siren heard for miles on an ambulance weaving in and out of traffic, flashing red lights, making sure people knew an injured person is aboard. It's a call for help too, letting others know an emotionally injured person was in trouble. But no one even glanced up or slowed to look, there was no rubber-necking to inspect the scene of the accident; they didn't stop to see how much damage was involved before continuing.

Until this point I hadn't had a problem with *custody of the eyes*, 'not looking'—consciously not looking into open doors as I walked in the hall, not looking at hand signs directed at others, backing away from snatches of conversations I wasn't involved in, and so forth. But this was some of the most heart-rending sobbing I'd ever heard. I would chance a quick look.

Gathering my courage, I waited until we reached the end of the Psalm when we would turn and bow while singing "Glory be to the Father and…" to sneak a peek. As we started our turn and went into our bow, without turning my head, just shifting my eyes, I looked over my office book and glanced from sister to sister. And there, holding an office book in one hand and a big wad of tissues in the other was Sister Lorna, looking the picture of confusion.

In a monastery, the right course of action, of course, is no action; no comforting, no offering help, no giving advice. I told myself to keep my attention focused on God and not let outside disturbances disturb my concentration; keeping custody of my eyes as the Novice Director said. And even though I believed this was the right way to handle the situation, it was extremely difficult, like standing on a cliff face leaning forward with arms rotating trying not to fall in. Whatever she was crying about, I didn't want to make it worse by getting us both in trouble so I would do the right thing and not offer help, no help whatsoever. I'd keep me helpful suggestions to myself, and my mouth closed. I thought it was a good lesson in self control and maybe after years of practice I would be comfortable not offering help too.

By worrying, I had once again blown another meditation period by allowing myself to become distracted. Keeping my mind concentrated on one thing isn't easy I was discovering. If I don't do better, I knew, I'll be in big trouble.

I followed everyone heading to the refectory for supper where a composed Sister Lorna was already seated. Could I have been wrong? Maybe it had been only an allergy attack, or a touch of a common cold instead of tears of sadness; whatever the problem was, it was good to see Sister Lorna piling on the quiche and eating heartily, at least her despondent mood hadn't affected her appetite. And because she wasn't sneezing, coughing, or wiping a runny nose, I ruled out a cold. (It stands to reason nothing brings gloom and doom on a choir more acutely than someone suffering from a cold. Instead of "Amen," it is "Ah choo," for days.) Preferring incense to mentholated ointments any day, I gladly excluded respiratory difficulties and bronchial irritation in Lorna's case.

Being a well-intentioned novice, I knew I had to do something.

CHAPTER

14

"Listen, my son [children], with the ear of your heart", begins the first line of the prologue to the *Rule of Saint Benedict*. Listening to your heart came easily in the desert. It was silence that filled the dawns and embraced the sunsets. Silence here did not talk, it screamed. Its indefinable perception spread over the landscape in decorated relief, embossing everything in its path with stillness. It was a "presence" continually bursting moment by moment driving away words from my head.

When I reached the end of the long downhill path for work that morning, I stopped and surveyed the whole of the garden. This morning everything seemed wonderfully still inside the contained oasis. As I walked the length to the opposite fence, everything had clarity. Calmness was drifting over the land like I was viewing a broad range of illuminated peace someone had plugged in.

The stillness made the usual vegetation look fresh and new as it acted as like a staged production of peace waiting for an audience to notice its performance. Ever patient, it persevered in silent repose. It was a peace hoping for attention, as if it knew we could both feed off this interconnectedness of appreciation.

My habit of staring into the distance was cut short by the familiar ankle cracking of Sister Lorna, only in the dirt, the variation was more like *crack*, silence, *crack*, silence, *crack*... I turned to greet her and was welcomed with a smile and a handle of a hoe.

Her eyes looked red and teary. She had started crying again. I asked without signing, "What happened now?" I was sure we were both cautiously scrutinizing each other, wondering if either of us was planning to inform our Superiors we were talking like we were supposed to. It was a risk that was always there because we were on our honor to tell the higher ups all intentional wrongdoing. Who knew when either of our consciences would get the better of us? Sister Lorna *should* report to Reverend Mother and I *should* report to the Novice Director.

"I'm just a little out of sorts," she said. "I'll be all right," using no signs at all. Her words weren't very convincing though. I was used to *hearing* part of her meaning by now; whenever she used signs, words slipped out and she ended up with *voicing* the entire sentence.

We walked to the other end of the garden and the gardener pointed at old and crinkled melon vines. I felt my arm muscles flex into action giving one a good swipe that ended in a tangle of withered vines wrapped around the blade of my hoe. Side by side we chopped at the dead vines. It felt good using my muscles I hadn't used in a long time. It made me think how right Thomas Merton was when he wrote, "Monastic life is very active, all in the name of active contemplation. There is a steady stream of things to do besides reciting the daily office, meetings, prayer, study times, along with work and more work. One *could* feel saturated with the pressure to perform and keep up."

It did make the monastery feel like it was a powerhouse of prayer with an exaggerated reverence for work. The systematic arrangement of duties helped keep me on an even keel emotionally. There was no homesickness. There was anxiety, but it was the right kind of anxiety; learning music, struggling with meditations, keeping the silence. It was the tight kind of worrying too, not like worrying about having to move again, or going to a new school.

One big difference from life on the outside, here there was no uneasiness about what will happen. With every hour of every day planned for me, I knew exactly what was coming next; routine work.

I was doing well up until Lorna and I started talking, every chance we had. Then I started carrying around guilt like I was its' caddy. I couldn't help feeling resentful, as a long time professed, she certainly should have known better. As a novice, even I knew talking was wrong. I was supervising an older professed. At least I was familiar with the role, reminding me how growing up in a home catering to someone who drinks too much, close attention and watchful supervision is completely reversed too; custody of the parent is placed with the children. Here I was, facing the same problem.

It was risky trusting Sister Lorna not to turn into an informer even though she assured me she wouldn't say anything. The pangs of remorse were with me always and could strike at any moment... for either of us. It made me feel discombobulated all the time. Knowing I shouldn't talk, I did it anyway; now I know how a drunk must feel. Time passed quickly as it always did when we were working. Before I knew it Sister Lorna and I were carrying the dead vines to the end of the garden and stuffing them in the compost cage, covering the new material with the old in a rotting mixture of banana peels, egg shells and vines.

As I dumped in my contribution, I decided today was the day I would *try* not to utter another word to Sister Lorna. Disgusted with myself, I questioned, what were the odds of being waylaid by guilt when I was overwhelmed with mistrust for the Novice Director like I was? As a new novice, I didn't know when Lorna's crying jags started or even if they were coming less frequently. For all I knew, she may have cried all throughout her novitiate. What's more, maybe our talking was actually helping poor Lorna not to cry, it was really beneficial.

I stored my hoe in the shed before clawing my way up the gravelly path. I thought of possible reasons for her tears: diet can affect people and was tempted to blame her mood swings on the vegetarian diet. With the mainstay here being fresh zucchini—baked, fried or raw, I didn't think singling out this one specific vegetable full of potassium, magnesium and vitamin A, would have such a sad effect on anyone.

One thing was for sure, Sister Lorna's crying wasn't due to a lack of sugar because our desserts were usually in generous portions, there was nothing to worry about in the sweets department; she had a constant supply of sugar coursing through her veins on a regular basis. It wasn't the diet.

By the time we reached the top of the hill, I had come up with at least five good reasons why I shouldn't be involved in Lorna's troubles: custody of the eyes (and mind) helps bring back what's really important, God. It helps teach discipline which will carry over and strengthen other aspects of discipline: chastity, modesty, temperance; I should be in control of myself and not allow curiosity to control me, controlling myself helps fight off temptation which adds to my self respect; if I am seeking God, custody of the eyes is the right thing to do because it honors God.

Standing at the refectory door, we took off our boots before entering the refectory. I picked up a nearby stick and scraped off the mud before placing my boots in laundry room near the back door. When Lorna reached in her pocket and pulled out a handful of moist disintegrating tissues to wipe her boots, I knew it was time, right or wrong, for me to say something to the higher-ups.

I showered quickly and waited nervously outside the Esmeralda's office. I closed my eyes and knocked. Even though I was fearful the Superior might think I had no right to butt into somebody else's business, I stood firm. I couldn't let Sister Lorna's crying go on without saying *something,* even if I was being a busybody. Lorna might have something seriously wrong with her like being a manic-depressive, or have one of a number of serious psychological problems causing her mood swings. Ignoring the problem wasn't the answer.

I was invited in the well-kept room that had a large wooden desk half the size of the room. Other than the few papers she was working on, everything was in its place. There were books held between bookends, pens and pencils in a holder, even the particles blown in by the wind were obliging; there wasn't a speck of dust anywhere.

I went straight to the point and told Esmeralda I was concerned about Sister Lorna's crying and how much I was bothered by it. She looked at me with wise, owlish eyes, eyes that seemed to be hiding mysteries of the Cistercian Order behind them and said. "I understand your concern. No need to worry though, Sister Lorna is seeing a therapist once a week. Her crying is probably due to menopause."

I almost fell over. Her reply was better than I could have I imagined. All of a sudden I felt nosy for butting in where I had no business. I was relieved at the same time, delighted Lorna was getting the help she needed. I was especially elated, because even though Reverend Mother was helpful and accustomed to doing right, she probably entered at a time when therapy wasn't widely accepted. But because she was all for getting Lorna help, I marveled at her progressive stance and having an therapist, a stranger, who may or may not be Catholic, know about a sister's personal problems and what goes on inside a monastery during revealing therapy sessions. Esmeralda could come out looking bad in the end.

She suggested we could help Sister Lorna through her menopausal time by being patient and understanding. I left her office feeling red-faced for my presumptuousness, but also with the knowledge that she was being helped by a professional; they were doing all they could.

Walking out of her office, feeling much lighter, I didn't get very far before the words of *Saint Benedict's Rule* came to me I heard during the last office cautioning:

No one shall presume to defend another in the monastery
Take care that, no matter what, no monk presume to defend or
    protect another, not
even if they share a familial relationship
No monks shall be permitted to do this in any manner, for it can
    lead to scandal.
Anyone who does shall be severely punished.

A feeling of remorse enveloped me. By meddling into something that didn't concern me, I didn't respect Lorna's privacy. I should have attended to my own affairs instead of those of others. I knew better, *now.*

CHAPTER

15

A day came when my usual good health had a glitch—a chipped tooth—both unlucky and lucky. Not because I enjoyed the needles, drilling and pain associated with going to a dentist, but my tiny piece of splintered tooth meant long drives into Tucson with two or three other sisters. All appointments were scheduled around Sister Lorna's counseling sessions to limit the number of trips to those that were absolutely necessary. With Sister Viola as our driver, Sister Dorothy sitting next to her, and Sister Lorna and myself in the back seat, we headed off for Tucson leaving a fresh pair of skid marks in the dirt.

Once the car doors slammed shut and the sisters invoked each person's patron saint for protection, we were permitted to speak openly and freely to each other—with no restrictions whatsoever. I had never read about any guidelines for sisters concerning road trips away from monastery, but then, I had never given any thought to where the milk, butter and eggs were coming from. At first I thought Sister Viola was joking about relaxing the speaking rule. Up until this point our conversation had been strictly according to the rules and only when necessary. After a few miles (as if they were waiting until they were *absolutely, positively* certain we were far enough away that we couldn't be heard... just in case) it was as if the signal had been given. We passed the five mile mark, and the small-talk began. Like a drawbridge had been raised, our thoughts and opinions spontaneously flowed between us it was obvious everyone was enjoying the traverse.

To prepare or the ride, the professed sisters put on tan veils and jumpers as traveling attire in an effort to be less conspicuous than the Cistercian black and white. The Cistercian reputation was one that was hard one to play down. Years of self-discipline and a life of sacrifice result in a thoughtful bearing and a patient demeanor, dead giveaways out in the world.

Our drive into Tucson was recreational learning for me. I asked questions about everything and learned the personal background of many of the order's abbots and abbesses. This was very helpful because it brought a continuity and clarity to the place and time in which I was now living. Background information on the other sisters in the car was gladly given, and they were just as interested in finding out about me too. We were a torrent of speed rolling along at 55 miles per hour, sightseers, talking and laughing.

As we drove through the southwestern desert passing yellow clumps growing on the ends of cholla cacti, my eyes went from cactus to cactus, greedily trying to capture each unusual shape in a permanent registry in my memory. Both sides of the highway paraded countless well-proportioned and clean limbs, as well as stumpy misshapen ones, but all were photogenic. I didn't want to miss even one. Secure in the back seat, I glanced at Sister Viola, a choir director with a passion for music, then down at the silent radio with knobs that were filled with dust. If it was alright to speak, I took a chance and asked; "Why don't we turn on the radio?" even if I knew the only stations we'd be able to pick up in this isolated area might be southern preachers or accordion music.

Sister Viola said that even though she really wanted to, all drivers had been instructed not to, so under obedience the radio had to remain off. She reminded me that the way to see God's will was through Superiors. Knowing that, turning it on wasn't even an option for her. "Like not running the air conditioner, you get used to keeping it off," she said, wiping her brow.

Seeing the logic in her words, something told me it would be futile asking if we could stop at a McDonalds in Tucson.

If our situations had been reversed and I was the one who hadn't heard a note from a radio in years, I did what I would have liked done for me; I described today's music the best way I could explaining how music had progressed. Her attentive focus immediately zoomed in. But describing music is like describing how chocolate ice cream tastes different from vanilla; impossible. So, to three cloistered nuns on a deserted back highway close to the Mexican border, I sang an example from the world I left behind, my rendition of a popular Rogers and Hammerstein song at the time:

My analyst told me that I was right out of my head.
He said I'd need treatment, but I'm not that easily led
He said I was the type that was most inclined, when out of his sight
to be out of my mind, and he thought I was nuts, no more ifs, or
ands, or buts.

My analyst told me that I was right out of my mind.
The way he described it, he said I'd be better dead than live.
I didn't listen to his jive. I knew all along that he was all wrong,
and I knew that he thought I was crazy, but I'm not.

They say as a child I appeared a little bit wild with all my crazy
ideas,
but I knew what was happening... I knew I was a genius.
What's so strange when you know you're a wizard at three?
I knew that this was meant to be.

Now I'd heard little children were supposed to sleep tight,
and that's why I got into the vodka one night.
My parents got frantic, didn't know what to do,
but I saw some crazy scenes before I came to.

Do you think I was crazy? I may have been only three, but I was
swinging!
They all laugh at angry young men.
They all laughed at Edison, and also at Einstein.

So why should I feel sorry if they just couldn't
understand the idiomatic logic that went on in my head?

I had a brain. It was insane.
Oh, they used to laugh at me when I refused to ride
on one of those double-deckerbuses
because there was no driver on the top.

My analyst told me that I was right out of my head.
But I said, "Dear doctor, I think that it's you instead,
because I have got a thing that's unique and new.
To prove it I'll have the last laugh on you

Cause instead of one head, I've got two!"
And you know two heads are better than one."

(*Twisted* by Wardell Gray and Annie Ross)
Co-publisher credit from RAYBIRD MUSIC. Reprinted by
Permission.

Their flushed faces laughed and smiled as the desert danced in waves of heat around us. With the sun pouring warmth like golden tarnish over the stark scenery, we pushed on as the scent of desert flowers blew in through our open windows. Here and there a tall saguaro sporting red fruit in bunches, pushed its dark green limb upward. From inside the car, heat was only a perception as we flew by, our happy mood overriding mundane things such as temperature. We came down out of the hilly portion of our ride where suddenly we could see everything all at once, including the horizon. We were now driving on the desert floor with no curves, contours, twists or bends. It was flat as far as we could see, blinding light fluttering in waves of heat on the road in front of us.

We joined the controlled chaos of a freeway. After an hour of high speed, we entered a large metropolis, culture shock of the highest degree.

Still hearing the flexible rhythms of the jazz singer's smooth voice in my head, Viola pulled the car in front of a single-story red brick building and parked. We dropped off Sister Lorna, right on time for her therapy appointment.

Tucson means "At the Bottom of Black Hill" because it is adjacent to volcanic mountain. It is second largest city in Arizona, behind Phoenix. It is the economic, political, and cultural center of the region filled with a concentration of people and businesses and/or development—a city where we were surrounded by an agglomeration of complex buildings, traffic; busses, taxis and cars: it's been some time since I heard the squealing of brakes; I hadn't missed it.

As a developing town with an expanding community, I should have felt more confident walking into the modern office to meet my new dentist. He baffled me. Dr. Dales looked more like a country vet who had just returned from a difficult birthing than a dentist. His tanned muscular forearms were evidence of the many hours he spent outside; his sun-lightened hair confirmed it. Thin lines radiating whiteness around his watchband stood out in contrast with his tan. I was relieved seeing how smooth and non-calloused his hands were. These were the hands of a pianist on the body of a farm hand.

I pressed back against the chair as he approached.

"Now, there's nothing to it," Dr. Dales said in his best reassuring voice. I forced myself to hold still, but dentist offices are like airport terminals, they house agitated energy. I'd always envied people who could stay relaxed under these circumstances. I certainly wasn't one of them.

Dr. Dales bent over my shoulder while he daintily fingered instruments on my teeth, probing, picking and pawing his way around in my mouth. He had outdoorsy physique that made it easy to imagine him ministering barnyard animals. Maybe to him I was just another animal that splintered a back molar when I picked up a nail with a mouthful of grass. I kept telling myself, if he worked on the sister's teeth, he must be licensed. I made sure a point to check his diploma on my way out, to make sure it wasn't from Tucson Veterinary College though.

With an instrument shaped like the neck of a pelican hanging from my mouth, he started up a one-sided conversation describing the many dentistry inventions he was working on, 'on the side.' I listened inattentively, nodding my head in a general approval at anything he said. I wasn't about to dampen his hopeful entrepreneurial expectancy while he was fashioning my tooth with a drill.

"Tongues", he said confidentially, "contain germs and diseases that are likely to transmit microorganisms." Dr. Dales was sure that preventative dentistry was marketable. As he contorted his body to work on my teeth, he told me confidentially, he had invented a small brush to use for cleaning the tongue. This convinced me that his 'on the side' really meant 'on the side of a stall' because the idea for a brush for a tongue wouldn't take a great deal of thought to invent, knowing how rough and sandpapery the surface of a cow's tongue is.

I ran my tongue over the roof of my mouth and hoped my tasting organ looked pink and healthy. With my face anxious and worried, I wondered if he had inspected it for signs of foot-and-mouth disease while he was in there.

It took the length of the appointment, but I had finally rid my mind of the images of livestock and barnyard animals.

Saving the best for last, at the close of my visit, he informed me, "I would like to take out your two remaining wisdom teeth. Let's do that next time. It'll give you something to look forward to." With a feeling of helplessness, I felt like one of his lambs being led to the slaughter."

On one hand, it meant another long trip into Tucson talking and sharing; on the other, en route I would be miserable, filled with the dreadful expectancy of another fearful visit trying to hold my mouth open as he angled his pliers at a back molar. One thing was for sure, I wasn't about to jump out and close the gate for him when I left his farm, otherwise known as his office.

Spotting the sister's white car in the parking lot I was glad to be outside away from the medicinal odor in the office and breathing the clean, dry, smog-free air of a city with few freeways.

I opened the back door and slid in the seat next to a subdued Sister Lorna. I wondered how her therapy session went but not wanting to pry, didn't ask.

Viola pushed on the accelerator and we were off with a lurch. I was looking forward to the return trip home through the countryside. On our way, with my mouth deadened with Novocain, I was content just to sit and look out the window at the smiling faces of the desert flowers we were passing, and wondered if they knew how lucky they were they didn't have to floss.

CHAPTER

16

"We already live in the desert. For heaven's sake, why would we want *more* time alone?" I soon found out it had its' advantages. On selected Sundays, I learned we were given 'Hermit Days' to use any way we wanted within reason. They were days for readjusting our emotional balance and physical stamina if we needed, free time for catching up on cleaning, letter writing, mending or taking extra naps and relaxing with no time restraints until Vespers. The sisters could also use these days for taking hikes, putting miles of space between them and the other members for a break. To my knowledge there is no precise scientific statistic as to when someone might snap, but being with the same people all the time could start to get on a person's nerves. These 'mental health' days (always a Sunday) helped to keep us from losing balance. These times apart caused noticeable changes in each each individual and raised the morale of the entire community.

Designated hermit days began after the office of Lauds with Mass, and lasted until Vespers, about 10:00 AM to 4:00 PM. We were still obligated to recite the office, but we didn't have to be in the chapel, we could read it outside under a tree, or on top of a hill overlooking the expanse of the desert, or in the quiet of an empty novitiate if we wanted. Where we recited the office was up to us, but it should be said as close to the usual times as possible.

I had my routine down pat. After Mass, the first thing I did was head straight to the kitchen. It was a free day for food too, food that was placed out on the kitchen counter for us, that is. It was *first come, first served* so when it was gone, and it was gone. It was always a mouth watering surprise to see donated goods among our usual staples, even if the donation was only a package of hot-dogs. A Hermit Day was a day for filling in missing nutrients our bodies might be craving, if any.

My second activity was sleeping. Getting up everyday so early would make anyone want to go back to bed! I couldn't wait, it would feel *so* good, my hands tucked under my bunched pillow, my covered feet thawing and I'd spend an inordinate amount of time stretching.

The desert mornings usually left my body a little chilled, even with heat blowing in from above, so after I finished my large brunch, I would drag my full stomach to my bedroom and start to insulate myself against the cold by putting on my two pairs of flannel pajamas and two sets of socks which I tucked into my maroon knit slippers. I wrapped myself in a heavy blue cotton bath robe, tied at the middle, and as the piece de resistance, I pulled a red knit ski hat tightly over my head like I had added a cherry; I looked like a proprietor of a used clothing store that had a limited rack-space problem; I knew no one would see me as I warmed.

Entombed in my bed with all the extra blankets I had, I could hardly move, yet all the bundling was worth the comfy heated feeling. Warm and full, I would feel so comfortable I would immediately fall into a deep sleep, until…

As the sun continued to rise, so did the temperature and corresponding heat inside my room. In my sleep, I knew I was too hot and was overheating. Fiercely, my eyes strained against the lids trying their best to open. With a Herculean effort I would pull myself out of my sound sleep to a sitting position, using every ounce of will and strength I had.

After reaching the full wakeful state, I would then grab the curtain cord and yank open the drapes and before I knew what I had done, bright sunlight flooded my room with all the intensity of a solar flare, blinding my already aching eyes. I never learned that just because I fell asleep in a cold and dark room, it didn't mean it would stay that way.

As the mercury in my room soared, so did my body temperature until I was at the point of spontaneously combusting. If there is anything worse than waking up drenched in perspiration, I don't know what it could be. If the shadow self wanted to contact me, these would have been the perfect times. Moving through alpha, beta, and theta rhythms was completely and utterly draining, both physically and emotionally, as I forced my eyes open even though I was still asleep! The next day I could feel the strain in my eyes. It would last all day like I had been looking at the end of my nose for several minutes.

Successfully pulling my body from a sound sleep to an alert upright sitting position took an enormous amount of strength. And after I pulled myself awake, I'd spend the next day wondering how I did it. Going from a sound sleep to wakefulness, like in dreams, may have messages from the beyond and kept trying to find the right message for me: be ever on the alert, don't let an unguarded moment go by, don't lose sight of my purpose. What *was* my shadow self trying to tell me?

Or was it a simple message coming from my overheated subconscious warning, 'any numskull would know better than to load her body under a hundred pounds of clothing then fall asleep?'

Awake and very overheated, off came the red knit ski hat, off flew the long blue robe, off went my flannel pajamas, pairs of socks and maroon slippers, until I lay on the bed in my thermals like a human vaporizer steaming as the hot condensation from my body met the cooler air in the bedroom.

This was the way I began every Hermit Day.

CHAPTER

17

I had been here for some time now and felt I had settled into the schedule nicely: Vigils, classes, music lessons, Masses and meals; all with the background of Lorna's crying. It was impossible to tell when she'd erupt and burst into tears. God really was testing how well I learned *custody of the eyes*.

But I was still learning the ins and outs of monastic life, like being allowed to speak on car trips, keeping myself awake during Vigils by pinching myself, or not looking with envy on someone's new sandals across the choir. I was astonished learning a married couple, staying in the guest house, had been given permission to prepare a special meal for us. It would be a treat for the whole community.

I couldn't believe it, first it was Uncle Van visiting, now this? Great!

Since we were off beaten track, special arrangements like this ~~didn't happen very often~~ never happened. People didn't usually just wander through; they had to know the monastery and/or the retreat center were here. The out-of-the-way guest house was an inviting place to make a retreat but because of our isolation, a retreat here was a genuine adventure. The number of hearty individuals willing to make the journey into ~~their heart~~ the heart of the desert was few. In a very real sense struggling toward personal integration and spiritual growth here was not for the faint of heart because of the aloneness, the heat, and the elements. It also depended on whether the roads had been washed out.

I went through the week wondering what dish the couple would prepare. Would it be real Italian spaghetti with French bread dripping with garlic butter with peach parfaits for dessert? Or homemade tamales with rice and refried beans that included spicy hot salsa? Or sauerbraten marinated in vinegar soaked in sour cream and spices? Or highly seasoned bratwurst with special mustard? Why, it could be anything! I looked forward to enjoying their gourmet dish with gusto. My mouth was already watering.

It was Wednesday at the best time of the day: mealtime. We were seated around the refectory table for dinner smiling. Reverend Mother, tapping a spoon against her water glass, announced—today was the day. A mouth-watering swoon went up from around the table. We were all ~~hoping it wasn't zucchini~~ anxious to experience their special dish.

I watched in expectation as the side door opened and the two visiting cooks entered carrying a large pot filled with some sort of exotic gastronomic fare and placed it on the stove. They fiddled in silence over the pot with salt shakers and herbs stirring in last minute seasonings like proud parents. I couldn't place the aroma. It was not spicy or pungent, but it smelled good nonetheless.

When at last it met with their approval they walked from the stove to the priests' table in the alcove so they could see our gratified expressions as we sampled their savory meal.

Reverend Mother said grace. Out of politeness, she motioned the cooks to serve themselves first and we watched with anticipation as they dipped a large ladle into the pot filling their soup bowls in one try. They were positively beaming when they took their seats. Mac was next. They were now in a position to monitor our expressions closely as we ate. They genuinely wanted to share their special course with the sisters who'd think they'd died and gone to heaven when they tasted such flavorful food.

Since I was the newest novice, I was first in line. Walking all the way around the long refectory table, I tried to distinguish an aroma that would give me an indication of what was in the pot. Closing in on the pot, I still wasn't able to detect a thing; maybe that should have told me something.

Using a pot holder, I eagerly lifted the lid revealing a light brown sauce. Whatever what was underneath was hidden. Picking up the ladle, I plunged it deep into the steaming liquid. Bringing it to the surface, to my amazement, I saw it contained bubbling onions! It was *onion soup!* There were big ones and little ones, some where the size of pearls and some as big as golf balls stewing in their own juice!

Assuming it was a delicacy somewhere in the world, I thought, here goes nothing and tilted the mixture in my bowl trying my best to keep an 'it looks delicious' expression on my face for the cooks' benefit. *Well, it could have been worse,* I encouraged myself. *It could have been liver.*

Staring at the mixture as I walked to my place, I couldn't help being amazed at some many concentric edible bulbs sitting amid fleshy transparent coverings. I never knew there were so many sizes of onions: pea size, marble, and ping-pong ball dimensions. I was grateful I wouldn't be the last person serving herself and be left with the heaviest onions the size of golf balls.

I kept a poker face as I walked. The community would have to wait till they scooped through the iridescent spots covering the thin skin on top to see what was in store for them.

I have always been a lover of onions, the stronger the better; onions in tuna with mayonnaise, onions alone on a wedge of cheese, onions diced into just about everything. I was really looking forward to my first mouthful of unusual ~~broth consommé bouillabaisse~~ chowder. The first spoonful *was* good and I smiled my approval across the room along with an appreciative thumbs-up.

It was after about the fifth mouthful I started having trouble. It wasn't long before I realized I had already reached my onion limit. At some point into an onion meal, the very thought of so many still to be eaten, is enough to turn the stomach. I looked at the other novices, who I noticed, were taking their own sweet time bringing their spoons to their mouths as well. In fact, we all were.

Not wanting to be wasteful, I ate as much as I could . Seeing a quick and inconspicuous hand sign from Esmeralda meaning 'wait', we stopped eating and started pushing the onions around in our bowls trying to make the meal last longer, like we were actually enjoying the food. (The sign for 'wait' had a variety of meanings: remain, endure, rest, to name a few; in this case it meant *'leave'* what you can't eat.

I suppose it was the right thing to do, but in the back of my mind were nagging doubts. Should I force myself to eat the remaining onions in my bowl? Then again, making yourself sick wasn't spiritual either. What was the spiritual way to act? This was what I was pondering as I sat pushing my discarded lumps of the now sickening tasting globosity around with my spoon. I was waiting courteously for the visiting cooks to leave before getting up. I didn't want to insult them by letting them see me making my way to the table in back to fill up on peanut butter and bread.

Spiritual lessons are learned in a variety of ways. This was why I entered the monastery in the first place, to work *my way free of all ties in this life*, paraphrasing Saint Basil. I saw the abbey as a place I could train spiritually while focusing on self-discovery and personal evolution. I couldn't remember reading anything about onions, though.

After a respectable amount of time, I got up and carried my dishes to the kitchen. Wiping my plate off in a trash can, I remembered gluttony was one of the seven deadly sins, but *wasting* food is just as bad. As the last onion rolled on top of the heap, as humbling as it was, because I chose to discard perfectly good food rather than eat the remaining onions in my bowl, I realized I was in no position to judge the spiritual behaviors in others. It was a hard lesson.

CHAPTER

18

Huge black and yellow bumblebees heralded spring in an ominous fashion. Three times the size of regular bees, I was ducking and dodging frantically, until Sister Lorna explained their interest was in my head was my hair color. They were seeking nectar by flying close checking to see if I was a flower, finding none, they'd whiz, unperturbed, on their way. Their deliberate flight from flower to flower, including me, looked like a living cartoon, and it was easy to imagine intermittent black lines penned by an animator marking their trails as they circled and looped through the garden. Because they were a lumbering kind of a bee and didn't fly in squadrons, I lost my fear of them and held still when they were skimming my hair in their touch and go flight patterns.

Warm spring weather thawed the ground, and with it, every conceivable insect known to inhabit a desert environment thawed too. The most unusual was a type of cricket that sounded like a firework spinning slowly at first, grow in intensity, and fizzle out like they needed to be re-ignited. As soon as one stopped, another would start, so there were always a few buzzing from their hiding places in weeds all day long.

The garden became a living kaleidoscope of color. While I was watering, I'd rest alongside a wire fence draped with twisting morning-glories and climbing sweet peas letting my eyes blur in the prismatic rainbow refractions and watch monarch and tiger swallowtail butterflies collide in their eagerness. When I looked at large circular round heads of gigantic sunflowers capturing the sun, filled with hundreds of seeds growing on rough, hairy stems, it felt like the whole garden was giving birth.

Sister Lorna came alive also with all the new activity also with few hands to help; organizing, planting, weeding and watering, it was more than a full time job. As it was, she spent both work periods here, plus numerous trips climbing up and down the hill to change the sprinklers. Not having enough food to last through the next winter was a real concern. As if the picture of our starved and wasting bodies loomed always in her mind, she bore the responsibility of keeping food on the table as a high priority.

Maybe it was due to the increase of summer work, but Sister Lorna's weeping bouts became few and far between. It didn't happen all at once, one day I realized her crying had stopped altogether. Mentioning this excellent development to her in signs (long time, no cry), she tilted her head in thought for a second, pointed a finger at me and said, "You're right!" and smiled. Without using signs, she said, "You know I never used to cry like this; the abbess would never have allowed it," and from the tone in her voice, I had the feeling there was a lot of truth in the statement.

It was a relief being in the garden with someone with whom I had friendly rapport. Even though I knew it was against the rules, I encouraged Lorna to speak and in no time we didn't go through all the trouble of even pretending to make signs. Because we were out of earshot from the monastery, down the steep hill, we talked freely. In a monastery of strict observance flaunting the rules made me feel guilty because I was the one who encouraged her start talking in the first place but I did so hoping it would make her feel better and she'd stop crying. Rationalizing it this way made me feel better but I still knew speaking was wrong. Sister Lorna being a willing story teller didn't help matters.

Getting her to talk was so easy; something I learned having my habit made in my dress making session. Asking a leading question such as "Were things much harder back then?" could branch out in a hundred different directions. I knew back in the good ol' days it wasn't just harder it was a *hundred* times worse prompting the saying—*"the good ol' days", may they never come again"*, I'd heard more than once.

She sat in the dirt with obvious relief as if she deserved a long break for all she'd been through. Glancing around to see if anyone was listening, she told me about the time she was in motherhouse in the East coast. "You don't know what strict is," she said, leaning on the hoe for support. "This monastery is a cake walk compared to how hard we had to work there. Life was different back then," different meaning stricter, I knew. Doing her darnedest to convince me in a serious tone, she widened her eyes saying emphatically, "There is no comparison!

"How would you like to see your relatives through a heavy wire mesh?" she asked, watching for my reaction.

"That depends on the relatives," I smiled, letting her see the lighter side of a painful experience, hoping she wouldn't start crying again.

"The mandatory fasting might be the worst part," she said remembering. "It was quite severe during seasonal times of the year. One piece of unbuttered toast for breakfast, ONE," she said sucking in her cheeks for a gaunt effect. "That's all. I can remember sisters fainting from hunger, but I never did," making sure I knew she wasn't a lightweight. This fact hadn't escaped me, not with about twenty years already under her belt. She was one of the pillars of the community.

"It's probably hard for you to believe, but our workload used to be much harder than it is here. One time I actually fell asleep in the chapel…"

"Oh, I believe it," I said. If I had learned anything during my time here, it was how incredibly hard Trappistines worked, each Sister willing to put hand to plow in a moment's notice, which may have literally been the truth in Sister Lorna's case.

"It's incredible when I think about it, everything changed within a matter of months. Back then we either entered as a choir-sister or a lay-sister; the choir-sisters chanted the office; and the lay-sisters did most of the physical work. I entered as a lay-sister," she confessed while looking beyond the garden for anyone near to hear us talking. "I didn't have a contemplative temperament but was made to chant the Office and it just wasn't me. I knew milking machines, not contemplation," she said, indignant over the loss of her calling. "It was a shame. My vocation disappeared from under me," she said, her voice trailing away like the horizon she was staring at.

For the first time I understood her deep sadness. It *was* tragic; I would cry too if the lifestyle I loved was pulled out from under me through no fault of my own and replaced with the guarantee it was *for my own good.* I wondered how many other sisters this new change affected, and if the Superiors knew how much pain it caused when they phased out the 'working' vocation of the lay-sister *for everyone's good.*

I had a good taste of monastic chanting by now. It is not divided by bars in the manner of modern music, its rhythm is not indicated by time signatures, such as 4/4 and 6/8. Chant has a flexible and irregular rhythm that closely follows that of Biblical texts. Knowing how difficult it is to learn, I felt for her, I was almost at a hopeless state myself."Novices today have it so easy," she said again. Her easy-going tone was replaced with a serious intensity as she told me about the dreaded Chapter of Faults. Even the name has a sinister ring to it bringing to mind hair shirts, girding ones' loins, or sleeping on the floor without blankets as a way of punishing oneself.

Before entering I made it a point to learn all I could about monasteries. My eyes opened wider recalling Rumer Godden's novel *In This House of Bred* and her realistic description of the toil, short sleeps, and scant food at times of cloistered Benedictine nuns. I read how it was customary for the monks of Saint Benedict to gather for the "Chapter of faults" where members were both corrected for infractions against the community's rule or accuse themselves of their faults and receive a penance for offenses. Either way, it didn't sound like fun. Lorna threw up her hands impatiently. "Coming clean about your faults with Sister Drusilla in the privacy of her office is nothing like the public confessions I had to go through. How would you like to get up in front of the entire community and tell everyone what you've done wrong during the week?" It's not easy, let me tell you."

She was right, my acknowledging offenses during private meetings with the Novice Director, is nothing compared to her public admissions of wrongdoings, however slight. This long-standing monastic practice, a lesson in humility, has survived as "Is there any misconduct you would like to tell me?" My daily missions to the Novice Director are, in my humble opinion, much better. But really, how many wrongdoings could I commit in a monastery? Not that I was perfect, but the faults I committed were so minor they didn't seem like faults at all—breaking Sister Lorna's favorite hoe in my zest to weed; being late for Mass because I was scraping mud off my shoes so I wouldn't leave tracks on the carpet in the chapel; compiling a how-to meditate handbook for newcomers.

It didn't take long before I discovered *admitting* faults wasn't as hard as coming up with new ones. I felt I should disclose at least one a day, or else I would look like an arrogant snob. Maybe I was. Is this confessable?

In the privacy of the garden with only tall winter rye grass hiding us, we would talk about work as usual, but then the subjects would branch out. If there is any consolation to breaking this rule, it was in knowing at least we kept most of our talking to religious/spiritual matters and didn't stray *too* far off course.

Holding a hoe tightly to her breast like a security blanket, she asked, "So you think trying to find transgressions is difficult here? Try attending a *Chapter of Faults.*" Grimacing, she recalled an incident that happened back in the *good old days* when monastic life was much stricter.

It was during our ride to Tucson and we were allowed to talk that I learned about her original monastery. It was founded by a group of Irish nuns who set the high standard for monastic life in America. As the first Cistercians nuns in the United States, they grew to about 50 nuns, Lorna included. As she was describing life back then, time and time again, the word severity came up in context with penance, self-sacrificing and mortification. It didn't sound fun.

Crouching in the bean patch I was weeding, I listened as she proved her point.

"Know that whenever someone was taking the blame, it wasn't easy to do, so these exercises were conducted in the deeply thoughtful and serious atmosphere of self-reflection.

On this one occasion the entire community had gathered and we were waiting quietly in the large church. In those days we were more formal. We had to go up one-by-one. The confessing sister would walk to the main aisle in front of the church where prostrations took place. I could feel the tension and sat fidgeting in my seat. When it was my turn, I got up and lay in my ankle length black and white habit, arms out from each side; face down on the tile in front of all the sisters. I then declared my shortcomings of the past week. This public humiliation was supposed to be a deterrent to help with backsliding during the coming week."

"With my chin still on a tile, I came to my last sin, one that was personally embarrassing so I resisted telling about it." With a trace of a smile, she told me she had to admit to the others she was guilty of the sin of vanity because while she was alone in the barn, she weighed herself on the animal scale and confessed weighing 137 pounds."

She told me she heard the muffled laughter of the sisters from around the church in a quivering ripple of giggling. I could almost see the sisters shooting her flitting glances of disbelief and chuckling to themselves as they pictured her trying to get an accurate reading of her weight on the scale. There didn't seem to be any embarrassment on her part recalling the incident. In fact, she acted happy she had a funny story to tell me.

The gardener wasn't finished yet and continued recounting the memory. She said she was through accusing herself, she got up and went back to her place on the pew, repentant after owning up to her wrongs.

She said when the next sister came forward and was admitting her failings Lorna sat brooding as remorse took hold of her. The more she thought about what she had done, a growing guilt took over in the form of the seemingly unpardonable sin of lying. She had failed to reveal what had been truly bothering her conscience during her first prostration. But was it worth getting up and going through the whole ordeal again on the same day or should she leave well enough alone?

It was a losing battle. Her conscience getting the better of her, she felt compelled to go back and totally clear her conscience by setting the record straight. This time as she lay prostrate, she confessed to falsifying her first confession; instead of just the sin of vanity, she was also guilty of lying because instead of weighing 137 pounds, the scale really read 147!

She said the sister's stifled smirks exploded into gales of uncontrolled hilarity as the church erupted in loud, boisterous laughter. I didn't think she cared if anyone around could hear her or not and laughed with abandon stopping only to wipe her eyes.

I put my trowel to the side. It was hard making out her words as she fumbled to get her meaning across while gasping for air. She whacked the dirt with her hoe in exasperation and admitted when it was over, she was glad that, once and for all, she had set record straight.

Holding her sides, she relaxed in a slump on the dirt and went on telling me the first person she saw when she pushed herself from the floor, was the red face of the abbess, Reverend Mother Seraphina, trying to control her own laughter. Laughing as she told me, she said when she was walking back to her pew she heard the low forgiving voice of the abbess say to her kidding, "I think the second one took."

It must have, because here was Sister Lorna years later, hoeing happily, talking freely, accumulating the very actions she should report to Reverend Mother, maybe not today, but as soon as her conscience gets the better of her, because old habits died hard.

As I watched her now, swinging her hoe erratically at a bee, I guessed her weight to be about the same.

CHAPTER

19

From the earthiness of the garden to the sanctity of the spirit, even in the midst of the unvarying schedule and monotony in the monastery, I never knew what to expect.

One afternoon I learned Father Wyss, Uncle Van, was coming back to visit! The experienced retreat director guiding us spiritually would once again be giving us a weeks' retreat to aid in our spiritual growth. When he wasn't giving us talks, as a writer, his free time would be spent working on a book in the uninterrupted quiet of the guest house.

Uncle Van, as a frequent visitor, was seasoned in the practice of contemplation, and valued silence and solitude as much as the sisters did. And from all the excited preparations from cleaning to baking, I knew the priest was one of the sisters' favorite visitors and were really looking forward to his company. *Any* company here was exciting, but as Reverend Mother Esmeralda put it, "His reflective talks' will be like a burst of oxygen. Plus, he brings news of current events." Mac kept us abreast of major news stories, but there was only so much room in his daily homilies during Mass for news bulletins.

Father Wyss arrived midday in a taxi at the parlor door in a cloud of dust. He was greeted by the portress who checked him in before he climbed back in the taxi and was whisked to the retreat center, the one story trailer standing on it's own a few hundred feet away.

I watched from the refectory window as he unlocked the trailer and stagger inside with his suitcase. The next week would be highlighted by his retreat talks, morning and afternoon. A diversion! I couldn't wait!

It was late spring, sweater weather, and all the sisters were waiting in expectation in the chapel. Father Wyss walked in through the side door wearing a dark brown cardigan. I noticed again what a good looking man he was with soft facial features with wisps of brown hair hanging across his forehead. I was looking forward to hearing his beautiful accent again I found captivating. He stood at the podium gathering his thoughts before straightening up. Pointing a finger at us, he began: "The human heart is literally a mystery, unfortunately even to each one of us." His demeanor was calm and gentle, and his speech slow and thoughtful, as if he were receiving heartfelt and profound instructions from somewhere moment by moment that only he could hear.

I soon found listening to him could not be rushed, for his long pauses interspersed throughout, kept the listener at a very controlled pace. He distributed probing thoughts in scattered intervals that made it seem like he was absorbed with an inner listening and was intent on sharing exactly what he had heard (or felt). He wasn't about to settle for anything less than an accurate rendition. With his preoccupied and interruptive speech (or because of it), he summoned full attention.

Of course Uncle Van was invited to join us again for meals in the Community room which had been turned into a dining area for the duration of his stay. Out of politeness, we were allowed to speak openly and freely with him again, but only to him, not to each other. Like his first visit, he liked to give the new novice, me, a hard time with lighthearted kidding. He put me on the spot several times, but I was adept at redirecting his attention to the other novices to their discomfort.

Because of his many retreat visits, the sisters shared a comfortable and familial relationship with him. They assured him that he was really a Trappist at heart, instead of a Jesuit, and Uncle Van agreed. They took his good natured ribbing in stride. Tonight, Father Wyss entertained us with story after story of exciting travel adventures ranging from the back alleys of Burma, to the 1,500-mile-long Great Wall of China. His verbal travelogue took us through flooded rice paddies and rooms made of paper. We explored pagoda towers and met with Buddhists as he described the dark colored dress of the priests. He narrated places and territories that were each more exciting than the last, taking us out of the cloister and into foreign lands with his words. His descriptive accounts ranged from frightening to humorous, but were all entertaining.

Once he was detained in Communist China. Officials forced him to stay by himself in a small wooden detention-cabin that had a bed and nothing else. He told us how surprised he was the first morning to be awakened by something moving about his bed. Opening his eyes, he saw the biggest rat he had ever seen staring back at him not a yard away. "Some welcome!" he joked. "Ach, mein Gott!" he thought. Horrified, he knew these large rats could be vicious, he lay rigid, not wanting to startle it into action. He told us he very slowly took hold of a wooden crate from beside his bed to try and capture it. After much chasing about and many failed attempts, he said he finally trapped it, but it had not been without a fight. Uncle Van said that to this day the fear of these creatures has never left him. With his next breath, he brought it to the sisters' attention he could hear the definite sound of scurrying at night in the quest house. He gave a shudder as he thought little creatures were sharing his quarters.

The very next day the sisters formed a rat brigade and descended on the guest house ready to eradicate the field mice with traps, snares, poison and buckets. The sisters assured Uncle Van that the buckets half-filled with water would lure the critters in for a drink, and providing no means of escape, would drown. His apoplectic look showing what he thought of the sister's fool proof method for rat removal needed no translation; "Ach du lieber!"

It was refreshing having another activity added to our day. After Mass, I was an enthusiastic listener when Uncle Van gave retreat talks to the community, including our priest, Father Macintosh. The visiting retreat director used quotes taken from one of his books, *The Call From Beyond*, enlightening us with his spiritual expertise.

Our retreat had begun: *It happens almost without our knowledge. A reorientation sets in, and from a state of confusion, we step into a territory which is clearer to our mind. We begin to see a connection with God which we did not see before, and we start to arrange our priorities. We move certain things away from our center so that a free space develops which allows God to come into our heart if He so decides. God can never be forced.*
(Long pause.)

It was a pleasure listening to his beautiful accent. He was born and raised in Vienna, Austria, and had been a teacher, missionary, interpreter, spiritual director, culminating in author. But to me, he was a retreat director par excellence. Granted, my experience in listening to directors and Jesuits was very limited, but I could tell from his ability to make me think and ponder his meanings, he was a great teacher. He left us with a parting thought—*God connects Silence with Knowledge.*
(Long pause.)

Every afternoon we would rearrange our chairs across the front of the chapel facing the altar and Father Wyss, looking very dapper in his dark turtle neck sweater would stand at the podium. His daily talks invited us to enter his quiet world of wordless prayer in the form of extended pauses in a style uniquely his own. When his long pauses started, I thought he was waiting for someone to settle in their seat or he had taken ill. It finally dawned on me these quiet times were intentionally spaced so we could integrate parts of his talks. Because this unifying was left to each of us, it felt like a very personal retreat experience; he didn't run interference or conveniently pull the ends together in neat little denouements; he let us come to our own conclusions.

I knew this had to be the sign of a good retreat director. Without realizing how, I was on spiritually deeper levels that were previously inaccessible to me. Father Wyss made this possible with his *thinking* intervals, giving us time to 'ponder' what he had just said. His style didn't bombard with words, but with quiet times. I didn't write everything he said in a journal; I didn't check out his references; there was no assigned reading involved. Therewas no busy work involved at all. He wanted what he said to sink into us and develop our spirituality.

In Stillness, I find God; with Inner Stillness, I allow God to find me.
(Long pause)

Uncle Van followed through with examples of daily reflections that could be both practical and prayerful. He encouraged each one of us to look at our past, face our hurts, sorrows and pain, to become whole again. He explained that our trials were graced moments. In his words; "What do we learn when everything is going right? Nothing."

He didn't overcome us with loudness and pride, but allowed us to search deeper into our inner stillness in a very personal way, profound way. We were nurtured and nudged by his authentic spirit. His wordless intervals allowed a deepening awareness of God's presence and let we participate in his patience and even temperament of a man practicing what he preached. Because he was prayerful, centered and disciplined, it was easy to feel connected to him. He knew God could never be forced into our hearts.

Nothing in creation is so like God as Stillness.
(Very long pause)

As the days went by, it was with regret that his writing sabbatical came to an end, and so did our retreat. We were saddened to say good-bye to his retreat talks, scholarly insights and his absorbing discourses that never sidestepped his spiritual prowess. But most of all we'd would miss his gentle humor and kindred spirit. He had pushed our dormant spirituality. No wonder the sisters cherished his time with them.

He left us with one final thought to hold us until his return and assured us he would be back again next winter for he loved the Trappistine solitude and silence. And the Trappistines! His parting thought—

In silence I temper my tongue,…in stillness I temper my heart.
(End retreat.)

On the final day of his retreat, I was surprised to see an envelope lying on the end of my bed; it's the way the mail is distributed. It was a letter was from one of my sisters and a welcome sight because it represented beaches, palm trees, and familiar locales. I was excited.

Unfortunately it also brought back visits from my father's friend, John Barleycorn who caused so much disruption. To an outsider my family looked like a perfectly happy bunch and we were happy, but it wasn't perfect. Seeing the letter, brought it all back, the moving, the new schools, and I almost forgot, the obstinate refusal to acknowledge he had a drinking problem. But since all that was behind me, it didn't matter now.

Before leaving home, I mentioned all the novices have their letters screened by the Novice Director. With this in mind, I devised a plan with one of my sisters. Not knowing how thoroughly my belongings would be screened when I arrived, I asked her to send a sheet of paper with numerous holes cut at random and keep a duplicate copy so she could align my letters with hers and decode my messages by reading only the words showing in the holes. It will be a secret way of transmitting messages without the people in authority knowing… if I needed to be rescued. It was an ingenious idea and the fact I would be pulling something over on, namely the Novice Director, made it worth it the risk.

Sitting on my bed, I opened the letter. Out fell the sheet containing the holes. The problem was, she cut *way* too many holes and she had to fill most of them in with doodles and hand drawn pictures for my messages to make any sense. My return letter with pencil sketches throughout filling in the excess spaces looked ridiculously like this:

Theorists might postulate my sister was suffering from adolescent anxieties.

Father Macintosh might minister, "Pray for the sinner and do penance for her."

Uncle Van might teach, "Stillness is the reality of life; she must learn to still her heart."

Saint Benedict might correct with, "For the minor fault of picture-gram communicating, the sister should be kept from eating at the common table."

But I could hear my father's incessant need for privacy and keeping the outside world out with, "Shut the #*@ %$#+ gull darned door!"

It seemed I was not the only person in my family who needed lessons in trust.

CHAPTER

20

The wit and wisdom of Uncle Van was followed by the introduction of the latest member of our novitiate, Sister Dolores. Short, about five feet tall and a little stocky with straight black shoulder length hair. She wore thick convex lenses that looked like they had been taken off the bottoms of Coke bottles set in a black frame. She stood poised and self-confident in front of the community in the refectory fielding questions. If she was asked something, her answers were long and verbose, sometimes giving three or four possible answers to the same question. Her talkativeness was a welcome change from the practiced silence of the others, but it was in total opposition to Uncle Van: he made sure we had intervals of quiet; Dolores made sure we did not. When we were introduced by Reverend Mother Esmeralda, she was leaning against a hard wooden refectory chair like it was a cane, squinting her way around the refectory at each of us like a female Mr. Magoo.

I remember going through this introductory etiquette. I remember feeling out of place standing in front of everyone and how I wanted to reach in and grab a handful of chocolate chip cookies instead of just one from the tin being passed around in welcome, but holding back to show my good manners. I recalled my relief when I found there *were* certain times we *could* talk, and how regularly 'not talking' made the talking times feel *very, very, special.* Getting to know Dolores was one of these special speaking times. As I watched her becoming acquainted, I knew it hadn't been just dumb luck that brought her here; if anything, it was smart luck. It made me happy that out of all the people in the world, I too, had been chosen to be part of this special family.

Dolores was about thirty years old (a few years older than I), and like Sister Dorothy, the new novice had transferred from a semi-active order because she wanted to experience the hard core spiritual life of a Trappistine lifestyle.

The new novice enjoyed talking. I could easily picture her in a quilting bee gossiping about this and that, pretending to be shocked by a juicy piece of scandalous hearsay; relaying reasons why she knew the sensational account was true. She was a archivist with her previous order. Reading literature and studying well into the night could explain her myopia. When she was asked what type of work she saw herself doing in the monastery, she admitted she didn't enjoy working with her hands. In fact, she once took a dexterity test to see what occupation she was suited for. She looked at her feet and told us with a mumble, the test results showed her area of expertise is a professional dog walker! We all broke out laughing, including Dolores. I could see her handling dogs by the patient way she answering questions. But a dog *walker*, no way. She was too small; a 200 pound Mastiff could drag her anywhere it wanted.

Her speech was nimble and covered so much ground getting her points across she turned this question and answer session into mostly listening to her answers. Excessive talking can be a sign of nervousness, but knowing alcohol loosens the tongue, if it wasn't her nerves, my second guess would be she'd been nipping at the cooking sherry. Considering the amount of physical labor involved in 'active contemplation,' I thought it a shame she wasn't as adroit with her hands as she was with her tongue. During this whole getting acquainted session, I wondered if anyone else was thinking what I was thinking. Why would someone who obviously liked to talk so much, and took great delight in being listened to, want to enter an order where speaking isn't permitted? In any case, we welcomed her wholeheartedly, because it was refreshing having someone take the initiative for a change, not to mention, having another novice meant our workload decreased.

Outside the windows, a group of concurring crows cawed in unison like they were agreeing with me as they flew by.

Sitting around the refectory table listening to her abundant supply of words, reminded me of my father's love of words too, only his were administered one at a time, and not in long-winded discourses; funny how things pop into your mind.

He knew the value of a good vocabulary. I remembered how he introduced an interesting new word on a small blackboard to teach us each day. Thinking back, it was an excellent way of increasing our vocabulary. We watched as a display of miscellaneous words gallivanted capriciously through our lives like a living lexicon: Placate—to appease. Enigma—a mystery or a puzzle baffling the understanding. Indubitably—too evident to be doubted or questioned. Delectable—delightful or delicious. Enervate—to deprive of strength, force or vigor. Copacetic—excellent, first-rate. My thinking was interrupted when Esmeralda passed a tin full of maple bars around.

Peering into the container, I thought how whenever possible, my father worked the new words into a sentence. If he was here now, he might say: "It's not an enigma any longer; things are copasetic, we *are* having a delectable dessert tonight, indubitably!"

Many times I wanted to play him at his own game and write my own words I *knew* weren't in his vocabulary. Words like sobriety, abstinence and self-*control*. As I listened to the new novice, I thought, it's no *enigma* I never added any of my words to his blackboard to placate a sense of fairness because they held absolutely no meaning for him. It wouldn't have done any good, and boy, was it enervating!

Novice number twelve was as excited to be here as I was. Sister Dolores in her years with her other community had read and studied about contemplation and knew the full scope of the hardships of the Cistercian lifestyle in preparation for her momentous transfer; silence during meals, silence during work, silence between one another, silence all the time. Not to mention the approvals she needed to relocate from one community to another was no small accomplishment, the permissions, signatures and dispensations. It showed she meant business.

There are no practical manuals telling how to cope not just with silence, but with trying to hold a glass cutter in a hand blistered from hoeing, or eating a food that is personally repugnant, or how to draw from an inner reservoir of will to force a climb out of bed at 3:15 every morning. Reading objectively about this lifestyle is like entering events in a journal or drawing a caricature of the experience. Reading and writing about it is very different from actually doing it.

Events around the monastery were sure to be different with her added intellect and energy. I wondered what Dolores would think if Sister Lorna started crying. More importantly, could she sing as well as she spoke. But most of all I wondered what would happen next winter, when Uncle Van's yang met her yin.

As time passed we found Dolores was intelligent, caring, and full of sisterly love. What she lacked in dexterity she made up in perseverance; another fine quality to add to her abbess-worthy resume. She never gave up. Dolores was so determined to find the right note during her choir practices I had to admire her resolve.

Sister Patty and I recoiled whenever we saw her reach for the door of the music room because we knew we were in for another rendition of "I'll find this note if it kills me" practice session. Even though the door was shut tight, her off-note squeals were enough to set one's teeth on edge, like all novices do learning he sing-song way of chanting. I knew she was doing the best she could, but knowing this only made it harder not burst out laughing. It was impossible to concentrate on the *Arizona Highways* magazine I was looking at the reading table because the table was directly across from the Music room. It was even harder not looking across the round table at Sister Patty, who was also doing her best to keep from laughing too.

The funny thing about avoiding eye contact with someone is, at some point the very act of avoidance becomes hilariously funny. If I happened to look up and catch Sister Patty's eyes, I saw the pained look of an animal pleading for mercy. The same look I'm sure I had. The more Dolores tried, the harder it was not to laugh. I usually ended up holding an open magazine in front of my face while Sister Patty hid her face in a sleeve. At the point her head was on the flat surface, there was no hope of either of us regaining control.

Occasionally, a sister would walk by and see us squirming uncomfortably at the reading table. One note from the music room answered all their puzzled looks. After what seemed like hours, the door of the music room would open slowly and Sister Dolores's head would timidly peek around scanning the hallway to see if the coast was clear. Patty would instantly become interested in something in the view. I wouldn't dare take my attention away from the engrossing article I was reading; it was a nonchalance we had plenty of opportunities to perfect. Confident her practicing hadn't disturbed any of the professed sisters, the diligent novice would step lightly on her way, slinking away like an alley cat that narrowly escaped being hit by a shoe.

When we were sure she was out of earshot, then, and only then, we regained our straight faces. It was easy to work up enthusiasm for her efforts. I never knew anyone so persistent. With so much practicing, in a short time she was already better at reading the modes than me. I wasn't too discouraged though, it turns out she was way ahead of me to begin with because she already knew how to read music. Standing directly across from her in choir, I was able to hear improve day by day.

She added a radically new dimension to the choir also, giving us an uncomfortable thrill during our normally calm meditation period. To help with meditation, to keep her back straight, she used a custom made prayer stool she brought from her former community, a little wooden bench without a cushion about eight inches high. (There were a couple prayer stools in the back of the chapel for anyone to use.) Sometimes the professed sisters used them because they were a big help keeping the back straight and the energy in our chakras flowing. We would see her carrying hers from location to location as she sometimes meditated in her bedroom, sometimes in the novitiate, and always during meditation periods in the chapel. Carrying it around like this gave me the impression she was a professional traveling prayer with her own business card: *have bench, will pray.*

Once, when no one was around, I tried one to see what it was like. I guided both my feet underneath the angled piece of wood and cautiously sat on the narrow seat. It did make it easier to keep my back straight but sitting precariously perched on an edge like a roosting bird, felt awkward. To me, the bench was more work than it was worth.

In the early hours, it is always a battle to stay awake. Many times I had to fight the urge to curl up on the rug in front of everyone and sleep during Vigils. Since newcomers are assigned a position in the front row, Dolores was across from me on the other side. Seeing her nodding head, I could see she was having a hard time staying awake too. In fact, it was obvious she was losing the fight. As the novelty of Vigils wore off, about a month, looking over the top of my office book, I stiffened, not believing my eyes.

My short glances watched her position herself exactly how she wanted to sit on her bench during meditation; arranging her habit until it was just so, straightening the folds, stuffing her habit under her until it fit snugly, tucking in the edges, adjusting her legs so her toes reached a certain point beneath the bench; textbook. Now that everyone was settled and quiet, we were ready to meditate.

That's when Dolores began a gradual meltdown. Her drowsy head hung lower and lower until the very last second when she'd catch herself with a lurch and wake up. It was astounding! I never thought being a gymnastics spotter would be part of my spiritual job description, but keeping her from harm turned out to be big part of mediation periods. Uncannily, she always caught herself right before smashing her face in the carpet. The lurch was so violent, there were times it flung her glasses somewhere on the rug. The rest of us, watching in horror, couldn't help lurching back with her as she came close to smashing her face. She immediately pulled herself back to her original meditation position on her bench, sitting straight.

One would think that first near miss would be enough to jolt her into wakefulness, but evidently she was sound sleeper. This frontal collapse happened again and again during our meditation periods. I tried to keep my eyes to myself, but this dangerous profound bow from a sitting position was one of the strangest things I'd ever seen. It was astonishing how she kept catching herself just before her nose smashed into the fibers in the carpet. It was nerve-racking to watch, incredibly resuming her meditations as if no one had noticed. It made meditation periods anything but prayerful and peaceful. I kept watching out of the corner of my eyes wondering when sleep would win and she would fall square on her nose, glasses and all.

Because Dolores was the newest novice, she would have to clean up her own blood if she broke her nose on the rug covering a cement foundation; it was little consolation. I wasn't the one to criticize. I was still having trouble with my own meditations. What did I end up centering on last time? My aching back? An insert? No, the attributes of an abbess! I can't believe I ended so far from anything that had to do with the reading. I shook my head in disgust.

While it was clearly impossible to concentrate with Sister Dolores's acrobatic show going on, it was just as hard to avoid catching Sister Patty's eyes sitting to the right of Dolores. In the chapel I wasn't able to hide behind magazines. If I sensed Patty looking at me, it became difficult, if not impossible to not look back. And when Dolores would go down for the count, trying not to laugh was excruciating. It was of the utmost importance not to start, because like a contagious disease that spread from person to person, if one person started, there'd be two laughing. Some days entire meditation periods were spent trying to maintain composure. Between Lorna's sniveling obbligato, Dolores's dangerous calisthenics, and Patty's impish glances, my nerves were shot by the time some of the offices were over.

I had to give Dolores credit. Even though she found out first-hand how hard it is to work against the pull of a sleepy disposition, she never gave up. The spiritual admonition of keeping an ever vigilant eye open took on a new dimension with Dolores in our meditations.

Undaunted, I knew her indefatigability and stamina in the face of overwhelming odds were traits she could add to a tally in her bid to become abbess one day.

Our newest member's combination of intellect and court jester gave her a childlike appeal that made her entertaining. Case in point, after a month while standing in the glass shop in her new habit, a feeling of amazement overcame me as I listened to Sister Dolores trying to convince the work supervisor, Sister Gail, to assign a different stained glass project for her, as if she could beguile the supervisor with her rhetoric. That's what Dolores hoped would happen anyway.

The symbolism of the clown moved from periphery to center as the lobbying began.

"I'm a beginner. I can't cut circles for balloons," I heard Sister Dolores complain. She was funny even when was she was being serious. I opened my eyes wide at Patty and gave her a 'do you believe what we're hearing?' glance. Embarrassed by the new comer's forwardness, I was glad we were hidden by the dividing wall separating the pottery from the glass work. I was cringing inwardly at Dolores manipulations.

Sister Gail explained how clowns played an important role in many religious traditions. Holy fools remind people of the distinction between the sacred and the profane," the supervisor said. "So Dolores, it really is admirable to be working on stained glass clowns."

Worried she hadn't swayed Sister Gail in the least, Dolores continued, "But learning how to work with stained glass is an art that takes time to learn; I'm not experienced enough yet. I'm still trying to master the straight line."

The silver jubilarian had overseen enough novices in her day to know how to handle this exhibition of false modesty. "Remember, Saint Paul said those who are considered wise by the standards of the world, should become fools for Christ's sake in order that they may be truly wise." The reason was the only justification that allowed the abbey to sell clowns as a religious item. "So don't worry about what the others may think about your artistic ability; if your balloons come out irregular or misshapen. Who knows, someone might be looking for just this kind of defect to add to their collection of famous artist's first works."

Not buying it, Dolores, in her insistence to not be associated with the feeble-minded, said, "Yes, theopneustically, the fool during the Middle Ages was considered to have special protection from God and therefore something enviable, I know, but the straight lines of a Celtic Cross mounted on a beautiful piece of driftwood would be an item guests would be more likely to buy."

"Remember, there are many different degrees of fooldom," Sister Gail said, in a voice that tempering her strained patience. "We are all under the special protection of God. The early Christians realized God's wisdom was wiser than the wisdom of all men. That goes for you too, Dolores." And in the politest voice possible, told Dolores, "If you start filling in your pattern with colored glass instead of colors of hot air, I have every faith you will become an excellent circle cutter."

Dolores took a step back.

While it ended the discussion that should have never have never taken place, it was the beginning of a two hour serenade of loud unrestrained "WHOOPS!"

Dolores added extra incentive to our novitiate classes that had begun living up to their name—Repetition, based on the premise novices have to hear everything three or more times before remembering it. The other novices had long since lost their enthusiasm for adding comments or asking questions; two novices had been here over two years and had probably heard the same speech a number of times before.

One afternoon the Novice Director sensing our weary moods, hoping it would strike a cord of interest asked, "Do you think God has a sense of humor?" Without waiting for Sister Drusilla to finish her blink, Dolores jumped in with, "I know for a fact He does."

"And why are you so sure?" Dolores answered with such authority I lifted my head off my hand and sat forward; if she had proof, I wanted to know.

Dolores relayed an episode while she was with her former community with pride. The new novice had what Sister Drusilla was hoping for, new material.

"It had been one of those days," Dolores began. "I had spent the entire day delivering homemade wheat hosts to many of the parishes in Tulsa. Fighting the five o'clock traffic was bad enough, but realizing too late, I passed my exit, made things worst. All day I looked forward to taking a long hot bath and now here I was getting off on a side street in the dark wasting valuable soaking time. Backtracking, it took nearly thirty minutes to find the right freeway entrance. All the while picturing my tub full of bubbles and how good it was going to be to finally slip my aching body into warm water.

"Then, when I finally found our convent, a visitor was parked in my space. I had to walk up a hill carrying boxes of left-over of hosts! To make matters worse, my feet were hurting from my new tight business shoes. She stopped to remember the moment. Shaking her head, she went on. "All the while I was thinking how wonderful it was going to be soaking my feet in a nice hot bath." I moved to another position and stretched my leg when the new novice started again.

"Unlocking the front door of the convent, I went into the kitchen, opened the refrigerator and put the excess hosts on a shelf. As I picked up my mail off a table in the hall, I could almost hear the gurgling of water running in the bathtub on my way to my bedroom. I put my purse down and kicked off my shoes from my swollen feet with relief. Taking steps in my bare feet was painful, but after hanging pajamas on the back of the bathroom door, I sat on the edge of the tub and started running water immediately.

The label on the shampoo I placed on the edge of the tub read, Revitalize hair follicles. I wished it would work on my whole body. When I reached to open it, I guess I wasn't paying attention because it started wobbling like a one-pin in a bowling alley, just out of reach. My fingers kept trying to grab it, but it too late. It skidded out of my hand, landing in the tub with a splash. I pictured the green extra-body shampoo spreading over the bottom of the tub like an alluvial plain, ruining my nice hot bath. I stood motionless not wanting to look at the big mess I caused. Knowing it was it was costing me the valuable soaking time, I forced myself to look and saw the open bottle of shampoo in the center of the tub *right side up* as if it had been placed there. In my exhausted state the only thing I could do was look at the bottle in the obliging way it landed and burst out laughing. That's when I knew, without a doubt, God has a sense of humor."

Sister Dolores took a couple of long deep breaths before ending her story. "I laughed for a long time because I think sometimes you just have to let it out, right?"

Sister Patty and I looked at each other. After maintaining composure outside the Music room listening to her trying to find the right note, we knew she was asking the wrong people.

In the same breath we replied, "Isn't that the truth?" knowing no one would be more aware of the understatement than us.

CHAPTER

21

Looking back over the months, I found it hard to believe I hadn't experienced anything the least bit transforming, other than handing in my street clothes. It worried me. According to Saint John of the Cross, by now my soul should be feeling touches of sweetness and delectable consolations in my meditations; I should be feeling illuminations, not this spiritual aridity. By my calculations I should at least be experiencing perfect hope and charity.

I fidgeted uneasily as I sat in the empty chapel by myself. This wasn't the first time I was here way ahead of time before the others. I had been nudged by my little voice telling me I needed to practice meditating.

Today for the first time, I would try sitting cross-legged on the floor. Maybe my lack of deepening had something to with the way I was positioned. I took my office book out of the wooden holder in front of me to get me started with a word or a phrase. A card behind it fell to the floor. I couldn't help noticing the beautiful picture of Mary on the front with a large gold aura around her head. I picked it up admiring the crimson and blue colors. Turning it over in my hands, I wondered if it was an icon of Mary…

Wow, I thought, it's a new record. It only took seconds for me to be distracted! Disappointed with myself, I scolded: Sheese, I'm here to meditate, not look at pictures! I pulled my legs in the correct position and sat straighter. Attentive and focused, I began one more time; ready, set, go. Immediately, I thought, you know, these slats never hold all the material they're supposed to; hymnals, missals, bulletins, pencils, ribbons, something always falls out.

Suddenly alert, I became preoccupied with an incident that happened to me in childhood. I then proceeded to waste the entire mediation time thinking about something that had absolutely nothing whatsoever to do with with praising God in Psalms. Taking myself in hand, I thought, that was then, this is now. With the advent of crib bumpers it's no longer possible for babies to get their heads stuck in the slats on cribs. Remembering this restored my sense of well being.

The damage had been done though, from then on I was unable to think of anything else.

The accident could have been much worse. I didn't fall on my head and crack my skull or have something heavy fall off a shelf and knock me silly, nor did anything hit me in the face and blind me. In light of all these terrible misfortunes, being found screaming at the top of my lungs with my head stuck in the slats of the crib didn't seem so bad. It could have happened to anyone.

By now, the sisters were sauntering in for the next office.

With the bell ringer announcing the start of Lauds, as we stood, I could feel my throat constricting. Under these choked conditions I tried to sing but soon realized all I could do to offer my croaking up as a sacrifice yet once again.

Genuinely surprised, I couldn't for the life of me, understand why after all this time, I was still having trouble singing.

CHAPTER

22

I went into the long, spacious refectory and had a slight shock. Reverend Mother Esmeralda was unexpectedly waiting for me. I paused for a long minute then stepped toward her. The next instant, she asked, "Do you have time to see me in my office for a moment?" I stopped breathing. Why me? This must be important. The Superior usually doesn't ask novices to confer with her about anything; all exchanges are supposed to go through the Novice Director. This was a bad turn of events and my guilty conscience took over.

My mind rushed over my actions of the past week. Did I accidentally leave a light on overnight? How did she know I didn't eat all my Brussel spouts yesterday? My next thought was somebody heard me talking to Sister Lorna in the garden and my anxiety grew. I was convinced someone turned us in. Maybe even Sister Lorna. When word of my indiscretion reached the Sister Drusilla, how could I look the Novice Director in the face after telling her I had nothing to confess this week? I would be unceremoniously demoted in her eyes knowing I had been caught in a lie. I nodded politely to Esmeralda. There was no getting out of it; I tagged along guiltily behind her to her office like I was going to a hanging; mine.

The Superior walked across the room, opened her office door, and sat behind her desk where she folded her arms in what seemed to be stance of defiance.

I walked in behind her and took a quick glance around before sitting across from her at a desk that was uncluttered as the Novice Director's with no pins, coins, or erasure shavings littering it. The room had a glass sliding door on the south side. Athick heavy curtain to keep out the draft was pulled to the side to let in light at this time in the morning. There was a picture of the Pope, plus the President on a wall, and a rosary of worn beads piled in a polished wooden dishwaiting for use. The low pile brown rug looked new; vacuumed and clean with no bits of paper scattered about. And no wads of paper near the metal trash can in the corner from missed rim shots. I was actually disappointed not seeing a reproduction of heavenly hosts and ministering spirits fighting in an epic power struggle against cloven footed demons over a bottomless pit somewhere in the office of this professional religious. But other than a large crucifix with corpus hanging on the wall, this room looked like a standard business office. She sat looking past me at the closed office door. In one quick decisive action, she opened the top drawer of her desk and took out a sheet of paper. After giving it a once over, she slid it across the desk to me.

A letter, she wants me to look at some letter? I was flooded with relief. Is that all? My guilty conscience struggled to accept I wasn't going to be reprimanded for talking in the garden, or that I wasn't in any trouble whatsoever. Everything else she had to say would be of little importance compared to this.

She told me a letter came from somewhere California. *I* was from California so I might know who wrote it. She wanted to know if I recognized the name of the person who wrote it. I explained to her, California is a big long state with millions of people living in it. Realistically, what are the odds of me actually knowing one particular person?

I felt her eyes watching me attentively as I picked it up and read the first side slowly and carefully, not wanting to miss one detail. It was full of cursive handwriting slanted backwards in large *flowery* script that made me think it was the stroke of a woman. I had to read the first page over and over to understand its meaning, and even then, I still wasn't sure what meant.

I turned it over. The back side of unlined white paper was the same as front, written in a gaudy, flashy pen. As I read under the watchful eyes of Esmeralda, I wondered how I could give an opinion about something that made no sense, each thought flowing into the next making it incomprehensible; one rambling thought running nonstop into another. What's worse, the writer didn't bother to use periods and commas, so I couldn't tell where thought ended and another began. Pulling at my collar, I tried to come up with something to say, other than the writer should take a grammar class.

I was convinced my lack of understanding was a coherency problem of my own. Until I reached the end of the page, and saw the signature; Charles Manson!

As someone who used powerful hallucinogenic drugs during his murder sprees, being high wouldn't even begin to explain his dastardly actions. But it shed light on why I was having problems understanding the content of the letter. I felt confident any problems weren't with me, but with the psycho who was out of touch with reality.

A cool gust of air chilled me as it blew under the glass slider.

I stood motionless, knowing how the convicted serial killer manipulated his hippie cult known as *The Family* into brutally killing others on his behalf. Bloody images followed.

My thoughts were broken off hearing a small voice coming from somewhere far in the distance. It was the voice of Reverend. Mother asking, "Well, do you think? Should I write back?" I grabbed the arm of my chair for support. "What do you think?" I heard again.

I couldn't get my words out fast enough.

In a strong voice, I told her vehemently, "No, don't write back." And just to be sure I was clear, I said louder this time, "Don't *ever* answer his letter." Without going into too much detail, I told her about the gruesome murders. "He's probably trying to use you for a reference, but don't have anything to do with him. Don't give him any reason to want to drop in and look around. Let somebody else *save* him."

Living at the abbey, we weren't exposed to grave threats. Our threats came suddenly, like coming across a rattlesnake sunning itself in the dirt, or coming face to face with a skunk, or running for cover in a rain storm hoping the next bolt of lightning misses you. Weren't we cheating death in the summer each time we stepped into the intense heat of the blazing sun? *These* were our threats. I was comforted knowing prayer, like an impenetrable shield, defended us better than our guard dogs on patrol.

I walked from her office with a clear conscience. No one had seen me talking to the gardener. After this near fiasco, my resolve had been strengthened. I was more determined than ever to act honorably, truthfully and live by the rules. I had come too far to let it all slip away because I couldn't keep my mouth shut. I was more confident than ever that nothing was going to keep me from seeing my vocation to the end. In fact, I saw myself in twenty years being one of pillars of the community. Everything was going according to plan.

Morning work had never looked better. Nothing is more conducive to bringing me back to the center of humility than being on my hands and knees and near the earth.

I inched my way down the path to the garden. I could hardly wait to be near the earth smelling dirt at close range. Pulling open the garden gate, I looked up and down the garden. Sister Lorna was nowhere in sight. This wasn't the first time I had to work on my own. Today it was a welcome relief.

I chose a pair of gloves from the shed then went to an area needing attention, the rows of lettuce. I began weeding between long leaves of Romaine. I thought again, how being on ones' hands and knees in a garden had an instinctive way of humbling a person. As I moved from place to place, brushing rocks and dead weeds out of the way, I thought of an incident involving kneeling that happened not long before I entered; visiting my the Catholic Church that was next to the elementary school I attended for four years. It was years since I'd been back and it would be a good opportunity to reminisce.

I walked up the familiar cement steps to the entrance and went inside the hushed silence of the large church. Because it was the middle of the week and the middle of the day, I expected to have the church to myself with no distractions. At first I did, there wasn't a soul around. The empty rows of pews were a welcome sight.

After genuflecting, I sat in the last row to have an unobstructed view of the altar. I placed my purse beside me deliberately marking my space; no one was going to sit next to me to disturb me. I came for the quiet, not conversation. Nothing was going to take me out of my peaceful state while I sat on this unoccupied pew in the very last row on the end of the aisle in the back of the empty church.

It felt strange being back in my old church after so many years. In no time I was reliving pleasant memories of my school experiences: the afternoon visits from school; the funny distorted face a friend made during Mass that makes me laugh even today; the sound of sparrows chirping from nests under the stained glass windows; the sweet scent of incense when I made my first Communion; the sound of our youthful voices echoing through the church from the loft in daily choir practices. All was peace until…

I cringed when I heard the door in the lobby open followed by two sets of steps. Then the door beside me opened and a man and woman entered. They took one look at me and hurried back into the lobby.

I couldn't see them through the glass partition because it was behind me, but I could certainly hear their muffled remarks, which unfortunately went on for some time. They were in a heated discussion. They didn't sound wild with anger, but whatever they were saying they destroyed my peace and quiet. Of all days for them to visit! It was mid day, why weren't they at work like everyone else?

At one point they went into a side room in back and closed the door but even with the door shut, I could hear garbled words and muffled shouts; they were definitely agitated about something.

My eyes moved when I heard the inside door of the church open beside me. It was the man. Oh good, I thought. They stopped talking and he's coming in to pray. But to my amazement, instead of choosing a pew and sitting, my peripheral vision saw him move to the center of aisle where he stood looking at the large corpus in the front of the church. Without turning my head, I watched him kneel on the hard red tile floor where he proceeded to inch his way up the center aisle to the altar on his knees.

Was he planning to work his way all the way to the altar?! I sat dumbfounded. My peace was shattered now that someone wanted to display his religious zeal in a way that way hard to ignore. While each step barely moved him closer to the altar, for me, each step moved me farther from the peace of mind I came in for. I sat calculating his forward progress and knew because it was a large church his undertaking was going to take a long time.

When he reached the halfway point, it came to me that *I* must have been the object of their discussion; he was trying to decide whether it was better to get it over with or wait until I was gone before performing his attention getting act. Whatever the reason, his conspicuous act of devotion ruined my peaceful afternoon.

With my calm now destroyed, before he reached the altar to start on his return trip, I stood, picked up my purse, and left, closing the heavy door behind me blocking out his dragging gait.

And now, crawling through the garden on my hands and knees during morning work, I tried to come up with reasons for his actions. I was confident it was a voluntary act of self-mortification. No confessor would ever impose the pain and joint swelling of arthritic knees as a penance for anyone. As I moved about weeding, I had a new regard for his feat, only I was luckier then he, I had an old army blanket to use as a kneeling pad. But either on cold hard church tile or cold hard ground, one couldn't help feeling contrite. It was a far cry from the egotistical madman of this morning and the way I began the day.

Hearing the bells signaling the end of work, I took off my gloves and placed them in the shed along with the kneeling blanket and scrambled up the gravelly path for dinner. I showered and walked to the chapel for midday office followed by dinner, where I sat in the refectory in my place eating my mashed potatoes. Looking around the table at the sisters, people who only a short time ago felt were strangers. I now felt they were friends, and wondered how this could have happened in such short time. Sisters with whom I thought I had nothing in common, I found myself bonding with on some underlying level. I was grateful to see the same people; sleepy, hungry, tired, happy, or sad. Getting to know someone without contrived accouterments was a way to speed up the intimacy process because a person is seen for whom they are, and not because they are wearing New York labels and Gucci shoes.

Somehow I had changed; I realized it was due to picking up subliminal facts about a person without the usual mutual exchanges of speaking which had allowed close bonds to form. Little things like a smile, a look, or a laugh came to mean a lot. That's why it was hard to hear about Sister Cathleen. Served like an aperitif before the noon meal was the announcement, Sister Cathleen had decided to leave. It caught me off guard, but wasn't surprised. Even though she smiled, she never looked really happy, she looked more bewildered than anything else.

There is a big difference between keeping trim the low-fat way by turning down cakes, pies, and cookies, and having the gaunt and frail look of a sickly person on a restricted diet, and Cathleen had lost this distinction. Her inability to maintain her weight made Sister Drusilla concerned for her health. Choir, prayer, classes, work, being busy is a good stabilization of temperaments. Cathleen hadn't responded to any of them. Not even confiding to Mac, the monastery's priest, who was available in weekly confessions, helped. By mutual agreement it was decided Cathleen would leave. There were no fraudulent claims of blame; no demands of 'one's due,' no grievance of alleged harassment; and no hard feelings.

Arrangements were made with her family, and the next day she was driven to Tucson, where she boarded a plane, and was gone. Waving goodbye, I hoped airplane food would be more to her liking. I would miss her.

CHAPTER

23

The rest of the week at dinner Charles de Foucald was read but not really heard, and dinner was clouded with the heavy feeling of someone missing. This feeling of abandonment was quickly dispersed in the fast paced monastic routine that didn't allow for self-indulgent bad humors. Mac was always available if we needed him and a one-to-one reconciliation acted better than a therapy session to relieve stress.

Thinking a change of scenery would help lighten my mood, I walked to the end of the plateau in back of the monastery where I had spotted a herd of about twenty cattle sauntering single file up a mesquite lined path near a cluster of large oak trees. From this distance, the cows looked like small black dots moving imperceptibly up the hill. Most likely, they were heading to the river bed on the far left side of our property, not realizing summer had left it waterless and full of dried branches, stones and tumbleweed.

Scanning the trail ahead, I calculated that if they kept at this pace I would probably beat them to the trees. Intrigued, I walked faster. The question was; which of us was going to reach the top of the hill first, me, so I would be able to hide, or the cows seeing me, would scatter in all directions?

When I reached the end of hill, I stood next to the oak trees looking down in a gulley. I could see for both of us, the path lipped the rim of a hill and shot down sharply toward a bunch of large bushes. From there, both our trails couldn't intersect at the bottom because of a 3-wire fence running the width of the property separating man and beast. I was relieved seeing the trail on my side T'd at the fence. I had to hurry though, if I wanted to secure a place to hide and not blow my cover. I was determined not to draw attention to myself.

I didn't know if it was true that bulls charged seeing the color red, but not wanting to find out, I whipped off my red garden scarf and stuffed it in my jeans pocket. With a sense of urgency, I trekked down into the gulley through brush like I was a sure-footed Indian; stepping over cacti, moving branches, and side-stepping rocks. Picking my footing carefully, I kept my eyes open for a good vantage point where inconspicuously, I participate in the spectacle of beasts parading by like a parade.

I was raised in the city and never had the opportunity of seeing large slavering animals within petting distance. I thought it would be a good way to participate in their ferocity; steers, bullocks, cows, shorthorns or longhorns, it didn't matter. If I was able to get close enough, I could look in their big eyes, hear them snort through large nostrils and get a good whiff of their cowliness. I'd be able to see if each one had a different expression, or if they had expressions at all.

It sounded like a good plan. I couldn't see them yet; they were still trudging up their side of the hill, but calculated if they kept this pace, I would probably beat them in a foot race to the top.

I found a secluded spot at the base of the oak trees and crawled in quickly, pulling branches in front of me. I was in a niche hidden by spreading branches at the bottom of gulley. Nestled in, I felt protected. With my eyes trained on the top of their hill where the trail crested. I waited for the first head to appear.

It was exhilarating putting myself in harms' way! There was a real adrenaline rush being so close to wild and dangerous creatures. They had no idea I was invading their private walk, and in a few moments I would be close enough to touch them. If all went according to plan, I could come back and do it again whenever I needed to add a little excitement to the daily routine. Grabbing my ankles, I pulled my legs in closer. Luckily, I remembered in time bulls charge at the color red so I whipped off my red garden scarf and shoved it deep in my jeans' pocket. I sat still barely breathing.

It wasn't long before the first black and white head appeared. Here they come, I swelled excitedly. Then the next one appeared, and the next causing me to go into an even smaller crouching position. I was ready and waiting to encounter nature in all its bovine glory. Up close they were truly spectacular.

It was fun watching their heads pop up one by one over the top of the hill. They didn't moo. They let out grunts with every step. They had cloven hooves on wide feet as they shuffled down the narrow path in front of me. Crammed in the side of the hill like I was, I hadn't counted on something; they were massive! With every step they seemed to double in size. The lead steer looked as big as a Brahma. The sheer bulk of this slavering brute was getting closer with every step!

Something else I hadn't counted on either, the front runner had **horns!** Seeing the hard bonelike projections lumbering toward me, the image of it crashing through the weak inadequate three-wire fence, getting tangled and going berserk flashed through my mind.

What was I thinking? My nerves of steel melted as the first animal pulled in even with me. It was huge! It must have weighed two tons! I couldn't contain my cowardice any longer. Seeing its large horns, I knew in a split second it was better to jump up and run rather than wait for the whole gargantuan herd to get any closer. Hoping I wouldn't be trampled as I jumped up, I broke for freedom.

Thrashing through the branches in panic, the sudden movement of the green branches, as I blasted out of hiding, jerked and shook them in a violent rustle. I frightened the lead animal so badly it nearly fell over; and it may have, I didn't wait to see. During my frantic efforts, I happen to notice when I frightened the first one, the whole line of cows shied to the right, like they were connected by a thread of instantaneous fear; their pleasurable sauntering at an end. As I made my out of the bushes, the image of them trampling me in self-defense in a wild stampede came to me, goring me as they ran in panic, stumbling over me as they bolted to safety. I saw them easily tossing me over the fence like a rag doll, the only means they had of protecting themselves from the dangerous intruder. Because I was afraid the angry group of spooked cattle was right behind me, I ran for my life, streaking across acres in no time. I ran hard for some time without looking back, jumping over cactus and thorny shrubs of mesquite, hurdling tumbleweed and bounding over pointy ends of agave plants. Sweaty and red, I didn't have a choice but to keep running.

The moment I realized I didn't hear them thundering in from behind, I stopped, and catching my breath, I started laughing. It was uncontrolled, happy to be alive, laughing. With my heart thumping like a bass drum, I had to hold my sides to steady myself. Bent over and gasping for air, I thought, now I can tell the Novice Director I found another way of relieving tension.

Standing there, I suddenly felt sorry I'd startled the poor animal, animal, actually the whole herd. They were sure to approach this same spot with caution every time they moseyed through in a conditioned response to this part of trail. They might even avoid it all together. Their fright was so great I wouldn't be surprised if their grade-A milk turned into buttermilk.

On the hill in back on the monastery feeling the steady beating of my heart and my heavy breathing, I wondered what *did* the sudden burst of adrenaline do to their systems? It *must* have had deleterious effects on their bodies. The next time one of them has liver fluke or listeriosis, not to mention meningitis or encephalitis; it would be my fault for impairing their immune systems. Now I really felt responsible for the lingering health defects in the poor cows and was filled with guilt.

My hysteria over, I walked at a normal pace. It came to me fear is fear in any species—I had had the same reactions every time I was forced to move; the effects weren't new to me by any means. I went through the list again: heart rate increases, blood pressure rises, nerve impulses alert the body to a state of alarm. Adrenaline is released. Activity in the digestive tract ceases. The mouth becomes dry as saliva thickens. Breathing increases and sweat is produced. Blood vessels constrict causing paleness. Accelerated air in the lungs makes the removal of waste material increase. Liver and muscles provide sugar for fuel for a flight or battle. To think all this goes on in my body every time we become fearful. Holy cow!

A change in my thoughts overtook me. Fear is fear in any species. The alarm I instilled in the bovines is similar to the conditioned response began every time my father walked in the front door carrying a paper bag; if it contained alcohol, it started a domino effect: loss of job, moving, and changing schools. Going through this again and again wreaks havoc on a person's system.

I stumbled when I realized the body is like a straightened bent aerial, it may look strong, but weaknesses are there so if any kind of pressure is applied it gives way to a variety of maladies and more than likely, breaks. It's common sense; the repetitive strain of going though an unpleasant experience over and over makes someone commensurately weak too. Unseen kinks in childhood, especially children of drinkers, hide in invisibility at first as lifelong scars left in the vertebrae as fear, guilt, anger, shame, distrust, depression, anxiety. The buried hurt eventually has to come out, and when it does, it is no longer invisible. It's now seen in the guise of illness; ~~ulcers, colitis, obesity, anorexia, suicidal tendencies, paranoia, insomnia, back problems, hypoglycemia, nervousness, stomach disorders, lumbago, asthma, hysteria, respiratory problems, heart problems, back problems, neurological problems, headaches, arthritis, skin problems, fingernail biting, performance anxiety, agoraphobia, xenophobia, emotional problems~~ a list I knew would be too long to finish before I reached the monastery.

How can any drinker (and their spouse) think otherwise? Buried hurt has to leave a damaging effect *somewhere* in the body. I was lucky in this respect. I was always was the 'strong' one in the family. I have nothing to worry about.

At the end of my cow adventure, I crawled back through the wire fence on the end of the property. I didn't have far to go and picked up my pace along with my agitated thinking. What is most unfair about living with a drinker is it only takes a short interval of sickness (one week or so of vomiting) to again resume a normal life. A drinker never sees the permanent damage left in those around him, he travels on lost in oblivion. What kind of a trade is this? A few sessions of shakiness and dramatic upchucking before resuming their lifestyle for the drinker, compared to his wife and children's' 50, 60, 70 years of being damaged by one or all of these alcohol related injurious effects? What must drinkers think? That it doesn't matter? I would gladly trade a lifetime of suffering for a lifetime of flimsy excuses any day. Tit for tat? Drinkers would never trade; they'd never have the courage. The problems they create for others last a lifetime.

Breathing heavily, I stopped in front of the glass slider on the refectory. With all these facts churning in me, I took hold of the slider and flung it hard against the wall. I saw Dorothy and Patty, watching from the reading table, jump, startling them.

The next second I was apologizing for my rude behavior making signs like, *it was an accident, I didn't mean it, the door got away from me,* causing me to add one more to the list of effects—convenience lying.

CHAPTER

24

It was one of those nights. I wasn't hungry but my stomach was making so many weird noises it actually woke me. My digestive tract was having quite a workout. I felt cold anyway, so I reached down and pulled up my blankets. Then I was too hot. Taking hold of my blankets again, I threw them off. I lay back down but now I was wide awake. I looked at the clock; it was only 10:00.

I started thinking of Cathleen on her way home. Then I began picturing Patty the novice, the one who walked to the dirt road on her way to the highway with a guitar strapped to her back. I couldn't get the image of her out of my mind, thumb out, hitchhiking to Tucson. She only lasted a year the first time. I didn't want their fate to befall me. The thought of it happening to me scared me more than I realized. What brought her to this lowly point? I bet they both had a hard time meditating.

This was too close to home. Out of fear of what could happen if I didn't learn, I promised myself, tomorrow, I'd go into the chapel at a time I knew the others would be busy showering after work, to hone my meditation skills. As one of *the* most important areas to perfect, it was my responsibility to improve.

I reviewed how meditation is really just focusing all your attention on one area. What is so hard about that? I made a concerted effort I wasn't going to fall to Cathleen's fate.

With no one in the chapel, I took a couple of deep breaths. I settled in: eyes closed, breathing deeply, stretching until I was relaxed. Ready, set, go.

The first thing that came to me was how disappointed my mother would be if I gave up my vocation.

My mother? Why would I start thinking of my mother?

I started over. Eyes closed; ready, set, go.

As soon as I thought I was squared away, insidious thoughts came through all the same disturbing me: I looked like my father's side of the family. I had straight hair. My mother had naturally curly hair. Right from the beginning, I was different from her.

I started over. Ready, set.

I remembered hearing the phrase chip off the old block more than once growing up. Did inheriting my father's genes influence my mother's opinion of me?

I started again. Go.

Did it mean I inherited his genetic predispositions too? Like drinking? If this were true, I would *like* the taste of alcohol, but I have to make myself put the disgusting taste in my mouth.

Did she blame me for all the trouble my father caused her family; the moves, the upheaval, the unlimited suggestions of how to stop it?

Instead of clearing my mind, I proceeded to fill it with all the different locations we lived. That house was close to a grocery store; it was fun running across the street to buy candy. That house had a huge den with two bath rooms and fit the size of our family. We were able to ride horses in that house making it was one of my favorites. That house was…

Way before I made it to end of the list, the bell ringer pulled heavily on the rope in the hall outside the chapel. Soon the sisters would be coming in.

CHAPTER

25

"Anne, bring the shovel!" I heard Sister Lorna's commanding voice plead from the other end of the garden.

Unfortunately, roadrunners, coyotes and boars weren't the only desert occupants forced into cohabitation with us on a like-it-or-not basis. Discovering a rattlesnake always brought loud shrieks from anyone unlucky enough to happen upon one. Noiseless and slithering, it was always with a silent 'sudden appearance' that they were found, and a shock when it finally dawned on you the eyes staring back, were not the friendly eyes of a gopher. And right now, Sister Lorna was in a showdown among the cabbages and cauliflowers.

Like a human pinball, I bolted into action, zigzagging and pivoting my way and that through the maze of vegetables, racing to the tool shed for a shovel, or a blunt instrument, with a harp edge good for cutting. Without a moment to lose, I grabbed the nearest shovel and ran back to toward Sister Lorna s l o w i n g my pace way down as I approached her. A few yards away, I heard the menacing warning of the snake's rattles for the first time, sounding like steam escaping from a radiator pipe. Choosing soft loose dirt to step on if I could, I was more than careful to be noiseless. I didn't want to scare it and have it find another hiding place. I couldn't have been quieter without becoming invisible.

The hissing snake never slowed its menacing warning at any time, as if it was running on a flywheel. I took a solid grip on the scoop side of the shovel and offered the dirty wooden handle over leafy plant heads to Lorna. She reached for the shovel as if in slow motion. I took several steps back and listened. Its horny rings at the end of its tail were still shaking. Neither of us said a word. I watched as Lorna painstakingly positioned the sharp end above the rattler's neck. There was no other way; slaughter among the dense white plants was inevitable. She held the blade poised and motionless above the snake's head for a few moments gathering courage for the deathblow. She then sent it down suddenly with all her might in one brutal slicing stroke. Immediately, the big snake went into contortions, twisting and squirming with Sister Lorna frantically jumping clear, both of us running until we were sure we were far enough away; about fifty yards.

It took a while, but the hissing eventually petered out, its rods now disconnected from its cold blooded gauges, until no more assaults were left in it. Since we would be on their level, we carefully chose a safe place we could rest and sat in the center of the walking path cleared by thousands of our boot tracks. She wiped her face with her blue scarf/ veil in relief. Clearly the role of executioner had taken a lot out of her.

"Th-th-that was the biggest rattlesnake I've ever seen!" she exclaimed." She let out a long shuddering breath as if she was trying to expel any floating snake particles she may have inhaled. We sat in the dirt, both of us with our hands tucked securely under our armpits in clenched protection, a natural reaction to avoid another silent ambush in our bivouac. And even though we could clearly see there were no other snakes around us, involuntarily our eyes kept searching the edges of our 'safe' space. We were always on the alert, constantly guarding the little area on the path; the only place in the garden with no weeds.

I followed a trickle of glistening perspiration as it ran down the middle of the gardener's dirt-smeared face until it hung like sap at the end of her nose. Color was slowly returning to her face, but her voice continued to shake realizing what she had done. To my distress, in a trembling voice she explained how the larger rattlesnakes were not as lethal as the smaller ones because their venom was not as potent, so we were lucky. Staring at her in amazement, I thought, is that supposed to make me feel better? I hoped this bit of snake trivia had more of a soothing affect on her than it did on me.

"Forget the venom," I said, "the bigger the snake, the bigger the fangs."

In an effort to settle herself, in a quivering voice she continued, "Remember, even a dead snake can bite from reflex."

I looked at her incredulously. My heart was just beginning to slow its thumping. Even though I could see the stilled rattles between the stalks, my eyes were now fixed unwaveringly on the perimeter for other venomous vipers that were crawling imperceptibly in the bosom of the garden.

The gardener, and long time professed sister, was a nun *first*. She felt it was her duty to direct and train with every chance that came along. This afternoon's events were too good of an example to pass up. She said, "Everyday we are in the garden, and everyday the snake speaks." I wasn't sure what her point was, other than being a reference to the devil. With my guilty conscience, I wondered if she connecting the appearance of the snake to our breaking the silence for months. Then I realized we had ended our tête-à-têtes long before the snake slithered into our lives.

Knowing her psychiatrist would have a field day with the imagery, in a nervous laugh I told her, "Be sure you mention this to your head doctor the next time you go to Tucson."

We sat uneasily in the dirt, both of us stunned by her daring, forcing a strained calmness. We played down the danger we nearly avoided. We tried hard to believe she/we acted bravely. We almost believed it too, if it wasn't for Lorna's trembling hands, my slight nausea seeing the gory killing among the white flowers, and our constant head-turning surveying the area giving us both away. We were sitting on their level. We couldn't help it.

As I sat in the dirt, I questioned; why did it have to happen near the cauliflowers? I was just starting to like the taste. Now every time it was served at dinner, I suppose the image of the dying creature would come to mind. Why couldn't it have happened near the broccoli? There was no chance of me starting to like its flavor.

A nervous ten minutes went by. "Well, I guess I better drag it out of the garden and get it over with," Lorna said, attending to the job at hand. "It will make a good meal for the coyotes anyway."

"You might as well put out my dinner for them as well," I instructed, repulsed as I was by the events that took place on this hot afternoon. We pulled ourselves up. Lorna went to the tool shed. I wanted to a better look at what was coming next and clawed my way up the trail home.

From the top of the hill I watched undetected as sister exchanged the shovel for a steel rake. From above, I saw her toss the shovel over the fence before cautiously making her way through the growth of vegetables pushing leaves and stalks aside, making sure another reptile wasn't lying in wait. I could tell she had done this before.

Using the prongs of the rake, she approached the dead snake with the tool like she was holding a spear and had a wild animal is sight. Lowering the curved ends, she pulled the long carcass over the mounds of potatoes passing the strawberry patch, through the yellow and white daisies lining the chicken wire fence, and finally dropped it along the fence surrounding the garden. She threw the rake on the other side. Picking her steps carefully, she walked through a low gate near the oak tree and was now in the desert. From the other side, I watched her struggle to catch the reptile on the prongs again of the rake and drag it completely under the fence. With some maneuvering, she managed to pull the lifeless corpse onto a road tractors use once a year, and continue moving it until she found an appropriate place to leave it. I found it disgusting to watch, but couldn't turn away from the indelible image of a long line made by the lifeless corpse in the dirt.

From my vantage point at the top of the hill, I saw her jerking the rake trying to the free heavy corpse; I suppose inadvertently making its tail rattle in a final farewell to life. She wiped the rake's metal teeth in the dirt cleaning off whatever secretes from a body that's had all its arteries severed at once. She walked away leaving it to decompose in the sun; a meal for some lucky desert scavenger.

From on high, I saw her walk back to the shed and replace the rake with a shovel to carry out her next unpleasant task, finding an out-of-the way place to bury the poisonous head. I knew what was coming next, hunting for the head in the garden. When she scooped it up with the shovel it turned my stomach but I couldn't look away. I should have because she held it up in front of her like it was cake on a platter. Face to face with the little skull, she inspected the hideous thing at close range.

Avoiding cactus and clumps of weeds, her arms strained as she struck the hard dirt in the adjacent field repeatedly until she had a hole the size of a watermelon. Tilting the shovel the diamond-shaped head awkwardly rolled off and into its final resting place. On top the hill, I saw the lone figure of Sister Lorna fill in the hole, patting the grave with several broad stokes of the shovel making sure its slit-like eyes were completely filled with dirt. But before she walked away, she stopped and looked at the grave site, like she was saying a few words on its behalf. The deed done, I got up and walked away from the butchery. That night, sitting in the low light of my bedroom, I reflected on the gutsy actions of Sister Lorna even though she was afraid. I wondered if I had it in me to do the same. I lay in bed seeing Sister Lorna's trembling hands, and knew it could have turned out much worse; she could have fainted!

Being involved in the decapitation of the embodiment of symbolic evil while living in a monastery, a symbol of goodness, I was afraid to fall asleep wondering if my subconscious was planning a nightmare of epic proportions; being chased by snakes, falling in sake pits, puncture marks caused by fangs over my body. Fear, snakes and evil are not the best subjects to dwell on when trying to go to sleep. But no matter how hard I tried to keep my mind from reconstructing the day's events in vivid detail, I couldn't stop thinking about it.

Lying in bed wide awake knowing the last bells had sounded long ago, and the grand silence had begun, I thought again of Lorna's quivering voice and pale face when the physiological affects of fear kicked in. It brought back examples from my life, like when I scared the poor cows or the fear I had when we moved; the same physical reactions surfaced. In the quiet of my bedroom, I thought how trying to get a snake to stop shaking its rattles was like trying to persuade someone to stop drinking; the closer you come, the more they defend themselves. But understanding this did nothing for my sleeplessness. I tried everything to try to feel sleepy but nothing worked; not counting sheep jumping over a fence, not getting a drink of water to dampen my dry mouth, or praying a couple decades of the rosary. I was aware of the minute hand on the alarm clock turning seconds into minutes, and minutes into hours, and there was nothing I could do to feel sleepy; I was the only one in the entire monastery that was awake. Until, I had an idea.

Knowing my knit slippers were beside my bed, I held the bed down with both hands to control its release, and stood slowly. I slipped the yarn slippers on my feet, not for warmth during this hot summer month, but for their muffled affect. At this time of night every squeak would be magnified. The room was so small, with one step I was able to grab the doorknob and ease it around. Finger by finger I let go, hoping the hinges wouldn't creak as I pulled it open leaving it ajar so I wouldn't have to reopen it on my return. I poked my head out. I looked right in the hall, I looked left; no one was around. Except for a couple of yellow nightlights throwing strange shadows to disquiet me, everything was still and calm. No one was up; success so far.

I stepped into the hallway. Beyond the bedrooms were the offices, and the refectory, and then the kitchen. The shadows cast from the nightlights near the floor, made me jump. I was still on the lookout for snakes.

I made it past all the closed bedroom doors. The offices were next. I paused only when I reached the magazine table in the refectory seeing the moonlight filtering in the window. I took a few moments to look outside at the moonlight spreading widely before me. My fear of being caught dissolved in the beauty of the desert panorama. The moon was so bright it looked as though everything was awash in silvery light, hills and far off mountains, gullies and washes, all looked evenly colored in the bright moonlight. At the end of the refectory, I stopped and listened; no traffic noise, no alarms, sirens, or horns; I didn't hear an airplane engine, or a television blaring; only intense, concentrated silence that let me slip effortlessly back into the enthusiasm and eagerness I had when I first arrived.

Suddenly remembering where I was and I wasn't just strolling around the monastery looking at things; my night walk had a purpose,

I made myself get on with what I was doing; I would be in a lot of trouble if I was caught. This was no time to dawdle. Trying not to make collateral noise bumping into the refectory table, I felt for a chair on the end, and then searched for the next on down the line, moving silently in front of the massive stone fireplace like it was a petrified cafeteria monitor. At the end of the table, I stepped forward to the kitchen and took a glass from the cupboard. With a slight tug, I opened the refrigerator and like a spot light, out flooded the cold bright refrigerator light throwing illumination over the entire room; the chandelier, the empty table and chairs, the fireplace hearth, and the counter, the light pinpointing my location made me hurry to my objective. Hunting through jars of mayonnaise, gallons of milk, pitchers of orange juice, jars of homemade pickles, cartons of butter, that's when I spotted it…altar wine!

I reached in, and wanting to make the most of my cat-burglary, I poured a generous amount into the glass. I replaced the bottle on the cold shelf and closed the door, glad to stop the glaring beacon coming from within. I am not a connoisseur of fine wines, in fact, I dislike the taste, but when I sniffed its heady aroma, I could tell it was the same wine used during Mass. I knew it hadn't been consecrated and hoped God wouldn't mind my imbibing this one time for the sake of calming my nerves. I held the full glass high watching the amber liquid glisten in the moonlight, and for an instant, I had a thought that could have distracted me from my mission, that children with a parent who drink too much, are likely to model their behavior. I thought if this is the case, then the past can work in the opposite way too, by showing how *not* to act. There was comfort in that. Standing in the empty, dark refectory in my robe and slippers wasn't time to linger over a debate and pulled my thoughts back to the purpose at hand.

I placed the full glass of wine to my lips and gulped. I didn't stop until the vile liquid was all gone. Knowing full well fermentation produces a solution used to make cleaning solvents, as the cold liquid tore down my throat, I wondered which part of my innards the wine was eating away first. In a low grumble, I asked, why do people like this sour stuff? I stood there a few moments in a chilling sense of isolation until the building settled startling me into action. I looked over the dark refectory and knew I better get back to the safety of my room without delay. I wiped out the glass and returned it to the cupboard.

Retracing my steps, I walked past the long wooden refectory table, past the thick stones on the fireplace, past the moon-drenched magazines on the table, past the offices, past the yellow glow of nightlights, and finally I was in front of my slightly open door.

In the security of my bedroom, I slipped into bed aware my mission was accomplished and I had gotten away with it. It wasn't long before I felt the wine invade my body relaxing me. Lying there a little tipsy, I wasn't proud of my actions, but if the alcohol worked to ward off nightmares of headless snakes chasing me, I guess it was worth it. I closed my eyes and fell into a deep sleep.

The next day during morning work, Dolores and I were told to bring our gloves and meet Sister Viola on the west side of the garden. We found her waiting for us in the white pick-up and climbed in the cab. She drove us over roads that had lost any resemblance of their former state with weeds higher than the truck's bumpers.

At a certain point far from the monastery, Viola stopped the truck and we all got out. She reached in back and handed us both a huge blue plastic bag from among many that had been donated to the monastery by a hospital in Tucson. While Dolores and I followed the driver walking in a determined gait, I wondered what she had in mind. It didn't take long for me to realize the obvious; we were singled out from the others because of our excellent work habits and attention to details. We had been hand-picked for our noticeable attention to duty and personal sense of obligation. News of our accomplished work ethics must have gotten out. I tried not to smirk. It wasn't often novices were invited to go on special assignments in the truck. I felt flattered.

Sister Dolores and I tagged along the sister closely, eager to prove they had picked the right crew for the job.

Finally, she took a few steps and stood directly in front of something the size of a manhole cover. Pointing to the ground, she told us to spend today's work period scouring the countryside for these valuable compost fillers, dried cow pies, "They're much better than chemicals to enrich the soil."

"Oh," I muttered, feeling deflated.

As I pressed into service, I thought, it could be worse, at least we have gloves.

She tossed a gunny sack stuffed with the bright blue bags off the truck and reminded us matter-of-factly, "Watch out for scorpions; they like to live underneath dung during the hot part of the day. Their sting is often fatal, so be careful disturbing their hiding places."

With that last bit of advice, Sister Viola climbed back into the truck and drove away, leaving us in a cloud of dust.

Maybe I deserved this because of my alcohol run the night before, or maybe it was just a coincidence, I was never sure. But I couldn't think of a more fitting penance for my devious actions than having to pick up large heavy plops of manure scattered up and down the hillsides in the hot desert sun all afternoon.

Waiting for the dust to settle, I looked up from my kneeling position before my respective cow pie, and with a deadpan expression said, "Well Dolores, we've hit a new low."

Her laughter, I was sure, could be heard in Tucson.

CHAPTER

26

Her reputation preceded her.

Over the months I had developed a larger than life image of the abbess from the eastern region not even the Queen of Sheba could have lived up to my expectations. Like all Cistercian abbesses, she was elected for life by 12 professed sisters. To gain this honor, I knew the visiting abbess must be a remarkable person in a spiritual league all her own. As a gauge of her spirituality, she was well-loved by this community and enjoyed a God-like prestige among them. As a model and example par excellence, she played a major role, not only in the formation of their Cistercian lives, but her power and vision went well beyond her jurisdiction to the surrounding male communities as well. I am no biographer, but it wouldn't surprise me if a cathedral or a string of priories was named after her one day.

As the founder of our desert monastery, she remained its' official Superior until the abbey demonstrates financial self-sufficiency and be a prospect for new members. In today's' world, not many people are looking for a ministry rooted in vows or joining a house centered in silence. Self-sufficiency could take several lifetimes.

Getting a foundation running is not an easy task. Some foundations never take hold and grow by adding new members. Keeping them running is not an easy accomplishment either. With the concept of cloisters slowly disappearing and vocations few and far between, it's rough, if not impossible, to keeping them afloat. I am reminded of the life of Saint Franca, an abbess who was elected at 23, founded a new convent at 43, and was dead at 44. There's a lesson in there somewhere.

I wasn't surprised learning as a woman Superior, she has administrative authority equivalent to that of an abbot of a monastery, but didn't exercise the rights and duties of priesthood. I realized the very structures of patriarchy in the Church, not to mention, male chauvinism, comes with the territory. The original 12 Apostles were men. That is enough of a reason for me. In a place were you freely hand over your will to superiors, the transition was easy; being a hostile woman's libber defeats the purpose and was a different agenda entirely. If I wanted to show anger, I would have entered politics instead.

Preparations went on for days. Waxing floors, shining woodwork, polishing cutlery, when at last we saw the monastery's dusty white sedan pull out, knowing it wouldn't be long now, the entire monastery squared is shoulders in anticipation.

It was mid afternoon when Reverend Mother Seraphina, or 'Sera' as she preferred to be called, arrived at our door, anxious to see how the abbey progressed since her sisters took over. Sera was a petite woman just under five feet, but because there was something purposeful in her walk, a strong determination, she gave the impression of being much taller. Her veil, pulled back over her head, gave her shiny grayish white hair a slight pompadour while the rest of it stayed tucked neatly under her veil, I suspect, by her strong will.

As her old friend, Reverend Mother, invited Sera in the refectory for coffee and cake, but Sera would have nothing of it. She had more important things she needed to do. Before anything else, Sera asked to be pointed to the chapel so she could make a visit. *How commendable*, I thought. I was on my way to my bedroom to change into my work clothes anyway, and decided to peek inside the chapel to see if she needed anything as the hospitable thing to do. It seemed odd after the four hour fight, she wanted to sit in church and pray, she must be weary from the trip.

With the professed sisters already at work, it was the perfect opportunity. I moved quietly in the hallway stopping at the door. I looked left; I looked right before turning the doorknob and peered inside without her knowing. My skepticism turned to praise for there was the abbess, not sitting on a padded chair, but kneeling on the rug, stone-like, deep in prayer paying respect to what was most important to her, God.

Satisfied she was the authentic in her spirituality, I backed away closing the door gently. Seeing her living her spirituality like this, meant more to me than what people said about her. I had a firsthand glimpse of her practicing spirituality that convinced me God was her primary concern. It was not just a rumor circulating around the order for the betterment of all. I went to my room and changed into my work clothes.

I plodded my way down to the garden, picked out a hoe from the tool shed and went to work next to Sister Lorna weeding another section of the pea patch. Lorna, aware her former superior was visiting she was holding her finger to her lips. The middle-aged nun looked furtively round the garden. This action let me know Lorna was aware of the all-seeing powers of the visiting abbess.

Time flew by. Special guests deserve special treatment. I looked forward to supper with the hope the 'no talking' rule would be relaxed. When the end of work bells chimed, we hurriedly picked up our hoes and stored them in the shed. Once the door was closed, our nonchalant act ended. We rushed up the hill slamming the garden gate behind us.

Like always, because it was quite warm, the glass slider was open. We slid the screen to one side and walked in the refectory where we were overtaken by the smell of a roasted blend of brewed coffee. I showered and went in early for Vespers trying to hurry what I hoped would be a very inspiring evening.

When I opened the chapel door I was surprised to find I wasn't alone, Sera was already kneeling in prayer in front. Her presence startled me. I didn't see her walk in ahead of me. I was somewhat taken aback realizing she must have spent the whole work period on her knees! Aware of disturbing her, even trying to be quiet, I clumsily took my seat sending apologies to her in my mind.

Ten minutes later the sisters began to enter gradually filling the chapel with their black veils.

We sang Vespers on our best behavior with no laughing. Meditating was useless, how could I meditate with this special visitor sitting among us? I tried anyway: back straight, ready, set go. It was no use; I never did think of anything else other than what was going to happen. As we walked through the hall to the refectory, again I sniffed the heavenly aroma of *perked* coffee. It was worth having her visit for this reason alone.

Supper was the first of many informal gatherings around the refectory table. We sat and ate in silence at first, then, as soon as Sera started speaking we knew it was okay for the rest us to speak to her, redirecting our comments through Reverend Mother Seraphina instead of Reverend Mother Eleanor, who I sensed was glad to temporarily relinquish the authority.

The novices, me especially, sat and listened with keen interest.

It surprised me again how the sisters, even after being in a cloister for twenty some years, were filled with spontaneity and quick wit.

You'd think they'd be uncommunicative and reserved. It was just the opposite, Cistercians loved to laugh. Despite Sister Lorna's occasional menopausal moments, these were some of the happiest, most accepting and well-adjusted people I've ever known.

The conversation around the refectory table painted a history of the community I joined. After founding this desert monastery with volunteers from her own community, Sera visited periodically to reassure those in charge she hadn't forgotten them and they could count on her for support. Her next visit may not be again for several some times, years perhaps. And because the desert sisters had spent their formative Cistercian years living and training under this respected leader of the Cistercian Order, they treated her with the utmost respect and love. It was easy to tell they were delighted being reacquainted with their former abbess and friend.

The second night was the same. We had delicious perked coffee and then the conversation began. Our talk was intermixed with chuckles building into hearty laughter. I realized again, because we weren't used to speaking, when we were allowed to, it made the talking times very special.

The conversation didn't lag. Comparing the present state of her monastery to when Seraphina entered, she told the usual stories of severe Lenten fasts consisting of only bread and water that I expected to hear. As an abbess first, she added insightfully, "A sister's life should always be like a Lenten observance, shouldn't it? Atonement and expiation, isn't that why we're here?" strengthening our resolve.

Sister Dolores and I looked at each other blankly.

Listening to the abbesses' accounts of the past, I was able to connect the past and present of the order like the across and down of a crossword puzzle. She described the mandatory long work dresses they wore back then: heavy ankle length cotton habits with deep pockets, under protective aprons tied at the back to double the weight. Information about their apparel developed more importance remembering she was talking about Massachusetts where in the summer, humidity hung in the air like dirt on a windshield. "Back then, exhausting field work was done by the sweat of our brows instead of machines. And I mean sweat. Those of you who entered there remember by the end of each work period, we didn't have a dry thread on, isn't that right Esmeralda?" Reverend Mother Esmeralda nodded her head wearily, as if just thinking about it made her tired.

The visiting abbess brought a deeper dimension to our desert monastery just being here. I could feel it. She had an interiorization about her of someone who spent long hours in prayer and Describing her being 'spirituality personified' wouldn't be far from the truth. Not many people can say they've met a living saint, but feeling the strength of her quiet intensity, I knew she was as close as I was going to come. After talking so much, Sera cleared her throat a couple of times and went to the kitchen for a drink of tap water. I watched her as she stood silently in front of the window at the sink. Her eyes searched the landscape at length under the darkening sky maybe wishing things were back the way they were with her former sisters still under her watchful eyes. I heard her give a soft sigh, as if hating to pull her eyes away from some faraway thought. Reenergized, she turned and came back to the table ready to relate more stories of the *good old days*.

Picking up where she left off. "Remember? Back then it was *real* work, not like today. Haying, before the machine operated fork was backbreaking, pitching and scooping hay. If you were lucky, you hitched a ride in from the fields in the back of the work truck. We didn't just pick corn," she said, smiling knowingly toward the novices at the other end of the table. "We cut the stocks down, collected them, loaded the husks and took them back and shucked them," in a tone of someone who knew what having hard thick calluses felt like. "You have it easy!"

And to prove it, Sera pointed out, "There were no private bedrooms like the luxury suites you have today."

Considering our bedrooms anything but luxurious, she made her point; we didn't have to share. Sharing a bathroom with one other sister was bad enough, but having to sleep in a dormitory with a number of people who were snoring, wheezing, sneezing, or coughing, was much worse.

Across the table Dorothy, my next door neighbor, was shaking her head in full agreement. I guess it was bad enough trying to beat me into the bathroom, let alone 30 others.

The abbess told us about the hours spent on hard wooden kneelers instead of the cushioned kneelers of today. Visiting family members were seen through a thick metal grate one at a time (if they were lucky enough to obtain permission). Imagine being introduced to a new member of your family, a baby, and not being able to hold it."

She made a convincing argument.

She was serious when she said, "Yes, you novices should be grateful we paved the way to your easy, comfortable lifestyle you have today." With all the professed sisters nodding their heads heartily agreeing, she said, "The life you are living now is cruise-like compared to what it was." I knew she was right. When I entered I had the same feeling about the easygoing life style in comparison to theway some hermits pushed themselves.

I heard Dolores exhale a "Thank God" in the form of a groan I'm sure everybody heard. I noticed too, no one took the opposing view to Sera's statement: *monastic life is not easy.* It summed it up for all of us.

The abbess, knowing novices were present, taught, "Sometimes difficulties are of our own making and they usually have to do with giving up your will. Handing over control with an attitude of non-resistance doesn't happen overnight either; it's forged in the practice of obedience. Going along with the intentions of a Superior isn't always easy, sometimes it's downright painful. But if you work at it, eventually you will 'come into your vocation'".

With proof sitting at the table with us, I was convinced I could shape my will by beating it into submission too. Considering I was in my first year, I knew I could do it. I didn't doubt it for a second. What would prevent me? The dignified abbess showed no sign of letting up, explaining how much more grueling her novitiate years were back then. Holding a shock of her pure white/grey hair in her hand, she said, "This is the proof, it used to be black."

I wasn't about to argue, I knew if anything could turn a full head of black hair white, the severity of strict observance could. Not to mention the shock of conversion of manners: poverty, chastity, renunciation, obedience, solitude and prayer. Living here was enough to make anybody's hair turn white.

Mother Seraphina exchanged stories with the professed sisters about the hardships of those early days. I listened to a number of; *"do you remember when?"* stories about how hard novitiate life *used* to be. They ended with a list of who had made it, and who had not. Protecting an 'image' isn't something these sisters are concerned with. I listened to story after story of personal misadventures and hilarious situations, until we were all in tears, including Mother Seraphina. Leaning forward to face the novices at the far end of the table, she said in a serious tone, "One sign of a vocation is a sense of humor," which produced the appropriate response, a round of giddiness from all the novices.

Always the first promoter of Cistercian life, she gave another example about a mysterious visit one of her sisters had.

"On this one day, late in the afternoon," Sera began, "a day like any other, one of our sisters, a long-time professed, I'll call Sister X, was convinced she had been visited by the Virgin Mary. Sister X told me she was doing nothing out of the ordinary during the morning, it had been another typical day working and praying, until Vespers. And according to her, she had gone to her room to change into her habit after the afternoon work period when she looked across to see there was someone else in the room with her. Sister X admitted feeling bewildered not knowing how the woman got in her room unnoticed. The woman told her she was the Virgin Mary.

I looked at Dolores but her eyes were looking at Sera, not wanting to miss a word.

I thought of the basics from Saint John of the Cross: **Corporeal** visions are seen with the eyes of the body, **imaginative** visions are those seen without the aid of a visual organ; and **intellectual** visions perceive the object without a sensible image. I didn't know if reviewing this would help me understand, but it couldn't hurt. I guessed it had been a corporeal sighting, but a lot of good that did me.

Sera continued, "Sister X remembers looking at the hem of the woman's dress trying to see if she was wearing shoes. If she wasn't, it would explain how she was able to enter her room undetected, but her feet were covered by her dress." Sister X didn't panic. She thought being visited by Mary was the most normal thing in the world and was nothing out of the ordinary. "Now *that's* faith," Sera challenged. Sera told us Sister X said Mary spoke briefly to her and she was told not disclose what the woman said to anyone, except her Superior.

I thought corporeal vision then, with eyes *and* ears involved; I *knew* reading the works of Saint John of the Cross would come in handy one day.

Sera told us this wasn't all Mary said to the sister, but the rest of what she heard she was told to keep to herself to use for her own perfection.

I knew Sera would follow her own council and not reveal important personal insights regarding Sister X. I wondered though, about the other spiritual counsel the sister received. Custody of the eyes was far-reaching. I didn't mind not being told the particulars of the rest of the conversation between the visitor and Sister X. It wasn't as important as knowing Sister X had a mystical visit. The others felt the same way. Nobody asked for details. Not even Dolores. What struck Seraphina about the incident

"One thing I will tell you," Sera went on, "Sister X remembers in particular how peaceful and calm the incident was. There was nothing frightening about it. There was no ghostlike figure, no doleful cries or lingering chills. On the contrary, it was perfectly normal.

Using the supernatural visit as an example to encourage us, the abbesstold us God bestows such things on people who are inwardly strong.

The fact that incidents like these were occurring in the confines of monasteries reinforced my decision to enter. Being familiar with Saint John of the Cross, a saint who had to be held down when his body went into ecstasy, the sister's encounter didn't surprise me. On the contrary, after living in the desert monastery all these months, I had been expecting something like this would happen to me too. Frankly, I was offended I hadn't been caught up in an enlightened state of rapture yet myself "to perfect me too." It was the first time Sister Dolores was at a loss for words, all except for the "Oh, mama!" she exclaimed under her breath.

Bringing her point forward, Mother Seraphina said resolutely, "Cistercian life does work."

We were still gathered in the refectory, all of us sitting quietly in our places with the two Superiors at the head of the table. The peaceful atmosphere of the room mirrored the still desert outside at this time of day, and a hush had settled over everything.

Outside, the sky was alive with color. The sunset had descended around us in yellows, gold and brilliant reds, imbuing everything with scarlet light you only see at twilight in Arizona. The fiery red of the sky worked to color the entire refectory in a rosy glow and made this eventide look and feel special, like it was a going away present for Sister Sera, a beloved person, as a final tribute to send her on her way.

Supper was finished. With our bodies replenished we sat like regulars in a our favorite coffee-house listening to Mother Seraphina's unique blend of humor, religiosity, and teachings, helping ourselves to seconds and thirds on the *good* coffee, trying to make it last as long as Sera's stories.

The room had a subtle distinction to it tonight, other than the attentive consideration given to us by this powerful abbess. It may have had something to do with the rosy color of the room altering our moods. As the sky slowly shaded the desert; the room's mystical tint heightened our spirituality too. Even the faces of the sisters seemed permeated with an indefinable knowing.

A slight breeze drifted the dry heat off the desert into the refectory through the many open windows. There wasn't a sound from the darkening desert to match our reflective mood. The sun had continued to set and by now it was difficult to see the person sitting directly across the table. Sister Dorothy, as the portress for the week, rose and switched on the wagon-wheel lights as the hospitable thing to do. As she crossed back to her chair, Sera commented on how nice it had been sitting in semi-darkness while we were talking.

With that cue, Sister Dorothy rose again, walked to the light switch and carefully dimmed the lights a little more. She glanced at Mother Seraphina before walking back to her seat this time. We all looked at the abbess, and then back at the novice. I felt sorry for Dorothy, not knowing what to do, but wanting to please the superior. "A little more," Mother Sera politely suggested.

Sister Dorothy slowly lowered them again, and looked back at the abbess in case there was another instruction. We all looked at the abbess with her, and waited.

"Just a little more please," she repeated.

Turning our heads to Sister Dorothy, we watched as she dimmed the lights one more time, slowly turning the round knob, proceeding to lower the light. With another slow turn of the knob, we all heard the **click** and looked at Mother Seraphina.

"That's fine. Perfect," she said, well satisfied.

For the rest of the evening we sat and talked in total darkness, listening to the gentle Arizona breeze murmur occasionally through the tethered bamboo blinds.

CHAPTER

27

The next day during meridian time I was sitting in the dirt far out in the desert where it's easier to think and put things in perspective. I had picked a spot next to a wiry shrub of mesquite, the only shrub in the area. It gave little shade but I was grateful for *any* shade. I cleared a space with my boot making a circle with them. It was very hot as usual, but because I had an agenda, I didn't feel the heat at all.

I wasn't disappointed by the visiting abbesses' visit, far from it. I was full of admiration, inspired anew to emulate her spiritually. I was lucky to meet one of the Cistercian leaders in the Order. It was quite a revelation knowing her spirituality wasn't an act. With Saint John of the Cross setting a standard of excellence for me, the bar was set pretty high.

The severity of the desert showed; there as not a ripple of a breeze anywhere. It was dry, still and quiet. I thought of the serious look on the visiting abbesses' face when she looked at us novices and warned, "Remember a vocation is for life." Sitting here in the dirt on the alert for snakes, I thought back on my world-shaking decision in enter. It wasn't an overnight decision by any means. A monumental decision like this that included giving all my possessions away, was not the kind of thing you rush into. Mine was years in the making. I remembered when I told my mother. She was delighted of course. My father with his sporadic bouts of drinking had lost all his say in the family long ago;

he *had* to go along with my decision. My siblings looked at me like I was crazy, and maybe I was, time would tell. *Making* the decision was the hard part. But when I finally made it, there was no turning back. After meeting Sera and seeing her virtuous behavior, it made me feel if the Cistercians were good enough for her, the Order was good enough for me. Still, I was having a hard time imagining why anyone else would choose to enter a monastery that was as primitive as they come. A strict monastic way of living affording meager rewards fashioned for reclusives, attracts all kinds of seekers. It was bound to be a pull for spiritual triathletes out there. Maybe the lackadaisical attitudes of the other novices were just a front. Only God can read the heart.

I thought back on my adventurous car ride and how hard it was even finding the place in the middle of the night. Without seeing anything remotely suggesting 'that-a-way' to the abbey, it was a wonder we even found it without help to navigate the back roads. During my time here, I learned this was intentional; by *not* marking the way in glowing red neon lights, MONASTERY AHEAD, or well placed crosses in dirt along the way, only people God wanted to find it, actual knocked on the monastery's front door.

With hindsight now, I knew the arduous taxi ride was a precursor of things to come. It let me know the entire novitiate would not be a walk in the park too. The time frame goes like this: an observership for least one month so the individual can see if it's the right monastery for them, and also for the community to see if the candidate is someone *they* want too. A postulancy of six months minimum is next. Then two years as Novice. If all goes well, the novice makes Simple Vows. At the end of that time, they make Solemn Vows for life.

The length of these stages didn't bother me as long as I still had the inner conviction this is what I should do. I knew I was in it for life, so what's an extra year or two either way? I always had the deep-seeded belief underlying my choice that 'God is bigger than family' to back me up. What really scared me, was knowing I had to pass an interview with the Superior if I wanted to continue after my observership. Sitting in the dirt fingering pebbles, I remembered my rigorous screening process and how nerve-wracking and intrusive it was. It has to be;

taking a total stranger into the enclosure to live with the community, they have to be careful.

I was happy learning the interview would be conducted by the Superior face to face, and not in front a panel of ~~judges~~ sisters. When I was asked, "Did you date?" I knew my interview was underway.

All candidates are on their honor to tell the truth. Right at the start I was at variance with one aspect, and wondered if other prospective novices had the same problem; wanting to shield someone who had been behind enclosure walls for decades. Realizing the Superior hadn't been desensitized watching television and hasn't seen outrageous fads, or witnessed the decline in morals, or seen plummeting necklines known as *'lo and behold'* dresses, I held back. Not because I was full of immodest behaviors, but wanting to protect the interviewer was a concern. My reckless times were innocent fun, but a cloistered contemplative nun who didn't get out might think differently.

A monastery being the least permissive of all groups in existence, the interviewer has to ask personal questions. Prodding someone to talk about dating or the lack thereof, is uncomfortable on both sides. Asking anything with a sexual connotation makes both parties uncomfortable as a natural reticence kicks in. It makes the subjects of purity, chastity and abstinence easy to gloss over. I stretched my stiff muscles and moved to the left before continuing reviewing my interview with all its imponderables. I started second guessing myself right away thinking I should have substituted the word "dating" with the word 'court' knowing the difference our ages. And when I told her, "Yes, I've dated numerous men," I regret not making it clear that it was over time. And as the idea of me entering grew stronger, so did the line "Where your heart lies, there is your treasure." I knew I couldn't have both marriage and a contemplative vocation.

Preparing to enter, I familiarized myself with the *Catechism of the Catholic Church.* "The virtue of temperance disposes us to avoid every kind of excess: the abuse of food, alcohol, tobacco or medicine." This statement covers everything with the same reasoning. How can you give yourself to God if you don't own yourself? It's like handing the keys to your car to a friend with the stipulation, "It's all yours... after 24 easy payments."

Looking at the monastery in the distance I remembered I'd made a few good points anyway, but wondered what the Superior thought when I said, "It's hard to be completely innocent in today's world." There didn't seem much point dwelling on it because she brushed it aside.

Modesty, decency, decorum; I had made a few good points anyway. Elaborating more would have just gotten me in deeper. In retrospect, I decided, like talking to a police officer, the less you say, the better.

I guess it was okay I didn't mention my father's problem with alcohol. I glossed over that area in my life. But I was thinking, how *stupid* would I have to be to act in the same asinine way of someone who chooses to drink too much when I had the perfect example of how *not* to act right in front of me my entire life? I'm sure the Superior would have agreed.

I got up, brushed the dirt from my jeans and thought, *thank God all that nonsense was behind me now.*

CHAPTER

28

Weren't all contemplative sisters the same type? Whether it's verbalized or not I think people (myself included) know the answer already. People who choose a religious way of life tend to be shy, studious, introverted types with dry personalities. It was an interesting idea that must have piqued Proving this, or disproving it may have been the reason a student was given permission to test the personalities our entire community, thus beginning, I am sure, one of the most unusual weeks ever spent in a monastery anywhere.

"Ah hem," Esmeralda began, clearing her throat as she stood at the head of the Community room. "We have been offered a chance for some real learning about each other," but before I agree, I wanted to see how all of you felt about it first, since it concerns us all."

Curiosity ran through me, this should be interesting. Speaking for us all, any added stimulation in our daily monastic routine was welcome.

"A student from the university wants to conduct an experiment. She thinks it will be fascinating and in our best interests too to examine our personalities by giving each of us a personality test."

Groans of displeasure emanated from both sides of the refectory table.

"Now we must not be too hasty; this is a different kind of test, not one remembering facts and figures. This is a test to gauge our personalities. Getting along with each other in the monastery is critical and this test may help. It's important we stand together in camaraderie in a spirit of love. We must make every effort to be as harmonious outside the choir as well as in, and you know how much time we spend practicing hymns. (Another series of groans erupted around the table). "Shouldn't we spend time learning about our dispositions and why we act differently from each other? Isn't it in our best interest to take advantage of every opportunity to further this compatibility?"

We were all convinced. I had been here long enough by now to know that questions were really polite ways of letting us know what was about to happen.

I had my reservations. Testing our personalities? What if it turns out I'm all wrong for this way of life? I wasn't sure I wanted my personality laid in the open for everyone to see. I liked keeping my faults to myself especially if the new knowledge could somehow be used against you. The Superior sat back squarely in her chair like a demonstration of finality. We were on our way to finding empirical proof as to why we acted the way we did; like it or not.

The next day everyone was called to the refectory.

"Examining a hypothesis..." is how the student started explaining her motives. She was about thirty years old, around 5 feet four with brown wavy hair. "I want to see what type of personality joins a monastery. In essence, I want to test my supposition showing everyone in the monastery is basically the same type. If my findings are correct, I'll use the results in my doctorate."

Oh, the paper chase, I remember it well, I thought, glad I was out of that mindset. I presumed she thought all of us would be introverted, bookworm types. If she was lucky and her findings supported her argument, maybe she'd have enough material to receive a Ph.D, a noble cause giving her a God-like prestige; I'd like to see her try to bring the certificate to heaven with her, though.

Our desks had been rearranged in a large circle in the refectory with the table pulled to the side. There was a little packet of papers laying face down at each place I wondered how she managed to obtain the extraordinary permission from the higher-ups in the order to let her conduct a personality test in a cloistered community in the first place. That showed a certain amount of intellectual bargaining power in itself. "Classifying and defining differences will help you get along better. It will help you to be more patient with each other too," she coaxed. "By understanding how others communicate and by knowing where they're coming from, you can utilize this information in your dealings with each other."

First, she made clear what the words 'introvert' and 'extrovert' mean, if we didn't already know. An introvert is someone who turns their own feelings inward. An extrovert is someone who is outgoing. She told us usually a combination of these traits is what gives us a true picture. "Don't worry, if you're not pleased with what you find now, in time you'll change and evolve. For example, an introvert may become more talkative and so forth."

We breathed a communal sigh of relief.

"That's a bit of good news anyway," the Superior encouraged. Flashing an ingratiating smile at us, the student said, "knowing your personality traits is the key to a happy life."

The student passed out the tests and we dispersed, finding private places where we could concentrate without interruption. Thoughtful and serious, we began the test as if they were a matter of great importance.

I have always been a good test-taker, not letting my nerves get the better of me; not blanking out or becoming sick with worry. The fact we weren't being graded, made this test easy to take because of no pressure.

I didn't know how much confidence I should put in this test or in someone just starting her professional psychological career. Focusing on the big picture though, I admired her ingenious idea. It *will* be interesting seeing which traits were common to us all. I thought of what the implications would mean for us; will the Superior, knowing someone is a certain way, would she challenge her with the opposite quality? I was leery.

Even though the student burst in on us excitedly with wonderful ramifications concerning her test, I like to figure out my personality traits for myself; really, what will I find out about myself that I didn't already know?

A week passed and the well-meaning student had reviewed our tests. The refectory table was pulled aside and we each grabbed a chair from the Community room and arranged them in a circle in the refectory and sat waiting anxiously.

Undoubtedly, the enterprising young student had gone over her findings. She walked in and dropped the tests on the magazine table. And even though I was sitting way across the room, I can still see the growing redness on the grad student's face as she hung her head in dismay and said incredulously: "I can't believe it! If I hadn't conducted the test myself, I never would have believed it! Not one of you is the same type! You're all different!"

I understood why she was worked up. What she discovered was completely different from the information she had accumulated. All her work, down the drain! Instead of framing her award, it was apparent she would have to put her thinking cap back on and spend at least another year reviewing her conclusions; stopped when she was just getting started. The image of her throwing her dissertation and shredded hypothesis out the window came to mind.

Her findings were amazing really. To think we had extroverts mixed in with introverts: loud mouths with the closed lipped: non-conformists living with eccentrics: realists thrown in with dreamers: logical personalities, together with the nonsensical, yet we hadn't come to blows. As intriguing as finding out about our personalities was, the class was still stressful and I was glad it was over. We weren't handed awards or certificates for having completed it. It had only been for our own benefit. Now when I walked over the hills by myself it was with the knowledge I was an extrovert; good to know.

Out of everything, what stood out most in my mind, and I hoped the graduate student realized too, was the surprising fact that even with our differences, *we were all able to get along!*

CHAPTER

29

Kicking my way through foot high weeds, I was careful not to scrape against small barrel cacti interspersed with the straw-like weeds. As watchful as I was though, I always ended with the tiniest needles embedded in my ankles. The needles worked their way through my boots, my socks, and eventually my skin. They had microscopic barbs making removal extremely difficult, not to mention painful.

I mention this because as a stained glass apprentice, my range of design was limited. My work consisted of turning out numerous roadrunners, the same bird each time with a body cut from different colored glass, followed by soldering on a beak and spindly legs. The problem was, even though I followed the same pattern every time, each bird turned out differently. To redirect attention from my shoddy work, I relied heavily on using unusual looking cholla cacti for the bases to draw attention from a lopsided body, a short leg, or a bent beak. I *needed* to find the unusual shrubby stem segments. This type of cactus has hollow cylindrical bodies that look like it was wrapped in old Swiss cheese, crusty and hard. Each branch of cholla is unique. In fact if a prize was handed out for the most unusual species of cactus, my choice would be the cholla. The dried branches were like finding priceless gold doubloons, and I would pick them up and gingerly inspect every crevice and fissure, turning them over and over, examining them from all angles.

For many years the sisters working in the glass shop had thoroughly combed the hills and dry river beds in search of these valued commodities to use as bases for their stained glass projects. Because of their diligent searching, it was a rare occasion to be lucky enough to happen upon one, they were so few and far between. Stumbling on one was fortuitous and I would trek back to the shop like I just bagged an animal that would feed our village for a month. The working sisters would gather round and eye my trophy through their artistic visions of how they would mount a stained glass crucifix, a red cardinal, or figures in a manger scene.

The lure of finding the Holy Grail of cholla kept me walking on unfamiliar fields in back of the monastery. For the most part, I didn't need an extra incentive to hike. I loved strolling under the aerial show of white stratus in this open-air planetarium anyway. I was a silent sojourner, a woman in love with peacefulness and walked for miles listening to the wind whispering sweet nothings in my ears, my eyes holding the vision of small yellow and purple blooms on the fields around me like a romantic bouquet. I couldn't help feeling I was God's one an only. Stumbling on a piece of cholla was an added benefit.

I craved these peaceful sojourns into the desert. I absorbed the peace like a sponge through my lungs, eyes and ears, pushing peace into my soul and never getting enough. I was like a starving person without food feeding off this deep inner calm the rest of the day.

It came to me how certain words lend themselves to certain situations. Describing the colors of the Arizona sky as they stretch yellow, orange and red across the sky should be described as nothing less than 'spectacular'; or the spontaneous blankety-blank oath that erupts when I almost step on a snake. Finding a dirty old branch of cholla, I would involuntarily shout *Gadzooks* every time because an uncommon discovery deserved an uncommon response.

Walking in the heat under the cobalt colored sky reminded me how I used to see something in the blue of my father's eyes to confirm his conviction of lasting sobriety. He actually thought his family *believed* his mumbo jumbo of lame excuses, that we had faith in same worn out rationalizations, and justifications with the same worthless result, proof positive of his physiological slowdown; 'keep on drinking dad; burn out the last of your brain cells', popped into my mind.

I was almost home. Spurred on by my father's love of words, I *knew* there had to be a word to describe the utter ridiculousness of someone believing in the false hope and confident belief, that without doing a thing, and without altering his behavior in any way, things will *magically* be transformed in the future. To support the absurdity of his position was the fact the nonsensical person actually believes that others believe it too. As I fought my way across a weedy field, I struggled to find the precise word to fit this kind of illogical thinking and well-intended hope that metamorphosis happens overnight.

I had many words to choose from: delusional, ludicrous, wishful thinking, absurd, deranged, stupid. By the time I reached the wire fence behind the monastery, the perfect word came to me. It was one that was completely accurate in its ability to transform, foolproof in its power to restore, and when nothing else works, it was the perfect word for drinkers to use to use as a last resort to bring about change—'Abracadabra'.

CHAPTER

30

As I sat at the refectory table eating breakfast by myself, I was looking forward to all the festivities that go with my second Christmas at the abbey, not to mention the eats. I could feel the special excitement of the sisters as they went about happily making preparations, cleaning, painting, ~~mowing~~ raking. And oh, yes, the extra long choir practices which were always enjoyable. There were a couple of drawbacks that prevented me from fully enjoying this jovial time and it filled me with worry. I am not, and never have been, an orator. It caused me great concern learning the novices had to read a selection in chapel during Mass in front of spectators; ranchers and their families, relatives of the sisters, and people wanting to experience a more spiritually uplifting Christmas.

Like I said, I am not a public speaker and don't like attracting attention to myself, but I was scheduled to read a page about spirit of Christmas during not one, but during three different Masses; Midnight Mass, and two more the following morning. All the novices were asked to so this one *simple* thing. I was in the front row. Churchgoers were right around the corner next to me. It may have been easy for someone like Dolores, but it was nerve-racking to me. Unfortunately, the monastery is not a place you can get in your car, wave goodbye and drive away for a weekend. There was no escape. The strain of this clouded my entire Christmas season.

I practiced my part so much, what I was reading no longer held meaning for me; I couldn't tell what my selection was about if my life depended on it. As I practiced, I wondered if there were any orders where public speaking wasn't mandatory. If I didn't know Father Wyss was staying in the quest house on his Christmas retreat, I may have dropped dead from worry. His presence added a wonderful lightness to this whole ordeal. He, of course, gave us retreat talks twice a day while he worked on his books in the quiet of the guest house. His theme this Christmas was self-love. He put the pressure on me when he asked, "When will we ever become totally unselfish?" I felt was speaking directly to me; I *should* be overjoyed to execute like the others novices during the Christmas Masses. And like I said, I couldn't leave. There was no avoiding the inevitable.

Then the unspeakable happened. Walking in and out of the music room practicing my piece, the Novice Director noticed my hair was longer than it should be and needed cutting so I would look presentable to people coming for Christmas.

My first reaction was "Oh good, it means another trip to Tucson."

"Oh, that's not how we do it here." My eyes grew big and my stomach lurched seeing her walk to her desk, open the top drawer, and take out a pair of long bladed scissors.

My left lip pulled up immediately.

"Don't worry, she said, I've trimmed many a head." Somehow her admission didn't make me feel confident. Hair is very personal. Knowing she was actually going to take a pair of scissors to my head, my entire body tensed. I was doomed. I know *sisters*, of all people, shouldn't care *that* much about the way they look, but after spending so much time in the garden with the hot sun beating on my head, my hair had numerous blonde streaks, sleek and white any hairdresser would admire; I didn't wear my cowboy hat at times for this very reason.

I just knew she would go for them and cut them off at the root. I also knew this is why there is a novitiate, to weed out imperfections like vanity. I hoped she remembered I was still in the initiation phase, just a beginner; a neophyte who needed to be handled with kid gloves. (Shades of Saint Francis de Sales accosted me; his biggest concern about being ordained, was having his curly golden hair cut off making the bishop think he was conceited. I agreed.)

She pulled her hard wooden desk chair to the middle of her office. I gulped. I sat on it as rigid as a marble sculpture. I involuntarily winced when she started cutting. Clipping here, snipping there, I watched in horror as strand after strand of my narcissism fluttered to the ground like flower petals.

When she was finally done, she looked at me approvingly, wiped off the blades and placed the instrument back in the drawer. I patted my lips giving her a mandatory thank you before racing out of the room to my bedroom hoping no one would see me. As I hurried along the hall, I was quite sure I was feeling a lot more air in different spots on my head than ever. I flung open my bedroom door and bolted to the bathroom where I prepared myself for the worst—my head, bald in places, with only a few strips of brown hair left to cover my cranium. I'd be lucky if didn't faint straight away from shock.

She surprised me. To my relief, none of my scalp was showing. The hair cut looked decent. It was something I could live with. Knowing I wouldn't have to hide my head from the parishioners was a big relief. More than that, the feeling she was out to get me lessened somewhat.

First, there was no punishment for being caught signing with Cathleen in the novitiate, now this. Could I have been wrong about her? Maybe she wasn't the scowling martinet I was making her out to be. I decided to give her another chance because I will be living with her for the rest of my life.

CHAPTER

31

It was the start of another year for me. There was still so much to learn.

"Idleness is the enemy of the soul." Therefore, let the Bothers [sisters] be occupied according to schedule in either manual labor or holy reading." So reads chapter 48 of *The Rule of Saint Benedict* concerning daily manual labor.

Once a year the Superior assigned new work duties for everyone in the monastery. I waited apprehensively along with the rest of the community, because today was the day. The garden worker throwing cow manure on a compost pile could be directed to throw pieces of potatoes into a pot and be a cook. Sister Dorothy, the sacristan laying linens on the altar after washing and ironing them in preparation for Mass, might be asked to try her hand at laying white PVC pipe in the garden. The appointments were left to the Superior, assigning work she felt was best for each sister. Sometimes a sister's job wasn't changed at all. She could be asked to continue doing the same job for another year, which could be very trying, but instead of objecting the sister had to smile and accept it.

Huddled in the Community room, we sat grouped together in anxious expectation waiting for Reverend. Mother to arrive in the event the new jobs weren't what we hoped or were in fact something we dreaded.

Making her way to the front of the room, she stood without saying a word. Maybe she was playing with us or not but the longer she stood deliberating, the more tense we grew, each of us wanting to know what we would be doing for the coming year. I stopped drumming my fingers on the desk when she sat across from me.

"Ah, hem," began Reverend Mother as she glanced down at a slip of paper she was holding. "I would like to take this opportunity to tell you how much I appreciate all the work each of you do on a daily basis. It has not gone unnoticed I assure you. We know the work of God is the daily office but as we are now at the end of the year, new opportunities are on the horizon. As Merton writes, *the monastery teaches us how to take our own measure by accepting our ordinariness.* I hope you will keep this in mind when I distribute the new work assignments. Each duty…"

I wish she'd just get on with it.

"Sister Gail of course will remain right where she is as head of the art department for creativity is a gift. I also would ask you to take over as Sacristan. Sister Dorothy with her musical ability will spend time learning how to lead the choir in chant.

"No one is more qualified and conscientious than Sister Lorna to care for the garden and she will continue at her job as head gardener."

"Sister Drusilla, doing a fine job with the novices, will remain Director of the novices, and continue to teach our Cistercian ways to newcomers."

Trying to keep my lip from snarling, I glanced at Sister Paula.

"Who attends the horses better than Teresa? I will ask her to stay on in this position while continuing on in the role of acting facilities supervisor."

"And we are blessed to have Sister Viola as our music Director. Keep up the good work. We all know how lucky we are to have someone like her leading our choir."

"As for the Novices," turning to face us she said, "Sister Dorothy will begin accompanying us during the office. This means devoting more time practicing so you will no longer work afternoons in the garden. I'll ask Sister Patty to take over your place."

I heard a sigh of gratitude behind me from my next door neighbor. I gave Patty a smirk thinking, ha ha, more garden work for you. Have fun, picturing her slaving away digging up all the potatoes I planted.

As for our newest novice, Anne, besides her regular duties in the morning working in the garden and glass work in the afternoon, I will ask her to take over the responsibilities of Bell ringer. Sister Drusilla will explain this to you."

My eyes wide opened wide. I'm doing what? What's this? I didn't like the sound of this. Did this mean I was the one who walked through the monastery ringing a bell signaling the start of another office seven times a day?! I had to keep a close track of time for the entire next year? My mind reeled at the thought. Considering the full scope of the bell-ringing duties, it hit me, did this mean I would have to get up earlier than 3:15 for the start of Vigils?

Out of the corner of my eye I noticed Sister Patty smirking from across the room. She had been in the novitiate longer than I and knew the freedom that comes with working in the garden and the liberties that go along with scheduling your free time; basically doing what you wanted and when.

I was still in a state of shock when we were excused. I made myself stand and walk behind everyone crowding around the new work roster posted in the back of the refectory. I checked the duty list again. Maybe it was a mistake. Seeing it in print confirmed it. It wasn't a mistake. I will be keeper of the bell for the coming year. I checked the list a third time. I had read it correctly; my carefree days were over.

From across the room, Sister Patty flashed me another uncalled for smile. She knew very soon allmy time would be taken by conscientiously following the office's schedule. My time was not my own any more. I was now a chronometer, a human time piece. I sat in Sister Drusilla's office trying hard to keep my lip under control. In her words, she needed to teach me the finer points of being the bell ringer. Accepting my fate, I thought, after picking up dried manure for the compost bin for weeks, acting as Bell-Ringer wasn't beneath me by any means."All right then," Sister Drusilla started. "Being the Bell-ringer is a huge responsibility." I felt a muscle in my lip twitch.

"Follow me and I'll show you how it's done."

I followed her to the arch outside the back door of the chapel. Overhead, a large bell dangled its clapper still and silent. She asked me to take the rope and try ringing it. I grabbed the bristly low hanging knot in my hand and pulled. I admit it was fun tugging on it making the heavy cup like object above me swing. Loud metallic blasts jolted the quiet filling the canyons and river beds with shocking reverberations. Slicing through the highest cloud, the peals were a strong signal that drowned out whinnies, howls, and moos. "Besides calling the community together," the director said, "the sound of the bells redirect our attention on God by letting us know it's time for the next office. I held the worn hairs on the rope steady as Sister Drusilla stood next to me. She explained how I should ring it for the *Angeles*. "Pray along while you ring and you'll know how much time to give everyone to finish the prayers. Every morning, noon, you need to ring the bell in a series of three. You've heard it."

The hand-held bell was next. She handed the wooden handle to me and asked me walk down the corridor next to the bedrooms ringing it to practice. "Remember, you'll have to set your alarm at 3:00 to wake everyone at 3:15." I didn't have much trouble suppressing my excitement. I could see myself ringing the bell by the light of the moon. That alone was worth it.

When she was satisfied I learned the basics, she said, "One other thing, the bell-ringer is responsible for ringing the bell three times during the consecration. You have to keep track during Mass and excuse yourself early with a bow and watch through the window to see when Father lifts the Eucharist. When he does, give the rope three good pulls."

I was all set for my first day. When the alarm went off at 3:00 AM, I jumped out of bed. Time always seems to go by faster in the mornings, and at 3:15AM, it flew by. The disadvantages of being a bell ringer were soon apparent as I peered through the darkness trying to keep my half-closed lids open. Working my white jumper over my head and attaching the Velcro behind my head for the veil, by the time

I squeezed the ends of the straps together, it was already time for me to sound the bell. I picked up the bell, opened my bedroom door, and went in the hall ready to wake the dead.

I had been instructed to walk along the hallway twice swinging the bell; I didn't want to wake them any earlier than necessary. I made my first pass timidly tinkling the little bell. At the halfway point in the hall, when I realized faucets weren't turning on or doors opening, I began to swing it in wide arcs, back and forth, loud enough to wake the Priest on the next hill. I came to Sister Patty's room. When the thought of her smirking came to me when I was named bell ringer, I had to fight the impulse to ring it furiously when I passed her door, dropping it and kicking it against the door jam like it was a soccer ball. I controlled myself and kept walking.

Being a bell ringer is a lonely job. I soon found it has its good points though; getting up before everyone else pushed me into an intensely quiet world. It was a forceful nudge into world filled with animal sounds like the yapping of coyotes, a commanding bellow from a steer, the muffled hooting of an owl, and if I were lucky, a return call from another owl.

When I finished the return round, I went into the chapel and waited at my place. Following me, the Novice Director was first to arrive. All the other sisters walked in bleary eyed, and as always, Patty was the last to be seated.

Even though there is no forced activities at Vigils: no chanting, no singing, no music, no meditating, going from one of the loneliest times of the day, to the sounds of people coughing, loud yawns and throat clearing, together with the unintelligible back and forth recitation of the Psalms, it *felt* like nonstop talking; it's amazing what a year can do.

I couldn't help noticing the expressions of pleasure on Sister Patty's face, sitting directly across from me, when I had to leave to ring the bell. Why did she find my being inconvenienced so cheering?

I noticed her gloating smile at Lauds too. I saw the same smug grin again during the Office of Tierce. I couldn't help wondering why she was taking such pleasure in my misfortune. Common sense should have told her not to provoke the timekeeper.

There were a few things I did as a novice I wasn't proud of but remembering the fearful expression on Patty's face wasn't one of them. Later that day, I was holding onto the rope and looking through the arched window, I happen to catch Patty's eyes as she ran across the yard trying to avoid being late yet again for another office. She saw me standing quietly with my hand on the rope watching her dash to the chapel hoping to beat my pull on the rope.

The image of her mocking smile this morning came to me. "Better luck next time," I thought. I gave the rope a good hard yank, making her scurry across the yard even faster. I smiled hearing the organ play starting the next office. Even seeing her pink and flustered face as she crashed through the back door out of breath wasn't enough to wipe the smile off my face.

My actions might be construed as childish, but actually I did her a favor. Up until then, she had trouble being punctual, from that time on, her promptness increased a hundredfold.

CHAPTER

32

The southwestern architecture of a monastery in a desert conjures up distinct images: graceful arches, the sun warming tiles of a cloister walk, a lone figure praying silently in a chapel, not men who looked like they belonged on a necktie posse.

Now and then our picturesque monastery needed help on its western façade and a contractor and his handyman sons, four in all, were called in. Wearing western attire, they repaired roofs, mended cracks, painted buildings among many other jobs. Their boots, minus the spurs, were covered in dust and their sweat stained cowboy hats looked like they'd spent years being slapped against their dirty jeans. The workers threw tools and equipment off their truck like saddlebags, then threw themselves off as well. I imagined hearing rodeo marks for a well executed dismount, as they tried to bring some degree of challenge to an otherwise boring day of work.

I soon learned Arizona received the seasonal reversing of wind accompanied by corresponding changes in precipitation known as monsoonal rain. In the summer, these storms traveled north from Mexico and give tremendous lightning shows unlike none I'd ever seen in the city. The discharge of atmospheric electricity in bolts was spectacular! I would hear a loud crack and see a flash of spidery networking across the top of the sky, hold a few seconds illuminating ghostly images only seen in this make-believe daylight. It was followed by deafening thunder that would put the fear of God in anyone.

Arizona is a thoroughfare for these storms so having the rain gutters in good working condition was a must. Some of them were in very bad condition with holes eaten completely through by rust, some were separated entirely from the buildings, others were dangling at odd angles, and others were missing altogether.

To prepare for the torrential downpours, the contractor and his handyman sons were called in. They drove in riding an old Chevy truck, confident they could fix the gutters. The violent heat, fierce and red-hot, didn't deter the dedicated crew who were obliged to keep their faces full in the sun while attaching the gutters to the roof. Watching them work, I couldn't help wonder what these rugged men-folk, with shirt sleeves rolled up on their muscles, thought of these churched-up sisters and their religious goings-on. Why on earth would these homesteading sisters, with eastern imaginations, want to stake a claim in such defiant territory?

Whatever they thought, they kept to themselves; they were here to work.

A couple weeks later they were finished, the gutters were draining properly. The cowboy carpenters drove off into the sunset, leaving another satisfied customer. But no one could foresee how the metal necktie they strung around the buildings was almost our undoing.

When wanderlust gripped me, I headed out with the sense of excitement I always feel walking on mile after mile of serious desert. I looked forward to seeing the desert's unique beauty, hiking over crawling weeds that seemed to grow like low pile on the desert floor. Even the scratchy bunches of tumbleweed on a faraway hill looked as soft and textured as velvet from this distance. But unquestionably, the overwhelming attraction Arizona has to offer is the deep blue canopy of sky stretching from here to eternity.

True to Arizona's reputation, the temperature that day was bringing the ground to a boil; the forecast, as always—hot to sweltering. Alone to survey the range, I watched waves of heat roll across the desert floor like an invisible tide.

I was walking on a slight downhill grade on my way back to the monastery hiking in from the interior of desert. It was late afternoon when the sky was reddish-gold, but time enough to climb back under the fence at the far end property for Vespers without hurrying. With my hand on the top wire, I stood still waiting for my heart rate to slow, realizing my rapid breathing was the only sound I heard.

Facing the monastery, I did a double-take as my body stiffened. Hanging directly above the abbey was one lone very **dark** cloud and nowhere else. It was nestled on the roof as if steeple was keeping the cloud from advancing. Its cameo appearance baffled me because it was light and cheery outside, not dark and stormy; I wasn't even wearing a sweater. It wasn't raining, nor did it feel like it was going to rain. I searched the sky for other clouds, but it was a perfect pastel blue, clear and bright, all the way to Mexico. I felt afraid. How could one dark cloud form when the sky held only the wispiest traces of condensation? It was hard not to see the improbability, the disbelief, the under-estimation which was naturally followed by the inevitable spiritual symbolism, dark vs. light; good vs. bad.

I pushed my way under the three wires and slunk back to the abbey keeping a low profile trying not to be noticed by the angry looking cloud I was approaching. Nearly there, I started running jumping over cactus, crashing through tumbleweed, hopping over rocks. Two minutes' of running and I'd be home safe and sound. As I ran, I thought, of all the places it could have settled on, it *had* to be the monastery. I felt it wasn't here by accident, it had singled us out.

I hoped I could make it before the cloud burst in a deluge causing more questions: what would the cloud scatter?

Drops of water? Or would it shoot hard ice pellets, like nails? No, the temperature wasn't that cold. That's what made seeing it so unsettling; it was still hot outside.

When my hand grabbed the handle on the back door, I stopped and thought; do I really want to enter a building that had this ominous dark presence suspended above it? I slid the door open, and crossing myself, I went inside anyway, happy I made it back unscathed.

I walked to the safety of my room where I threw my cowboy hat at the closet. I sat on the edge of my bed wiping the trail dust off my boots. The slow thumping of my heart was the only sound in the room.

Suddenly, there was a tremendous blast that almost knocked me to the floor. The doors and windows shook in one gigantic spasm, and at the same time, I thought I heard the puzzling sound of a faraway bell. What the was that, shot out of my mouth. It was the loudest thunder I ever heard! A nervous thirty seconds passed while I steadied myself on the bed for more explosions.

Fortunately, one monstrous blast was all the little cloud had in and it was over; it had exhausted all its pent up pressure. I wouldn't be surprised if the monastery was jolted off its foundation!

I was shaking when I stepped into the hall. I looked up and down to see if others were near. No one was close, but I did spot the Superior standing in the kitchen with sisters Viola and Teresa. They were gesticulating excitedly to each other.

I hurried to join the safety-in-numbers-group. As I approached, I caught what Sister Viola was saying: "The thunder was so loud it knocked the plate I was washing out of my hand to the floor," holding the two pieces of the broken dish in each hand. "Then I heard the doorbell ring. Look, the cover was blasted clear off the wall and landed on the other side of the table." She took a few steps and asked, "Can you believe the doorbell's heavy metal cover shot all the way over here?" She picked it up and passed it around to let us feel how heavy it was.

"But are you all right?" Reverend Mother asked.

"I'm fine," Viola said with relief, "but I've never heard anything so loud in my life!"

We stood dumbfounded, happy to have cheated death, our nervousness slowly diminishing.

Satisfied no one was hurt, Esmeralda left to check on the others and make an anxious inspection of the buildings, ending our impromptu emergency conversation; when she left, the permission to speak went with her.

A minute later Esmeralda returned with a report.

"For some reason the chapel is filled with smoke. I'm getting Sister Teresa. Maybe she'll know where it's coming from. You come too, Viola." The three of them left for the chapel to check for the origin of the smoke.

I was curious too. A few seconds later, I went to see for myself. Opening the door, I stopped short; she was right, the chapel *was* filled with a heavy black smoke. Sniffing, the vaporous matter smelled like a cooktop element had been left on the stove for a week. This didn't make sense since the chapel wasn't anywhere near the kitchen; it was beyond the foyer, after two right turns, down a hall and past the refectory.

I walked to my bedroom still shaking a little, leaving the three sisters wandering around in the smoke searching for its source. It *was* baffling. Out of all the rooms in the monastery, it was the chapel that took the brunt of the cloud. No where else and spoke volumes.

That evening when we went to Vespers, as each sister entered, she stopped, took a deep breath and scrunched her nose scrunch in disgust before taking her seat. Unable to discover the source of the smoke, the sisters called in the cowboy carpenters. The next day, like Red Adair and his crew capping a gushing oil well, the carpenters threw ladders, hoses, ropes, and flashlights over the side of the truck like rodeo gear.

I heard the foreman father report to Esmeralda, "We'll git to the bottom of this," while directing his sons to start looking for the cause of the smoke. The cowboy carpenters spent the day looking *under* the house, *in* the house, and on *top* of the house conducting thorough searches. Clumping boots were heard throughout the buildings.

After the carpenters' exhaustive investigation, the father announced triumphantly, "I apologize, it's our fault! We accidentally connected the lightening rod to the rain gutters. When the lightning hit the rod, it sent electricity around the buildings in a live circuit."

It was an honest mistake by these dedicated workers. Still, why did the smoke accumulate only in the chapel? It left me with an uneasy feeling.

The carpenter continued, "It's dang lucky the electric heater t'wert on. Your whole spread would 'a been on the stagecoach to kingdom come!"

I could see the headlines now: Nuns sent to heaven the hard way; film at 11:00. Thinking about it, what better way could there be for me to meet my end: I would most likely be in a state of grace; I wouldn't be alone since my spirit had zoomed to heaven with the whole community; I would be buried near the abbey with sacred ground covering me till the end of time?

One day with the chapel windows wide open, the smoke was gone; not so the anxieties the close encounter caused.

That night it was hard for me to sleep. I lay awake worrying whether the rain gutters and lightning rod had been connected properly this time. If another bolt comes cracking down on us, would the doorbell cover be blown across the room again; would the chapel fill with heavy smoke to overtake us, and God help us if the heater happens to be on.

Hoping a change of position would change my thinking I rolled on my side and slipped my arm under my pillow. It occurred to me, not for the first time, having insomnia *inside* a monastery is harder than having it out in the world. There are no sleep aids to help with drowsiness, no magazines to flip through by the side of the bed; no getting up for a glass of warm milk, and no television with its continuous drone of noise to lull me to sleep.

Here, there is only the desert silence pounding in my in my ears letting me know I'm still awake while everyone else in the monastery was sleeping. Commanding myself to sleep is a losing battle; my body didn't fall for my pretend yawns.

Lying here, I wondered if sleeplessness was hereditary. My thoughts carried me back to my father's sleep routine. I would see him at 2:00 in the morning, drinking coffee, his head buried in a newspaper, reading; smoke from his ever-burning cigarette funneling through the top of the lampshade, swirling a yellow haze to the ceiling. I don't know what made him get up so early, but after drinking so much coffee, I never understood how he was able to go back to sleep at all filled with so much caffeine. Nicotine is a nerve stimulant too. By all accounts, he should have been doing handstands off the recliner.

Still restless, I lay in bed worrying about the next lightning strike. Similarities surfaced between a bolt of lightening striking a house, and what happens when drinking hits a household and both become ~~intolerable~~ inoperable: sparks fly—angry flair ups occur; electricity short circuits—family roles become hazardous; currents malfunction—negativity peaks; fuses blow—tempers flare; power is cut—parental leadership dissolves. Unfortunately while trying to feel drowsy, whenever I thought of a similarity, I was jolted into wakefulness.

I turned on my other side thinking it was too bad families don't have people like the cowboy carpenters to come in to repairdamage. Most families catering to a drinker do have however, a finishing crew consisting of one woman, a disapproving wife shaking her head at the deplorable antics of her husband. She has no need to wear gloves because her hands never touch a squeegee, or scrape at sill decay to clean his messes. This is someone who is galvanized by the need to feel in control and actually looks forward to the times when the household is turned upside down, when she's in the best position to methodically 'right' the disturbed household. They even consider suggestions how to right the situation long-term, insulting.

I was wide awake now. Who is sicker, the drinker or their partner? I looked at the square electric alarm clock by my bed to see the green glowing hour hand mark another hour. In my half-awake sleep state, the realization came to me these *helpful* wives are wound in counterclockwise direction. It gave me a ~~practical~~ *great* idea. Instead of going through all this rigmarole of setting things right, wouldn't it be easier for family members to ~~hogtie lasso bushwhack~~ wait for a drinker and confront them with their actual ~~smart-alecky disturbing~~ childish behaviors to convince the drinker they have a problem? If the drinker is unwilling to believe one person's hair-raising story of what a drunken side-winder they've been, maybe a whole corral full of ~~wranglers~~ family members and friends describing harrowing instances, would jolt the drinker's memory. The stories might not be as dramatic as shooting their way out of a saloon in a drunken rage, or downing a snootful of firewater and running poor Billy-Bob down with a horse, or accidentally shooting someone in the back with a six-shooter when they were aiming at a spittoon.

Then again, the accounts just might be enough for the heavy drinker to finally admit to a problem—being bailed out of jail, starting a fist fight with a neighbor over trash cans, parking a maroon car next to a car already parked, so close, it actually left a long lavender stripe on the other car. Maybe personal, embarrassing instances would be enough to make the drinker aware they weren't fooling anyone; it was time to get help.

The last thing I remember before falling asleep was the boisterous exclamation: Yippee-Yi-Yo Ki-Yay!

CHAPTER

33

The colors of a spectrum are always the same, and always in the same order: red, orange, yellow, green, blue, and violet. It's the complete color-coding arrangement made by God. Nothing displayed this order more perfectly than the prismatic window dressings in the sky—rainbows.

This was my train of thought as my eyes skimmed the disorder of the stained glass workroom. There is no hand sign for 'craft' or 'art,' but there is one for glass, and with a quick rub of an index finger across the smooth surface on the enamel of a tooth it let someone know immediately you where probably talking about the "glass shop".

Art rooms are very interesting rooms, and this one was no exception. Without any fastidious attempts at neatness, we let the chips fall where they may: glass chips, bark chips, ceramic chips littered the floor along with shavings of copper wire and drips of solder; artistic mulch spread around our chair legs like they were nourishing our minds with creative ideas.

Each of us who worked with stained glass had an assigned work station and it was up to the individual how clean she wanted to keep her area and tools. If person didn't want to spend much time wiping off her equipment for the next day's work, it was only fair she should work in her own mess, as one sister so aptly put it.

I looked at Sister Dorothy's station brushed clean, with everything placed just so. Sister Patty's work space had a 'what's the point of cleaning when I'm coming back tomorrow' look, as did mine. Although I hadn't been here that long, my space was already covered with silver splashes of solder that burned pockmark-like scorches into the square yard of carpet I worked over, evidence of my sloppy amateurish work.

In the center of the table, like a bouquet of flowers, leaned our glass cutters soaking in lubricant.

With practice, I learned how to use a soldering iron, a gun-like tool that becomes extremely hot when plugged in, used to melt the solder at each joint. With more practice I learned how to use a glass cutter the size of ball point pen. It has a rolling carbide tip that 'scores' glass as it rolls across the surface. And with even more practice, I learned how to ignore the painful cuts made by the careless handling of a piece of glass.

Most of the copper wire we used for hooks had either been donated by a local resident, or old telephone wire the sisters found on their property. We never ran out of uses for it: our floors showed it. They were covered with the stuff. Before we could use it, we had to scrape off the black plastic coating making the floor of the glass shop

Large uncut pieces of glass stood against the walls. Especially exquisite were the large chunks of opaque variegated glass leaning against a wall that had swirls of color running through them. They were so beautiful, they were almost too good to use.

The biggest piece of furniture in the room was a huge wooden chest pushed against a wall perfect for storing thousands of pieces of left-over glass of every shape and color. It was a discarded card-catalogue from a library that had about 50 long, shallow drawers. Pulling one out was like peering into a treasure chest full of make-believe diamonds, emeralds, rubies and sapphires; a convenient way to keep colorful groups of phony gem-like pieces together.

As I looked at the large chest full of extra glass chips, it occurred to me we could put them to good use making glass mosaics. The art director, Sister Gail, liked the idea. It wasn't long before I was given an easy first project to work on: a fish that involved little detail work. The black lettering of "IXOYE" was painted across its body painted by hand. I cut a small piece for an eye. A grinding machine specially made for mechanically smoothing edges took the 'craft' out the work but when I looked at the smooth black finish on the glass eye, it was worth it. I could follow the same pattern used for the hanging stained glass fish. The word "IXOYE" was a Greek symbol for Jesus. It is the initial letter of the phrase, *Jesus Christ, God's Son and Savior.* Sister Gail explained that back in the time Christians didn't dare to wear any mark of their faith, the symbol of the fish easily conveyed to others they were Christian. It was used in any number of ways: tracing the fish in the dirt, scratching it on a tree or chalking the innocent little fish on a rock, let others know they were believers.

The next day at my work station I found a small wooden tray complete with handles and the pattern of the fish Sister Gail left for me. Flat and one-dimensional it was a good first project. I traced the foot long fish on the bottom of the tray and began gluing the light brown glass for the scales and blue glass for the water background.

I was looking forward to the next day when I would fill in the spaces between the pieces by pouring plaster of Paris over the entire image.

I protected the tray's wooden frame with masking tape in preparation for the plaster. Sister Gail showed me how much water to mix with the plaster of Paris making a paste. We then poured the gooey mixture, the consistency of cake batter, directly on the fish and put it on the windowsill to dry.

The next day when the plaster was hard, I wiped off the excess plaster, damped-sponged the mosaic clean careful not to scrape the plaster and painted the letters "IXOYE" in black. I thought it turned out well.

Someone else thought so too. Sister Gail informed me when the very next visitor in the gift shop walked in, she stood perusing the items a long time. Scrutinizing the entire shop, from the hand painted mugs, to the driftwood crucifixes, to the stained glass roadrunners, and packets of stationery with sketches of the monastery printed on them, complete with steeple and background hills. Sister Gail said the woman suddenly stopped looking, pointed at the tray and said, "I want the fish."

This was the beginning of my mosaic career.

Because it is customary for Cistercian monasteries to actually take time to make gifts for their other monasteries instead of giving impersonal store-bought items, my mosaics were deemed suitable. I started receiving requests for upcoming feast days from Reverend Mother for gifts prior to upcoming feast days we could send from the entire community. I was flattered, and welcomed the special work. I was even permitted to continue working during non-work times if it was a rush job.

Saint Benedict, one of the first fathers of the Cistercian Order, pictured holding a book of his rules, was the next project. I was delighted in spite of some reservations, after looking at his picture. His rounded head and long graying beard would be more difficult than a fish. Piece by piece the face of Saint Benedict took on a three dimensional look. When it was finished, I hoped it would be sent to Merton's monastery of Gethsemane, in Kentucky; or perhaps it would end up on a wall in Mac's monastery in Oregon; I would never know.

When Sister Gail handed me a holy card of the Lady of Guadalupe, I thought I was in over my head. The picture was complicated, with intricacies and blending of subtle colors and shades. Studying it, I knew it would be a project lasting weeks; rays of light exuded from her body and a small angel was holding her up. Her hands were held together in prayer and she was wrapped in a flowing chartreuse gown with hood that had a pattern of gold stars dotted on the material. I was intimidated.

The next day I found a piece of plywood leaning against my work station from Sister Gail, who had sanded it the day before. With the blank board in front of me, I drew on a grid, lined up a T-square, a ruler, erasers and tracing paper along the edge and started in. Patterns, color and order are what make mosaics. I reassured myself again I wasn't replicating the aurora borealis. I was simply copying colors which were anything but simple. I had nothing to worry about. After penciling in grid lines on the card corresponding with the grid lines I drew on the piece of wood, and I traced the woman's image on the board. I was ready to begin.

I have never been a good illustrator; drawing is not forte. Even the simplest outline of a horse looked like it had been drawn by a sixth grader, and let me know I was severely impaired in this area. I had every reason to feel threatened. I told myself to stop worrying because the sketch would be covered with pieces of glass and no one would see it. After convincing myself it was only a guide, I started in.

Beginning at the bottom, I sketched the wings of the angel first. As her image materialized before my eyes, the words on the back of the holy card passed through my mind. They gave intensity to my actions. I thought about the traditional story of the Lady of Guadalupe, the patron saint of Mexico, who appeared to a poor Indian named Juan Diego in 1531. After telling him she was the Mother of God, she instructed him to ask the Bishop of Mexico to build a church in her honor on the hill they were on. When the Bishop didn't believe him, Juan Diego asked the woman for a sign. She told Juan to climb a certain hill and gather roses in his garment. It was winter but when he reached the top he found a garden of roses, gathered the blooms and walked back to the Bishop. When Juan let the roses fall from his garment, instead of watching the roses fall on the snow, the Bishop was staring at his cloak. Looking down, Juan saw the image of the woman on his cloak, surrounded in rays of light. She was standing on a crescent moon being held up by an angel in the form of a young boy.

One thing was clear; this mosaic, with its shading, clouds, and two heads was going to be much more difficult than my first projects. I could feel the tension rising in me.

Over the years the sisters accumulated light-to-dark shades of every color in their collection of glass in the card catalogue storage cabinet. All the colors were here, finding just the right shade was the hard part. Pulling out drawer after drawer, I sorted through the glass and picked pieces of rose-colored glass and placed them on the table next to my glass cutter.

I started at the bottom piecing in the little angel dressed in dark pink holding the lady's hem. The angel was directly beneath a sliver of crescent moon, not holding it up as I first thought, he was holding the trailing ends of a light pink gown in his fingers.

Gluing the pieces on the grid lines was time consuming but pleasant working quietly in the hot desert afternoons. Beside me the other novices were scoring and cutting, along with me, working on their own projects.

Every day I was greeted by the lady lying under a scaffolding of grid lines; and every day I read the prayer on the back of the holy card asking for the gift final perseverance. I thought I didn't need any help standing fast. It is the one area I had confidence in. Even so, I never turned down the possibility of assistance from above to further my vocation; I welcomed all the help I could get.

Day after day, I continued cutting and breaking pieces of glass, making headway on the project. As I watched the mother of God fill in nicely, my mind began bringing up ideas on its own. I realized working on the figure of the Lady of Guadalupe made me feel like I was an attending parent, and I was processing my own emotional scaffolding.

As I meticulously placed piece after piece on the grid lines, a sense of doom surrounded me. My thoughts questioned the kinds of scaffolding wives create when living with husbands who like to drink. I began wondering why mothers adopt a particular kind of parenting. Common sense told me that if a child feels secure, it was probably because the parent was available; so the child grew into a confidant, secure adult. If a mother wasn't available, then a child grows into an anxious, nervous adult, due to the alternating intimacy and guessing if the mother will be there. If a child doesn't have any needs met, they'll probably have no confidence, and grow into a needy, emotionally unstable adult, going through life fearful most of the time. In the quiet of the glass shop, fitting in piece after piece, it was all coming together.

It follows, if a child is used in the role of a friend, the parent is a thief and a swindler. They have conned away carefree childhood days, and replaced them with problem solving and care-giving. As I lined little chips of brown glass around the edges for a border, the connection became clear to me. Having an emotionally distant husband forces his wife to elicit love, comfort and assistance from her children, thus making an unsuspecting child develop a support system strong enough to hold two people; the child and the mother. A heavy load, to be sure. Childhood is supposed to be a time of wonder, not a time spent wondering how the mother needs the child.

The mosaic taught me parents were artisans, constantly laying in colors of human behaviors starting with a blank pattern in the first days of life. They shape experiences in vivid segments, with each color, blending into the next, in a special mix of internalized color, making a beautiful new individual. It was all falling into place.

The solid brown crescent moon presented two problem areas: both ends tapered to very thin tips that were tricky; pieces this small couldn't be stored. Finding a piece of brown glass the size of a saucer, I placed it in a rag, walked outside, and struck it against the walk. Then I was able to sift through the shards searching for pieces small enough to use for the tips of the moon.

After weeks of scoring, cutting, and gluing, I reached the final section, and the most difficult; the soft colors of her face. But when I attempted to glue in the delicate features, it felt like an invisible force was holding me back keeping me from continuing. It was the oddest feeling. Hesitantly, I would stare blankly at the open parts of her face. For some reason, I was cautious; no reluctant, to start, and thought it was due to my lack of experience.

It became drudgery and I had no explanation for it. I felt so unsettled I was certain the religious anima, as mediator between the self and ego, was working on my spiritual awareness in some way.

I knew logically, that the religious anima reveals images to a person in the easiest way possible, dreams; but wished a more direct method of communicating would come to me. Instead, I was nudged by moods, inclinations and abstracts that didn't relent. By bringing my past into the present, I had eased unresolved feelings into my moods making me feel restless and uneasy. It occurred to me these bothersome perceptions were typical of the nature of the anima and remembered an idea from the well-known medieval text:

I am the flower of the field and the lily of the valleys. I am the mother of fair love and of fear and of knowledge and of holy hope. I am the mediator of the elements, making one to agree with another; that which is warm I make cold and the reverse, and that which is dry I make moist and the reverse, and that which is hard I soften... I am the law in the Priest and the word *in the prophet and the counsel in the wise. I will kill and I will make to live and there is none that can deliver out of my hand*.*

The mystical text didn't help matters, especially the last line. In a monastery where there are few external stimuli, problems are impossible to avoid. The reality of the monastic experience is that it becomes a site of awesome encounters of solitary struggles. Monasteries are good for just this sort of thing. By doing nothing more than innocently laying in chips of glass on a mosaic, I was forced to look at the reality of my life. Something had to give.

On one very hot day, I noticed how unusually quiet the afternoon seemed, more so than usual; no birds chirping outside the many windows, no novices around making work noises, no professed sisters with their black veils fluttering as they walked from one building to another. The stillness felt like someone had died, like a dead calm was hanging in the air.

Then all of a sudden drops the size of grapes started falling outside in a torrent of warm rain. It was as if the most basic level of my unconscious had opened in a sudden flash of clarity too. I had a strange sensation of knowing; peacefully, I just *knew*. The reason I was having trouble piecing together a glass mother, was because I didn't see my own mother as whole. My memory's eye wouldn't permit me to portray the essence of motherhood, because of the distorted perception I had of my own mother. For the first time, I saw clearly how wives, catering to husbands who drink too much, are as unbalanced as their husbands.

I now began to understand why I couldn't bring myself to put together a picture of motherhood. It arose from the dubious bearing of a mother who mistakenly thinks the word *submit* means to yield, or surrender to the will of her husband, instead of realizing its rightful meaning is to "commit something to the consideration of another". Submitting problems to a husband is seldom an option for individuals who let themselves be fused with another.

In an instant I knew why I was having trouble putting in the pearly chips of glass in the pale Lady's high cheekbones; they were an indication of having a strong bone structure. Having a backbone means possessing enough healthy self-esteem to be able to step away from fusion with another. It means not being afraid of being alone. I questioned the character of all mothers who were afraid to stand up and take risks. How could I piece together a bone structure from the model of incomplete self-love I had in my mind's eye? I couldn't.

I realized why I couldn't design eyes that are unable to see their own self-worth, much less engender a healthy 'selfishness.' When a mother's need outweighs those of her children, it leaves out large chunks of parental concern and vision is blinded. Knowing this, unconsciously it was holding me back. Just as sightless are parents who require resolutions of conflicts *from* their children, making it impossible to see how much damage is being done; damage remaining a lifetime. No wonder I was having trouble finishing the eyes on the mosaic; it was the perfect fit explanation.

Something inside me wouldn't let me position pieces for a mouth after having experienced communication that is geared to only 'safe times', and not when others feel like talking. How could I, after years of experiencing a mouth put together a mouth after years of experiencing a mouth that didn't have opinions and no voice of its own? After years of absorbing that one learned to communicate only when the imbiber feels like listening, and not when others need to speak; when communicating means listening to a barrage of complaints? Really, how could I complete a mouth when I knew only houses a silent voice mistakenly seen as a meditative spirit, and not as depression? Or when not speaking out is the result of fear? There were no colors for this.

It was when I was down to the last few pieces. I realized choosing to live with someone who drinks too much and not doing anything about it, corrupts healthy self-esteem and anyone who does is unhealthy as their spouse. From the beginning of the project, my unconscious, with its clear recognition, wouldn't let me put together her face, because it was the complete visage of the false self!

As soon as I realized all this, inspiration flowed; choosing red chips next to orange, yellow against green, blue touching violet: putting everything together with my hands, heart, and mind; until holes were filled, cracks were covered, spaces closed, and I was ready to begin the final phase: mixing the plaster of Paris in a bucket, and then pouring it over the mosaic, covering her completely. Working the clayish paste with my hands, I pushed the wet goo over the figure until all the cracks were filled and left it to dry at my work station over night. Before I put my tools away, I looked at my hands, tender and raw, irritated from weeks of glass cuts, and was surprised to see how each cut filled in with plaster too: like the mosaic, I had been through a process of becoming whole.

The next day standing over my dried work of art, I knew the art supervisor would surely give it away as a gift to another monastery. I would probably never see it again; I would have nothing to show for my weeks' of work except a new insight into my sub-conscious motivations; a new clarity to my life's purpose. These were a gift of a lifetime. It made me think of the legacy of a drinker's environment not bequeathed in wills. What will family members have to show after putting up with someone who refuses to get help? Inheriting money and property; even bills and debts, will never outlast the detrimental emotional effects a parent has on their children. What is the shelf life of hidden guilt? How long can the loss of childhood be locked away? Invisible mistreatment can't be kept in cartons.

Leaning over the hardened plaster I found it personally rewarding after all I had learned, composing a legal document, a make-believe will distributing a drinker's estate:

I, Mr. 'Today's the day I finally stop drinking' Smith, being sound in my own mind, in the event of my accelerated demise, do hereby bequeath the entire bulk of my misfortune to my children to be divided unequally among them.

I leave the label of 'stubborn' to those who refuse to be manipulated by the strings of motherly need caused by my being a poor hubby. Split between you, my life's work, years in the making. It might be hard moving such a mountain, but the rewards will make it worth your while. $.03 cents a can now, isn't it? I leave my responsible nature too. How could I *ever* forgive myself for placing the six-pack that flew off the top of the car when I pulled away?

I leave my charming personality too. "The open can of beer between my legs is not mine officer, it's my wife's. I know she's not in car, I was holding it for *her*."

I leave my wonderful sense of humor also. Who else would think this funny? "I'm not planning on drinking any more, I'm planning on drinking just as much"

And to my beloved wife and partner, I leave this one final worry, "Now that I'm gone, who's going to tell you what to do?"

With my work done, somehow I felt battered and bruised, but knew deep inside I was smiling a wide, impassioned, gratifying smile. I stood back and let myself admire the perfect balance and harmony now shining from the lady's eyes, which represented the enlightened universal soul of all mothers, endowed with the immeasurable power of motherhood; mothers who are at once the radiant center housing the voice of conscience, and the listening heart of gentle approval. The bonds of motherhood wrap the family in an indefinable warm glow of love connecting one with another in close relationships. It had all this to come together at last.

Sister Gail walked in to check on the kiln she had loaded with clay items from her mornings' work and glanced at the white slashes covering my hands. Thinking it funny, she said with signs, "Look what the mother did to you," acting surprised.

With the beautiful face now looking back, I signed back, "You don't know the half of it," and went to wash my hands.

CHAPTER

34

That evening during Vespers I was all set to meditate: ready, set, go.

It was no use. The hopelessness I felt for wives catering to husbands who use alcohol as pacifiers was all I could think about. How could I meditate with this feeling sadness overpowering me? Is this what depression feels like?

I started again. Back straight, head erect, hands open to receive. But my peaceful mindset had been destroyed by former troubles that had insidiously slipped in my mind unaware. How *do* wives of drinkers cope knowing they will again just go along with their husbands' *total lack of respect* for them and their families? I would despair too. I sat in my meditation pose full of belligerence. All that came to me was the feeling of overwhelming sadness for the futility of their plight.

I looked across the chapel at the Novice Director. She had no idea I was squandering the meditation period thinking of best adjective to describe a drinkers' uncaring behavior. What made it worse, was knowing name-calling actually makes these ~~assholes jackasses~~ husbands feel *special* so it defeats the purpose. It's actually better to ignore the ~~big baby~~ infantile behavior because negative attention is better than no attention.

Sitting in a room with a large crucifix, I wondered what Jesus thought of my meditation.

One more time: ready set go.

The image of a row boat on a lake came to me. The next moment I realized the depressed state of wives living with a drinker is like sitting in a row boat with a hole in the bottom. While simultaneously scooping water out with both hands, it's realized bailing alone is not the solution. Appreciating the fact that sitting in water all day is conspicuously unpleasant, they hope no one will notice. If it is, they divert all comments immediately to the color and shape of the vessel and not how the hole was caused in the first place. They never mention how hard it must be trying to keep afloat day in and day out.

With my meditation time running out, I thought of Sister Lorna and her therapy sessions. Was the water in her boat sloshing over the edges when it was decided she would get therapy to keep her from going under?

Hearing a knock in the back of the room, I felt grateful those in command ended her suffering. Sometimes depression resolves on its own in time, but other times it's necessary to hand the person a bucket. I was relieved Sister Lorna had someone to help her bail at least once a week.

Walking out the door, I thought, no wonder I hard time meditating with all this trying to get out of my subconscious. I felt a wave of sadness realizing I never drained the boat for my mother.

CHAPTER

35

It was a cold morning. I was sitting in the novitiate listening to the Novice Director talking about the great Carmelite mystic, Saint John of the Cross express the inexpressible in his book *Ascent of Mount Carmel,* when I heard it. As far as unusual sounds go, this peculiar sound was definitely in the top two.

The Novice Director was holding a Repetition class and all the novices were sitting paying attention to the nun walking around the classroom elucidating points about his lofty spiritual doctrine. As informed Christians, the director thought we should at least be familiar with his teachings; journeying to pure spirit like he did we could do on our own time.

None of them had flinched or made a movement to look for the sound. Puzzled, I knew they hadn't heard it by their uninterested postures. It was a sound unlike anything I ever heard before, but I've never lived in a desert before either.

With my hearing on the alert, I tilted my head to one side and listened with purpose, but all I heard were the words of Drusilla paraphrasing the saint about fanciful thinking. I sat back reassuring myself must have imagined it.

We were learning about two interior bodily senses, imagination and fancy. Saint John of the Cross is one of my favorite mystics/authors, but he can be difficult to understand, even with an instructor explaining his meanings for us. Sometimes it took several explanations and many re-readings before I would start to understand. For example:

> All the things, then, that these senses can receive and fashion are known as imaginations and fancies, which are forms that are represented to these senses by bodily figures and images. This can happen in two ways. The one way is supernatural, wherein representation can be made, and is made, to these senses passively, without any effort of their own; these we call imaginary visions, produced after a supernatural manner, . . the other way is natural, wherein, through the ability of the soul, these things can be actively fashioned in it through its operation, beneath forms, figures and images.
> Book II, chap. II, para 3; *Ascent of Mount Carmel.*

I thought, maybe it was an audible mirage, convincing myself I made it up. I looked at the other novices and wondered if they heard anything in-between Drusilla's remarks.

Wait, there it is again! I looked at the others; no reactions so I leaned back in my chair listening to Drusilla finish making her point. I concluded everything was normal and I hadn't heard a thing.

Was I losing my mind? I hadn't lived in the desert *that* long. I've read about desert hallucinations driving people mad brought on by a lack of water, but I wasn't lacking fluids. How could they miss hearing the strange hissing sound? It didn't sound like an engine or anything mechanical, it was more like a buzz. Ten seconds later; it was back, louder this time. I looked at the others. But there were no puzzled faces or looks of bewilderment; they were still just paying attention to the lecture. Was my mind playing tricks on me? I was too young to be cracking up!

Maybe this is one of those interior bodily sense communications the saint was talking about—imagination and fancies. Drusilla was explaining how they come "... *passively with out any effort.*"

One more time, from out of nowhere, the prolonged hissing shot through the silence sounding like steam escaping from a radiator. I was tempted to yell, don't you hear *that*?! Although it had been a very chilly morning, it was still Arizona; the temperature was bound to rise. Even so, this wasn't considered radiator weather. I was stumped.

Wait! There it is again! The furious hissing sound was noticed by everyone this time. We rushed to the window to look. Our searching eyes still couldn't mark the source, so with Sister Drusilla leading the way, the entire novitiate tromped behind the Novice Director in hot pursuit. We crossed a field and went up and over the next ridge and looked down at a hot air balloon! It was not where it was supposed to be hundreds of feet in the air, it was hovering over the pointy ends of a large cactus.

If 'right with height' was any indication, this balloon was in trouble as it huffed and puffed but still couldn't make it over the hill. We stood panting, not knowing how to help facing the crippled vessel hovering about 20 feet on the side of a hill. Up close we could see its grayish blue fabric billowing loosely because it wasn't fully inflated. A wicker gondola holding a two-person crew was furiously blasting a heater sending hot air up into the balloon trying to inflate it. The balloon hadn't actually landed; it was hovering unsteadily and losing altitude with every second. It was about ten o'clock in the morning and already starting to get warm. There was no wind to speak of. Maybe it was getting movement from a solar wind higher up. They were so low it was lucky they had avoided hitting jutting rocks, crevices and large tall soaptree yuccas.

Out flew the pillows. Out flew extra rope. Out flew their extra clothing in a last ditch effort to lighten their quixotic position of hanging in the air, aerodynamically unable to move from their dead air space.

They were in the precarious position of having to put it down on an uneven slant of the hill among cactus and rocks. They were so low, with the rising heat, it appeared they were fighting a losing battle. After about ten minutes of watching this bizarre sight, Sister Drusilla announced we had had enough excitement for one day. Who knew how long the craft would be hanging in the air this way? We marched back to the novitiate, occasionally hearing a gush of hot air sent into the balloon to work against the earth's pull. It was like watching a wounded animal suffer, it was a worrisome sight. I will say, it did give us one of the best all-time Repetition classes ever!

We staggered back to the novitiate trying to keep our habits from catching on cactus, turning our heads every so often hoping to see the wayward balloon air borne.

Back in the class room, I wondered how were we supposed to concentrate on anything other than the downed craft? It wasn't realistic, especially hearing the periodic blasts of air reminding us of its dangerous location.

Drusilla continued explaining the discourses of Saint John of the Cross:

The stairs of a staircase have nothing to do with the top of it and the abode towhich it leads, yet are the means to the reaching of both; and if the climber left notbehind the stairs below him until there were no more to climb, but desired toremain upon any of them, he would never reach the top of them nor would hemount to the pleasant and peaceful room which is the goal.

Book II, chap. II, para 5; *Ascent of Mount Carmel.*

Sometimes the most important lessons in life practically have to land on your head.

Because we were out of the balloonists' sight, they must have wrongly thought 'out of sight meant out of earshot'. As soon as our audience of sisters departed, they started blaming each other for their confounded luck; little did they know how far sound travels on dry desert air. Panic must have set in. One started to yell at the other. Paradoxically, it had taken the two of them to bring the craft in on the side of the hill, but only one now was to blame for the whole predicament. Overhearing their plans for extrication attempts sounded like an odd combination of Saint John of the Cross and Laurel and Hardy. They were not going to surrender to a complete defeat and were determined not to give up.

As we listened, we learned hot-air balloon recovery is not a process that happens quickly. The crew continued to blast in hot air while trying everything they knew to reach lift and right the problem.

Almost going aground somewhere in the desert with no phone, miles from their destination, with a group of mild-mannered nuns keeping track of their every move, must have been embarrassing. The only thing worse would have been if they actually landed. "Herb, if you had balanced it like I told you, it would have flown right," a deep voiced man yelled at the other man, "and we wouldn't be in this mess!"

"I never even wanted to go on the desert adventure in the first place, you talked me into it," the other man defended. "You talked me into it!"

"Well, my flight strategy was *perfect*. If you would have only listened to me," Herb returned. "Now we've lost all control, and it's all your fault!"

No response. The second man probably thought a retaliatory remark would do no good and kept his mouth shut. I bet he was wishing for a door to slam, I empathized. He did the next best thing, an extended gush of hot air was released that was like saying, "Just try and talk over *this*!"

We all laughed at this decisive measure, even the Novice Director. "It wasn't *my* fault the wind died, you know," the second man countered.

"Yes, I know", Herb scolded, "but you should have realized you can't control the wind. You should have taken this into consideration and planned accordingly. How we ever got so far off course, I'll never know."

I sympathized. Having stalled on the side of a hill was bad enough but if they had actually hit it; it would be an admission of powerlessness and neither wanted to take responsibility for this fiasco.

Hearing the litany of excuses coming to us on the desert air sounded so familiar. They were like the classic reasons used by binge drinkers to defend their crapulent behavior, foisting responsibility on convenient excuses—allergies, so-called predisposition, genetics, history, anything but taking responsibility for their predicament. It was a side show in itself. The more they shouted at each other, the more memories it brought back. "Herb, why didn't you just trust me? I've had more experience and more flight time than you," the dialogue started again.

"I'm sorry, but so far trusting you almost landed my ass on cactus." Herb complained. Even Saint John must have smiled in agreement at this.

From the classroom, Drusilla allowed us to keep track of the balloon during the hour class, one of us running over, checking on it, running back and reporting to the others. It came close to the ground a couple times but never did touch land. This, in itself, must have been a feather in their caps. "I'm been commandeering one of these babies for years and never had *one* unexpected touch down yet!"

When their squabbling stopped, we jumped up and looked outside. The balloonists were able to save face when a sou'wester picked up, and on the weakest of currents, were carried off in the deep blue Arizona sky, taking their barrage of excuses with them. I can still see the red balloon framed by the sun, as it disappeared in the white clouds. Once again a hush fell over the desert. With the bells for the next office disturbing the desert air like sudden metallic screeches of peacocks, I walked to the chapel with the balloonist's excuses still in my ears. I was overjoyed realizing it was the same with me. Like the balloonists, my father's lame excuses for drinking, were all behind me now too.

CHAPTER

36

To any other member of the monastery, a family visit I welcome event. The usual thoughts of loving exchanges and familiar hugs should have been enough to look forward to, but my thoughts were all in the form of questions. Will they laugh at my habit? Will they try to convince me to leave? And most important question of all, will my father be sober? How embarrassing would it be if he showed up roaring drunk, stumbling to the convent door? I started imagining the worst, "Hey, sister, shupposing you turn the blame heat down a little?" The suspense was killing me. I could hardly wait for them to arrive. Weeks before they were scheduled to visit, I tried to come up with a believable excuse to use in the event the head of my family arrived tipsy. I couldn't come up with one believable reason. There was nothing to excuse this type of uncalled for behavior.

There was a sense of relief though, as I looked forward to being able to escape the unrelenting train-schedule of the monastery's routine, even if it was only for three days. It had been over a year since I had seen my family and I missed the witty repartee that constantly went on. I missed them all, but I had never been doubled over under waves of homesickness. Being away from the family *problem* was a big relief. By stepping into the visitor's parlor with them, it meant stepping back into the familiar pecking order replete with hairpin triggering mechanisms. Still, it would be nice being around people I didn't have to handle myself while interacting with them. The monastery has its own pecking order too, from the Bishop to the priest to Reverend Mothers to Novice Directors, down to the latest face carved on the community's totem pole, the newest novice. But no pecking order is more acute as one's own family. In an extravagant way, when I entered the monastery, I broke free from all the *shoulds* from my kith and kin—which was freeing in itself.

The day of reckoning was finally here. It was during dinner when the reader, Sister Dorothy, reading about Saint Anthony, the classic model of the desert temptation experience, was interrupted by the sound of a car on the plateau slowly approaching the monastery. Dorothy stopped her reading. The sisters stopped their noisy eating, and I put my full spoon of sweet-potato soup back in my bowl.

Sheepishly, and without raising my head, I lifted my eyes to view the length of the long refectory table and saw Reverend Mother staring at me. In fact, they were all staring at me. We all knew; my family had arrived. I no longer felt hungry.

The Novice Director pushed against the table and rose, motioning me to follow. Like a warden leading me to the electric chair, I placed my napkin on the table and followed her out of the dining room to the guest parlor. I sat behind the counter next to her, on the edge of my chair listening to their station wagon slide to a halt on the gravel followed by the slamming of car doors. The heavy foot steps of my father were leading the way. He opened the parlor door and my brown headed mother entered with him, followed by my two brothers and a sister. The first thing my father rushed to say was, "What were all those blue things scattered over the hills?" We never talked about anything personal, so it was a good ice-breaker for people I hadn't a seen in over a year. Hearing his intelligible speech, with relief I thought, *thank God, he's as sober as I am!* Then my mother hugged me across the counter as she said hello.

"We've been collecting cow manure," I answered proudly. "I've been doing it for weeks. I like doing it," I said smiling with relief realizing he really hadn't had a drink to get him through the visit. His speech was clear, unimpaired and alcohol free. I was elated.

In an official capacity, Drusilla welcomed them and handed them the keys to the guest house, pointing to it telling them the refrigerator was fully stocked nut if they needed anything else to ask. I held my breath hoping my father wouldn't didn't ask if the monastery put out a special label for beer like *Nun Better* or the like; he liked to tease. They climbed back in the car to settle in the guest house. Now that the getting reacquainted part was over, I relaxed knowing I would be spending the next meditation period giving thanks my father arrived as sober as a judge.

Drusilla left the parlor leaving me alone to wait for their return.

I sat back in my chair thinking. Since my family seldom took extended vacations, I was grateful the higher-ups (I mean way up; chapter 53 in Saint Benedict's Rule advises monastery's to show guests 'every courtesy.') Room, board, a full refrigerator, I *know* made them feel *very* welcome! I was filled with gratitude the monastery had gone all out to make them feel welcome because Lord knows, my mother deserved the rest.

I sat picturing them finding the homemade loaves of bread immediately, the real butter and the flavored honeys. More than anything else, being given food, I know made them feel welcome; I wasn't so sure about the deafening silence with no phone or television set to drown it out.

It wasn't long until they returned and the parlor door opened again. We left it open to coax in a non-existent breeze. They sat on plastic chairs behind the counter set in the middle of the room. I was on the other side. The first thing I did was explain why the counter was here in the first place. "As a cloistered community, the nuns observed papal enclosure they weren't allowed to cross." And that typically a Cistercian parlor had grilles separating the nuns from the outside world, but we were lucky here, we only have this counter. The sisters voluntarily agreed to abide by the separation rule."

"Okay," they agreed. I could tell they were taken aback by the whole religious environment. Who wouldn't be? It still scared me at times.

They were shocked seeing my habit and veil. I caught them glancing at it like they couldn't believe their eyes. Even so, they only made complimentary remarks about it. They seemed visibly relieved when I told them during work periods I wore jeans, a shirt and a cowboy hat proving I hadn't strayed too far from my familiar look. I didn't need a bathing suit because we didn't have a swimming pool or frequent a local plunge.

"What, you pray all the time?" a brother asked.

"Not exactly, but we didn't play card games, volleyball, croquet or the like because we weren't here to have fun. My fun came in hiking and community get-togethers." As an example, I told him I enjoyed sitting on folding chairs outside the refectory with the community in a circle in cooler evening air, snapping green beans into bite-sized pieces, or shelling peas from pods while watching the most spectacular sunsets imaginable, all of us in total silence, of course, making his mouth drop open.

Their eyes widened in unison while they laughed. *Some* fun seemed to be the general consensus.

With the parlor's open door, I asked them to keep their voices down. I reminded them again this was a monastery where people didn't talk if we could help it. I told them we made hand signs and gave an example of a sign to show it wasn't so easy: I held out two fingers. Then I squeezed the fleshy part of my hand with the other. I asked them what I meant.

None of them volunteered a guess.

Why, 'SECOND HAND', of course." They all groaned because it was so obvious.

I gave them a couple more chances. This time I used the sign for 'sister': pulling on the end of my veil; no one got that one either. Or the sign for glass: scratching an eye tooth with an index finger; slick enamel wasn't exactly an obvious comparison.

To people who didn't know the reason for using signs, silence, their overall grasp could be summed up with the question, 'What's the point?' Without going into too much detail, I explained how silence promotes inner peace and helps us remain solitary, even in the community.

"Oh," I heard in response. It was enough of an explanation; I wasn't going to start compiling impassioned reasons for my point of view. I did tell them about Saint Anthony. As the first hermit, craving solitude, he chose to live in cave so he could fight off temptations of the flesh and attacks of *demons*. I believed these were the same 'demons' that were triumphantly stalling my meditations. I wondered if they would think twice about leaving the guest house.

Life in a monastery is not grave, solemn and serious. I gave them a humorous example of signing, one that happened not long after I entered. I was sitting at the dining table when Sister Viola gave a series of signs. This was unusual because we weren't supposed to make signs during meals. I knew the first sign was 'grass,' (both hands chopping simultaneously) but couldn't understand what the second sign meant so she had to make them a second time. I still didn't get the meaning. Exasperated, she picked something out of her salad. She was holding a leg of a grasshopper!

My smile went flat as I told her I finally understood.

Without using any signs at all, she retorted, "I *told* you we had fresh food!"

My family laughed. I was positive they would now go through their salads with a fine toothed comb.

Using the episode as a lead in, I told them about our large garden telling them I could grow just about any type of vegetable now, even rhubarb. I told them how tomato plants come with built-in worms, and if they wanted, I could bring one up in a bottle to show them because they'd never believe how large they grew. They passed on this show and tell.

I let them know how backbreaking it was picking peas, and how mounding dirt over rows of potato eyes was almost as bad. I let them know how sweet corn tasted when it's eaten soon after it was picked. With pride I told them we canned a large share of what we harvest to get us through the winter.

Puckering my lips for affect, I told them how much I liked homemade dill pickles cured from a previous planting. Scratching my head, I confessed I didn't know why head lettuce was so hard to grow in this soil. Not enough water? Too much water; it was a constant battle. Somewhat sarcastically, I told them hoped they enjoyed the fruit of my labor.

I apologized for not having many strawberries to offer, unfortunately, we only grew strawberry *leaves* this year with hardly any blossoms. On the other hand, we did have an excess of zucchini! I'd bring one tomorrow to show them how long they get, along with a few ripe melons. I wouldn't forget to bring up a couple tomatoes too because I wanted them to taste what additive, preservative and spray-free fruit tastes like, positive they'd tell the difference. Stretching, I told them how much stronger onions tasted than bulbs from a store that had been shipped in from somewhere on the planet that ended with them being stored in bags.

While they were here, I suggested hiking as a time-filler. With first-hand experience now, I explained how smaller rattlesnakes were deadlier than the large ones because their venom is more potent. I warned them to watch their step and not lift flat objects like boards, because snakes liked to hide under them. As best I could, I gave a rendition of how a disturbed rattler sounded, but think it sounded anemic. I laughed when the image of them high-stepping around rocks and cactus like ballerinas, came to me.

I stopped and caught my breath. They sat back in their chairs.

If they we going to hike, there was another caution they needed to know about besides snakes. I told them to be on look out for wild boars too. Somehow I didn't think they would be hiking much.

But if they *did* want to hike, I'd loan them my canteen because in 100° or more, dehydration can easily turn into heat stroke so it was probably better not to walk too long at this high altitude.

As is the case in hot sunny areas, I told them bugs are a problem. Understandably, the refectory, because of the food, attracted its share of insects and the occasional housefly scouting for crumbs. I was reminded me of a funny incident that happened to our chaplain, Mac, a good natured, friendly sort. Since the cooks put Mac's meal out ahead of time, he brought it to their attention how occasionally he found gnats and flies floating in his milk. They began covering his food with a napkin and placed a saucer over his mug of milk.

I told my family this gave the Novice Director an idea for a practical joke. Since all our mugs were the same color—off-white with black handles, she took Mac's mug to the ceramics shop and painted a big, black spider inside it on the bottom, glazed it, and re-fired it in the kiln. After it dried, she replaced it with the identical mug on his table. A large black spider on the bottom of a white mug would be hard to miss.

Relating the account, I told my family before going to dinner the next day, everyone had been told of the trick Sister Drusilla was going to play on Mac. We were told not to do anything that would give it away, like turning our heads every minute to see if he was drinking. That afternoon we ate dinner in an expectant atmosphere waiting for him to discover the phony arachnid in his milk.

We waited and waited. The longer he dawdled, the harder it became trying to keep our faces straight: crows cawed, horses whinnied, and bumble bees whirred passed the open screened doors while we watched the priest out of the corners of our eyes pick up his mug again and again, sip, and replace it, uninterested, back on the table.

"Then all of a sudden, there was a loud scream."

"What's this?" the priest shrieked. In one motion, he pushed back from the table making his chair screech while he stood; his eyes wide in disbelief. Not believing what he was seeing, we watched him stare fixedly at the grotesque creature clinging tight to the bottom of his white mug for a long time.

From the other side of the room, quickly the superior, Esmeralda, 'signed' the explanation to him letting him know the spider wasn't real. It had been fired a second time in the kiln and was now a permanent fixture in all his drinks!

Mac's sang-froid slipped to the floor with the drops of milk from his mouth. His face blushed a shade of red I'd never seen on a human before. Then he started laughing. We all started laughing. We laughed and laughed and laughed. I don't think he'd seen anything so funny in a *long* time. Neither had I.

Hearing the funny story made my family laugh too. I hoped it made them see the monastery in a different light other than reciting rosaries, walking in processions and performing penances.

I assured them there were difficult times too, like how hard it was struggle out of bed each day when the bell ringer jangled the bell in the hall at 3:15 A.M., even before my eyes had time to make a seal.

For people who set their alarm for 11:00 A.M., they nodded in agreement.

I let them know how difficult meditating is at times too, making sure they understood why I persevered. I told them the struggle in itself was purifying even if my wandering thoughts felt as annoying as someone poking me in the armpit at times. I put up with the pestering because I was certain meditative states were express lanes to God. I wondered if my talking about meditating would urge them to try sitting in a lotus position, and/or, meditating. I had a feeling my mother would, because living with a drinker for years she was probably already close to sainthood.

With the bells ringing for Vespers I told them if they wanted to hear us chant, they could go into the visitor's side of the chapel. They excitedly said yes, even my father who I was sure hadn't set foot in a church in decades.

Getting up, I'd told them I'd be back at 9:00 tomorrow. They shuffled out the parlor door muttering about the heat. Hearing the chapel door open, I started clearing my throat.

I went out the other door, stepped in the hall, and walked to the chapel where Vespers was about to begin. Sitting, I heard my relatives climbing into the pews in the back, but couldn't see them.

On the second day of their visit, my mother thinking I'd like to talk to my siblings without parental interference convinced my father to stay away with her. Considerate and kind, she always put others first. I *was* grateful to her for this bit of privacy that allowed me to sit and talk with my siblings without them. I think on some level she knew children raised by a drinker were like walking wounded, living veterans after a war who shared a unique camaraderie. She knew we could sympathize with each other in our shell-shocked states so I was glad she arranged this 'free' time but didn't ask her why she did it, I was glad she didn't go into complicated reasons involving blame. After all, they were on vacation.

I spoke again of familiar experiences, concrete external things they could relate to like the vegetable garden and told them how a creepy centipede managed to find its way inside someone's pant leg. I learned soon enough these strong toothed mandibles had jaws and sharp claw that are poisonous so having one on the loose was serious; 'all legs, feelers and jaws,' is a good way to describe them." Fortunately, after hearing a few thuds of a shovel, I told them, the offending reddish-brown chilopod lay dead, but they should definitely be on the look out for them.

Around lunch time, I went on about a subject that would interest them: food. I told them know how hard it was not being allowed to raid the refrigerator for leftovers when I wanted. No need to worry though patting my bulging stomach, I wasn't skin and bones yet.

I told them about *hermit days* and how we could eat anything we found in the refrigerator. Bragging, I confessed to drinking a whole liter of root beer at one time after a long walk.

I told them how special holidays were here too. To prove my point, I told them about last Valentine's Day where we had a heart-shaped meatless meatloaf dripping with spaghetti sauce, spinach with cashews and tutti-frutti ice cream for dessert. No need to worry, I assured them, I was getting enough to eat, I said, tugging at my tight cloth belt.

When the bells rang for the noon meal, they walked back to the guest house. I left for the refectory where I gobbled my food but they still beat me back in the parlor. I walked in and winced as my brother handed me a beer over the counter. It was of course, against the rules to accept any food, drinks, or presents. All gifts should be turned over to the Novice Director to be distributed as she saw fit. (A pair of sandals given to me, I might eventually see on the feet of another sister on the other side of the choir.) But since they went to all the trouble of carrying the ice cold beer across the yard, how could I insult their efforts by refusing it? I couldn't. I just hoped they'd remember to take all their empties with them. I know my mother was fostering her spirituality while she here, the sisters, the chanting, the emptiness of the desert, the whole holy shebang. How could she not? She already had long-suffering down pat.

I took the can making sure my back screened the door to the interior of the monastery, let out a loud cough, and pulled the tab. With a nervous look around, I guzzled half the beer and quickly handed the can back to my brother. On this hot morning, the cold bootlegged beer slid down my throat with all the force of a tranquilizer. As it made its way through my insides, I rationalized I kept *most* the rules in the monastery I just wasn't fanatic about it. I downed the rest of the beer. (I only did this, of course, because my father wasn't in the room. I didn't want to start him on a binge.) Pushing the empty can back across the counter toward my brother for disposal, I watched as he deftly collapsed it against the counter with his palm and put it in his pocket out of sight, disposing the evidence. His action reminded me how ingenious children are at surviving when they are forced to live with a parent who wets their whistle occasionally. We are stupendous survivalists and deserve our crest, a heraldic seal, maybe an **S** for long suffering. I *thought* about bringing this up, but I didn't. Instead, I told them how good it tasted, almost as good as a cold drink of pure mountain water.

Changing the subject, I turned and picked up a couple gifts from the display shelf behind me. The roadrunner won approval for its unique design. I knew it would, it was the only non-religious item we had left. I told them how my stained glass work had been up-graded from single objects to whole areas of space—mosaics. I told them it was a very exciting change, one I was looking forward to because, thank God, I had strong fingers. I opened and closed my fingers in front of the faces repeatedly. It was either rather that or a bout of arm wrestling and I hadn't pulled *that* many weeds to give me a muscle.

I told them about the time it seemed to be the general consensus of the Superiors that I should learn to make bread. I related to my family that it wasn't just ordinary bread, but the famous Trappistine bread that had been in the order for generations and generations. Anyone who tasted it fell under its ambrosia-like trance: especially when it was served warm with lots of melted butter over it. I felt honored to be chosen to learn the techniques from scratch. It meant getting up at 2:00 A.M., but the way I felt about it, if I was getting up at 3:15 A.M. anyway, what difference will another hour make? Both times took monumental efforts.

Sister Viola had spent several days taking me through the many steps, showing me how to measure, mix, knead, and bake this delicious full-flavored bread, both white and wheat. It was a difficult to drag oneself out of bed at 2:00 A.M., but it was worth the extra effort. I liked getting up before anyone else and moving about the shadows in the dark quiet and actually began looking forward to these once-a-week bread making sessions.

My family was all ears when I told them how one morning, after setting the large bowl of dough aside to let it rise, I joined the others who were saying Vigils in the chapel. At a certain point, I left to check on the bread. The whole refectory was filled with the delicious smell of bread dough that had turned into a white puffy mass bulging against the plastic cover. In order to get more of this aroma, I crouched down and put my face close to the bowl, lifted the cover, and drew a long deep breath. This was the wrong thing to do. I didn't know how the mixture, because of the yeast, emits a strong odor of *alcohol* that almost knocked me out! I lost my balance and reeled back, nearly hitting my head on the side of a counter.

Thinking back, I told them while laughing, if I had fallen, no one would have ever believed me if I told them the knot on the back of my head was from making homemade Trappistine bread!

Hearing the bells announcing the start of the next office, I was glad to leave them laughing as I sidestepped through the door and walked along the many windows to the chapel at the end of the day.

On the third day of their visit, it was 9:00 the next morning and the orange, fiery sun was already making the temperature one for the record books. It was extremely warm.

Bright sunlight was streaming across the fields of golden sand verbena, and I watched with a blurred vision the rippling heat rise from the ground. In extreme heat like this, everything is still. All activity remains for another day if possible. The sun was so bright it made the surroundings feel like I was in the still frame of a picture. Only the crickets in their whirling dervish-like buzzing didn't mind. On this day, one of the hottest of the year, my family decided to spend some time shopping in Tucson and would be late for our visit. It must have been something important for them to go out on their way like this, adding another hour to and from Tucson in this unbearable heat. Even so, I was glad they took the opportunity to see the southwestern architecture and experience its Indian art, maybe picking up a souvenir or two.

On their return, around 11:00, I watched their station wagon approach leaving a hanging trail of billowing dust behind their car. When they stopped at the guest house, I rushed outside to greet them, positioning myself behind the long chain that marked the front boundary of the enclosure. (This chain was lowered when the monastery's car or truck needed to leave.) I stood behind the chain lightly swinging it back and forth bringing the pleasant odor ofdesert weeds fanning my face. The motion of the swinging chain under the searing sun was mesmerizing. Squinting as much from the sun as from disbelief, I focused on the activity near the guest house. I could see they were now carrying something like they were a slow moving elephant, stopping and starting, staggering every few steps. It was a strange sight to see, so completely out of the ordinary; lift, carry, abort; lift, carry, abort. Peering through slightly closed eyes, I wondered if the heat had affected my eyes. Whatever it was seemed to be of some weight.

They managed I bring the object halfway over the clumpy uneven field before they collapsed again, their faces red from the strain. Then, with one gigantic heave, they picked up the box up one last time and clumsily dropped it in front of the chain. *What in the world*, I thought…

With faces slick with perspiration, my mom proudly stepped forward and announced, "It's a ping-pong table!"

I stood in disbelief until they opened the box and slid the cumbersome table out. My father unclasped the latch on top, opening it so I could see the whole table.

Smiling, my mother said, "You mentioned there was no recreation here, so we thought ping-pong might be one activity they would allow."

I was surprised. She had actually convinced my father to drive another hour back into Tucson, look for a shopping center selling sporting equipment and purchased the expensive item. Then tying it on top the car, they drove another hour to the abbey, and carried the heavy load in a joint family effort across the desert on one of the hottest days of the year! It *was* quite an accomplishment. And one I relived every time I saw the chain.

What would the Superior say? My face was immobilized knowing exactly what she would say: "Absolutely not! This is not a resort. Where do you think you are, Disneyland?" I felt helpless. I told them how grateful I was for the gift making it clear it was up to Reverend Mother Esmeralda to tell us if we could keep the gift. In my heart I knew there wasn't a chance in the world. I kept thinking positively telling myself, *you never know, we might be able to keep it.*

They folded up the table and left it by the chain until I had a chance to plead my case to Esmeralda. The bells started ringing for the noon office. I watched as my family trouped back to the guest house for lunch.

All through dinner I tried to come up with the right soft sell. I waited outside the Superior's office trying to find the right words to tell her about the generous recreational donation. The longer I waited, I was sure there was no good approach. After all their effort, I didn't want her to say, "Tell your family they have to take it back."After dinner, I motioned to Reverend Mother I needed to speak with her. I followed her through the hall and into her office where I began to get a sinking feeling. I didn't want to hurt my family's feelings by telling them the sisters didn't want the table. I knew a recreation period would not suddenly be inserted to the ancient monastic schedule on my account. She expected no chit-chat, so quickly I explained how much it meant to my family to have the sisters accept their gesture of appreciation, a ping-pong table.

I backed away from the inevitable disapproving tirade.

Immediately her eyes lit up. Without hesitating, she said with a big smile, "The timing couldn't be better! The Abbot General is coming for his *Visitation* this summer. You'll never guess, during his last visit with the monks in Utah, they played play ping-pong! Thank your family very much for their generosity, and tell them it is a God-send." As I started toward the door, she continued, "There's one more thing. I'd heard the Abbot General is pretty good."

I couldn't believe it! I couldn't wait to tell my family the good news. I made my way along the corridor besides the chapel looking out the arched brick windows into the monastery's backyard. The sisters were not much on ornamentation it reminded me and were keen on a plain, ordinary natural look; no hanging plants, no macramé's, no bird feeders or planters, only four arched brick windows framing the distant mountain. I remembered how drawn I was to this emptiness when I first entered. Feeling the same pull, every time I came to the last window, I still stopped a moment to look.

Remembering my mission, I went into the parlor where I found my family anxiously waiting for the verdict. I didn't keep them in suspense and blurted out: "It's okay! Esmeralda said we could keep it! On one condition: I couldn't leave the enclosure." This wasn't an insurmountable problem for my family, they knew what to do right away. They unhooked the chain, placed the table where the chain should have been and set up the net. They stayed on their side, and I stayed on mine. Making the most of this liberty, we played all afternoon. Lizards scurried by checking us out, road runners and rabbits stopped momentarily to regard us with caution, while overhead hawks circled at a safe distance eyeing the ping-pong ball like it was a juicy lizard egg.

As the sun rose higher over our table-tennis afternoon, it came to mew how ping-pong was the perfect gift from parents who didn't ***do anything*** to keep the disruption of drinking out of the family. With each back and forth motion of my paddle, words came to me: you're important/you're not important; you're worth something/you're not worth anything; we care about you/we don't care; you're good/you're good for nothing, over and over the remarks flew like they were well-placed drop shots, no one can defend. At some point, you'd think the players themselves would stop the game out of sheer ridiculousness.

Pounding the ball speedily across the table, I could understand why they didn't. Unconditional love is love without any limitations that turns into altruism when the welfare of others is ignored. Drinking affects the whole family. Some children are able to bunce back and learn to cope with the family 'problem'. I didn't think either one of them would ever stop their game-playing long enough to figure out something so simple. I was one of the lucky ones, I came it through it in robust health; how else was I able to walk for miles over these high hills?

Sweating and hot, I was happy hearing the end of work bells. We folded the table and pushed it to the side, ready and waiting for the next games.

It was the last day of their visit. After we said our goodbyes in the parlor, as sad as it was, I knew they had to go back to their own treadmills; I on mine. I walked down to the garden for morning work in a glum mood. Alone in the garden I heard the sound of their car edging over the gravel on the road, trail away and disappear.

I stopped hoeing and tried to see if anyone was waving from inside the car but they were too far away. I waved anyway just in case. I was left in the quiet leaning against the hoe thinking over the last few days. The image of them struggling with the ping-pong table over the field came to me; it was one memory I'd never forget. Even so, I knew my father's sobriety was the best present by far. I calmed myself with the knowledge they could come back next year, in the spring perhaps, when it wasn't so doggone hot!

I idly pushed the hoe. Something was nagging at me. I had the feeling something was missing and questioned why I felt their actions on one of the hottest days of the year wasn't enough. What was missing? It came to me with all the fierceness of the sun spiraling down on my head at noon. It was the lack of intimacy, intimacy that can't be bought or enticed into the open with specialty gifts because it fights forced captivity. Only absolute liberation allows its gradual descent.

As soon as I realized this, I took hold of the hoe with both hands and waved it in the air after them. With a sense of futility I yelled halfheartedly after them, "Come back you cowards!

CHAPTER

37

Father David could have been a king reviewing his monarchy and we were his loyal subjects; he was the Abbot General. He was accompanied by an assistant, Father Jaques and they were here in the official capacity of conducting *Visitations* that serve as a time of reflection and assessment for the entire community. There was no getting out of it and was perhaps the biggest drawback of living in a monastery; you can't just get up and walk away for a while. The Abbot General would be going from monastery to monastery speaking to each member of the community, priests and nuns, abbots and abbesses, novices and postulants alike. That meant me too.

The Abbot was tall and broad shouldered. It was easy imagining him wielding a sword in a defensive stance protecting the sisters against desert marauders. He was about six feet tall with a healthy tan that spread evenly on his serious face. He had the trim physique of an outdoorsman, not a pale complexion of someone who had been slaving away over books inside a church administration building. He wasn't wearing gold or silver cuff links; in fact, he didn't have cuffs at all. He wore the loose black and white habit of a Cistercian held together by a leather belt. I knew for him to be in such a high position, he did it the hard way through long periods of prayer, fasting, penances; he earned it. He deserved to be treated with respect.

His assistant was a clean-cut middle aged priest whose first language was French. He seldom spoke due to his limited English. When he did, he was difficult to understand because of his thick accent. Where Reverend Father had no detectable accent, Father Jaques had nothing but; he even laughed with an accent.

When I learned these important members were staying in the guest house, I was excited because *any* variation in the schedule was welcome. As soon as I learned the Abbot was originally from England, I hoped the hot dry desert sunshine in Arizona would be a welcome change from the wet rainy region of his homeland, at least for a week.

The more I thought about my upcoming Visitation, the more nervous I became. And in a monastery, there is ample time to think. It's all I thought about. I was not looking forward to my turn at all. What did I have to say that would be of any interest to a multi-lingual, well-traveled and well-informed Abbot? I was already intimidated. With all of us standing in the refectory, as the Abbott's right-hand man, Father Jaques with his broken English, attempted to explain how they had flown from a monastery in Italy. Father David took over telling us about the circumstances surrounding the monastery's name. At the beheading of Saint Paul the Apostle, when the sword was brought down, the saint's head bounced three times and from each spot a spring erupted, and eventually three churches were erected: Church of Saint Paul, Saint Paul and Nero after the Emperor Nero who ordered the beheading.

Excitedly, Father Jaques added, the springs, located in the sanctuary, still flow today.

As gruesome as this was, I remembered something about the order's beginnings that was worse. The reformed rule for Cistercians was due to a cleric discovering his friend's body in her room. When the undertaker's coffin wasn't long enough, he removed her head, wrapped it in a cloth and left it on a table. The cleric was unlucky enough to find it! Understandably, his gruesome discovery irrevocably changed his views on mortality and caused his extreme self-denial and asceticism. This is why the **O**rder of **C**istercians **S**trict **O**bservance, or OCSO, is so strict. You don't forget something so integral to the formation of the rule we follow today. In fact, it made me think twice about joining an order that had its roots based on mayhem and murder. Until I realized the discomfort I felt growing up with someone who drinks too much with its sacrifices, suffering and losses, actually helped prepare me for this strict life.

The visiting abbot announced he wanted to hold a getting acquainted session in the form of questions and answers in the Community room. We all walked a few steps to the room to the left and took our places in our desks. As long as he would be doing the talking, I had nothing to worry about and crossed my hands in my lap.

The range of questions the Abbot discussed included concepts of keeping the silence, the charism of communities, what it means to live contemplatively and the cosmic means of the Eucharist, addressing subjects of interest for the whole community. Because Reverend. Mother Esmeralda was fluent in French at times English and French were mixed into the conversation along with phrases in Italian, and of course Latin. I felt listening to these important dignitaries I was listening to powerful rulers conducting foreign affairs and pictured a crystal chandelier suspended from the ceiling instead of the wagon wheel. In place of our hand crafted wooden table and chairs, I was in a hall decorated with large tapestries instead of the smooth river stones making the fireplace. I imagined we were sitting behind white tablecloths set with silver and china with heads of state discussing matters of great importance. It wasn't until Sister Lorna broke in and asked a question in her very distinct eastern accent that I was reminded we were still in our Community room next the refectory with the Abbott sitting at Mac's table in front that had a saucer covering his mug to keep out bugs.

No one seemed surprised though, when Sister Lorna, the one person who could tell the difference between swill milk and raw milk, asked the Abbot one of her earthy questions phrased in the politest way possible: "What should be done when physical energies are awakened?" A hush fell over us all.

Reverend Father, having fielded questions of this sort innumerable times before from both men and women, answered "Many of you may know the reason already. Energy transforms into the divine energy that leads to a mystical marriage..."

His words were drowned out by the thunderous noise of a jet engine shattering our peace. It was so loud it was frightening! It rattled my teeth not to mention the windows on the monastery disturbing our peaceful afternoon. Then came the inevitable sonic boom in its wake shaking needles off cactus in a trail of noise as it zoomed by. What the hell?!, I almost said, putting me in danger of losing my innocent status.

Sister Esmeralda jumped up. We followed. Outside, we all searched the sky, including the Abbot and Jaques, for the origin of the sound. A low flying jet was moving at a high rate of speed parallel to the ground away from us. I had never seen such a low flying jet in all my life. It looked like was going to crash nose first into the trees on Mount Enright! The jet was so low we were almost eye-level with the pilot in the cockpit! We stood pop-eyed; gawking at him practicing defensive shows of strength hoping his space age controls told him to pull up soon. I wondered if the pilot felt he was in a time warp flying over Trappists from the past driven by outdated ascetic practices trying to bring peace to our souls. What he was doing was in total opposition to our way of life.

Yes, how peculiar we must have looked to the pilot as he sped through the sky seeing our veils flapping as we ran, necks craning as we searched the sky. We were contemplatives dating back to the 12th century and the abbey of Citeaux (from whose name Cistercian is derived) who spent hours in prayer trying to find inner stillness. We must have looked quite odd to him!

Reverend Mother said apologetically, "There's an air base in the area. The people in charge tell me they use this route to train pilots. It's called contour flying, flying below radar signals. They use electromagnetic contour probes…"

Her explanation was lost in the wake of trailing engine noise. Waiting until the noise was almost gone, Esmeralda explained, "Sorry everyone," shaking her head in disgust. "I've complained numerous times about this, but it doesn't seem to do any good. Air Force Authority said they were planning land-use more efficiently especially over noise-sensitive areas. They promised to send a publication showing flight maps to inform citizens of jet departures and landing paths, so there is hope."

With our heads tilted up, we watched the jet turn at the last possible second and bolted to the top of the mountain and went and over, then down, flying out of sight on the other side, leaving us in a heavy silence."That's all, shows over," Esmeralda guided. "Let's go back inside."

As I followed the group inside, I couldn't help wondering what the Abbot and Father Jaques thought of our peacetime maneuvers; jets practicing flight patterns at close range in sustained training operations. Or what they thought of the United States Air Force in general.

I think we were all glad to get back into the safety of the monastery. It was such a sudden change from the usual soothing quiet. The shocking display from the air force left me feeling demoralized until I realized our quiet life of prayer, in direct opposition to the loud show of might, was just as powerful, if not more. When everyone was seated again, Esmeralda told us this wasn't the first time jets flew overhead and the sisters nodded emphatically in agreement.

"That was *some* welcoming," the stunned Abbot said, and calmly continued his question and answer session.

With my nerves still rattling being audibly traumatized, it was difficult to pick up where the Abbot left off, 'how silence illumines a person in God'. Instead, I thought about the harmful effects of exposure to noise apart from the obvious, hearing impairment. I knew noise stimulates aggression and other anti-social behaviors. And how elevated levels of noise like jets create stress and may increase workplace accident rates. I made it a point to notice how many sisters broke their stained glass during work this afternoon.

There was only one thing that could have taken my mind off the fury we just witnessed. It was one that terrified me even more, my Visitation appointment with the head of the entire Cistercian Order. To say I wasn't looking forward to my appointment was an understatement. In fact, I was dreading it. I needed to come up with something like this that would steady my nerves.

After a day of hard thinking, I finally found one. I remembered something Sister Dolores told us about a piano recital she was scheduled to perform. She was extremely nervous about the upcoming performance and came up with an ingenious plan to break the rising tension that would take the focus off her performance. She set an alarm clock under the auditorium seats so it would go off mid-way.

The diversion worked to relax her so well she said even thinking about the bell sounding made it hard for her not to smile. I thought it wasan ingenious idea—bordering on inspired. I needed a plan such as this for my appointment with the Abbot General. I racked my brain determined to come up with something just as effective... until I found one.

The afternoon of my Visitation, it was a very hot as usual. It was the kind of invasive heat that turns your face red even if you're sitting indoors relaxing out of the sun; the kind of heat that saps your energy and effects motivation; it was Arizona hot. There wasn't much point changing into my good sandals for my walk to the guest house knowing road dust would not only cover the tops of my shoes, it would dust the inside of my toes as well. As a one time meeting, not knowing if neatness counts, I made the effort anyway and wore my good ones. The last thing I did was feel my hand again making sure I had my secret item.

I stood on the porch of the bricked trailer kicking my heels against the cement steps loosening the fine dust. I straightened my veil and knocked on the screen door. The words of the Novice Director came to me. "Make sure you ask for the Abbot's blessing when it's over." The door metal door squeaked open.

Won't you come in?" an enthused Abbot asked. I gave him my best smile before turning the metal door knob that was as hot as a branding iron. I was careful to cover my hidden contraband in the other. I walked in clutching the object tightly, keeping it out of sight during the entire interview I what might be the first smuggling operation in the history of the order. I followed him passed the kitchen and noticed a loaf of homemade bread on the counter and knew the sisters were keeping him well supplied. We went through the dining room into the living room that was filled with homey furnishings. A large framed print of flowers hung on a wall above the couch. A coffee table in front of the couch was clear of loose newspapers, magazines, dirty dishes, or anything else that suggested a person was making himself at home. He sat in a comfortable arm chair in the living room and I sat across from him in a chair with a floral design. Each time nervousness came over me, I gently squeezed my good luck charm hidden inconspicuously in my hand. It was like the inhalation-exhalation of a mantra, giving me a feeling of control.

He asked where I was from and when I entered. I told him it was stroke of luck I happened upon Merton's book *The Sign of Jonas* in a box in the garage by accident. I told the Abbot how I shared a love for Zen, same as Merton, and how I thought I would end up living like a hermit some day like he did. I wondered out loud how Merton was able to put into words exactly what I was feeling. I tried to convey he impressed me so much, it made me commit myself to the Cistercian ideal.

A trickle of perspiration rolled down my face. I felt breathless after having to arrange my frenzied words in some kind of meaningful order. But, I hadn't stumbled over my words, or made a fool of myself; my speech had been composed and confident. I knew it was due to the hidden advantage I was holding in my hand. It kept me from breaking out in a cold sweat, even though the temperature was close to 100°. The Visitation was only about 10 minutes but felt like an hour. When he asked all he wanted, he thanked me and let me know the Visitation was over.

I felt my insides collapse in relief.

As I was about to leave, I heard the Novice Director's recommendation in my head. So before I chickened out, I blurted, "Father, may I have your blessing?"

He marked my forehead with the sign of the cross with his thumb blessing me.

It's now or never, I thought. As I thanked him for his time, I brought up my closed right hand and opened it slowly like it was a warm bloom, deliberately, one finger at a time and asked, "Are you game?"

He looked at my hand for a few seconds and didn't say anything. Then as recognition set in; approval showed in his face. Realizing I was balancing a ping-pong ball on my open palm, his eyes crinkled in delight. I had my answer.

Esmeralda knew the Abbot was fond of ping-pong. She told me he probably wouldn't mind playing a couple of casual games while he was here and instructed the strongest sisters to bring it in off the dirt and set it up in the only room large enough to hold it, the refectory. This was no small undertaking. It took sisters Viola, Teresa, Dorothy and Patty to lift the heavy wooden table. They carried it across the yard, around the back of the monastery and through the open sliding doors. With everybody cooperating by moving chairs and place settings out of the way, we pulled the dining table into the Community room, replacing it with the ping-pong table.

What began as an afternoon of light recreation turned into a week of no-nonsense competitive games! Who would have guessed the mild mannered Abbot had a strong competitive spirit? It soon became apparent the winner would be the last person standing. That behind the quiet calm of his brown eyes beat the heart of a fierce competitor. This was the first time I ever had any personal dealings with a member of the clergy outside the pulpit. We had Mac, but it was in the formal capacity as priest performing religious rites in church. This was different. It was my first time just *hanging out* with superiors and it was nerve-wracking at first.

The Abbot, playing in his long habit reminded me of turn-of-the-century lawn attire, but his rolled up sleeves showed he meant business. He proved himself a gracious sportsman with Reverend Mother Esmeralda, coaxing her into picking up a paddle and showing her the basic shake-hands grip. During the game he picked up speed moving back and forth around the table, explaining to her, "Hold it like this." "No, the thumb goes here," in an honest attempt to improve her game. "This is the reverse penhold backhand grip, the freemiller grip, or you can use and the traditional playing style," giving her quite a workout!

With one game finished in his favor, he teasingly asked, "What? Only *one* game?" not believing she wouldn't want to try to better her game, the sign of a true gamester. But seeing she didn't have the drive, he didn't push her. We all sensed her relief.

Standing on the sidelines watching the Abbot, I hoped he didn't think we all had weak wrists. I thought back to the many heated game I had played with my relatives before the Abbot arrived. They acted as an excellent warm up.

As each person stepped to the table to take her turn, we heard time after time, "Game, set, match," accompanied by an obligatory apology by the Abbot for each of his powerful passing shots.

"Protect yourself Gail!" I felt like yelling. I had the feeling the bookkeeper was more at ease with a pencil. She gladly handed the paddle over to the Abbot's next opponent, Drusilla.

Father David had a definite case of one-upmanship. After besting the other novices, Drusilla was next but she never went beyond fifteen points against the visiting priest. Then she wanted to play me.

I had made my peace with the Novice Director long ago. Her character of a gifted and wise counsel had turned out to be true. Watching her swing the paddle now I could tell she had natural ability and coordination that showed in her flair with topspin. Even so, there was NO way I would let her beat me when we played. "This is for scolding Cathleen," I thought, drilling the ball by her. "This is for having better posture than me." "This is for the next mean thing you do." It felt good exacting vengeance on her. When she had enough of table tennis, and I was completely warmed up, the Abbot moved in and replaced her.

"In all fairness," he volunteered, "I recently gave a Visitation with a community of brothers, and we played a lot of ping-pong."

Was he trying to scare me? I wondered. I stepped up to face him. Teasingly I said back to him, "Say your prayers! Freeing any hindrances that could get in the way, he took hold of his crucifix hanging around his neck and pulled it to the middle of his back. He smiled at me over the green net to let me know he was ready. I smiled sweetly back, giving the impression I was an easy mark, but knew I would not go down without a fight.

Whiz went the first serve past me with rotating, off-balanced speed. We were off! I was lucky to even make contact, sending the white ball off the table and through the spokes in the wagon wheel hanging high in the air. We waited for someone to find the ball, which had ricocheted into the fireplace before we could continue. The goal of a smash is to hit the ball so hard the opponent cannot return it; ball speed is the aim. This was my best hope because the Abbot had longer arms than I, and he returned almost everything I hit. Even though I used sidespin effectively, smashed the ball hard,countered with drop-shots; lobbed, chopped, blocked; and even leaned in toward the net grimmacing menacingly. Nothing worked. My opponent out-played me.

The best excuse? God must have been on his side. It was as excellent justification, and one I could live with.

I had the feeling ping-pong might was more than a game to Father David. With every point he scored was a point for the entire male branch of the order. With every strong backhand or non-returnable service, it was a blow to feminine ideologies everywhere.

It was more than just a game for me too. On some level I needed to prove to myself-to the others. I was showing them I was good enough to be here and belonged here. Every passing showed that without a doubt, I had a vocation and was going to see my vocation to the end. If you didn't believe it, grab a paddle.

Each of us made valiant efforts, but after two days of hard play, the entire community conceded we were no match for the Abbot General, not even me.

In the middle of one of our afternoon competitions walked Annette, the latest novice. Reverend Mother had strategically planned the new novice's entrance to coincide with the Abbot's visit so she would have the privilege of meeting him.

Still holding our paddles, we wandered around the refectory waiting until all the introductions were over. Knowing Annette brought her oboe with her, Esmeralda asked Annette if she'd like to treat everyone to a music recital. What better way to break the ice? "Well, ah, the thing is, I haven't been playing all that long…"

"Anything will do," Esmeralda encouraged."I haven't mastered it yet. But if you'd like to hear what I *can* play…"

"Surprise us,"Esmeralda coaxed.

Annette slowly got up to get her instrument.

I knew the oboe is one of the most difficult instruments to play. I was looking forward to being entertained by the poignant sounds of the wood instrument. *This really is well-timed*, I thought. *Music played for the Abbot General should be like the royal music of the spheres to reflect his position. Too bad we didn't have harpsichords, lutes and bassoons as well.*

On her return, the new novice walked tentatively to the front of the room to face us. She fiddled with the mouthpiece to get the treble or soprano range just right, rubbed the wooden tube against her leg making it shine; everything was ready.

Taking deep breath, she blew into the woodwing intrument.

My eyes opened wide when I heard her play. "This is an 'A'. This is an 'E'. This is an……

Good Lord, she's playing one note at a time! My face felt hot with embarrassment for her.

When she was finished playing the notes of the scale, we got up to leave amid a smattering of applause.

We followed. But not before leaving our paddles on the table as a reflection of her ability—flat.

CHAPTER

38

A colonial farmhouse it wasn't.

It was inevitable, too many novices and too few bedrooms. The solution involving the least amount of disruption was to buy another mobile home, like the guest house. It would have a firm foundation and be bricked several feet high, so when it was finished it would look like a regular house built with wood framing, dry wall and stucco. The challenging part was moving the heavy oblong living space from Tucson by freeway, over highways, through a wash and up the curvy drive to the back of the monastery.

The higher-ups decided the best place for the new novitiate would be in back by the craft shop a few hundred feet from the monastery because the plumbing and electricity were already in the vicinity. It was the most logical place \on the property, and not because of our loud talking and laughing, she assured the insecure novices.

I didn't know how smart it was having the novices separated from the main monastery; as a deterrent, it's easier not to horse around with the threat of authority living within ear shot. I couldn't see us throwing wild parties till dawn with quests using drugs and alcohol; most likely all she'd turn up someone reading late into the night; we were real rabble rousers.

In any case, the chain acting as a boundary would be dropped for the trailer.

The preliminary clearing of the selected space, the leveling, raking, and rock removal had been completed by Mac, Viola and Teresa, not to mention the laying of pipes, putting in water tanks and plumbing in ground that was hard as marble. After weeks of linking drains and pipes, the converting was over. Cords were disconnected; power tools stopped, and blades fell silent. Sawhorses were moved away, pounding of hammers, sounding as loud as jackhammers in the quiet desert, were laid in a heap with the rest the arsenal of stilled tools. Once again we were able to listen to the peace in the desert. Its resting place was an outline of twine waiting its arrival.

The space remained empty waiting for the next few minutes when creaking and groaning our new novitiate with dorm rounded the last curve. What had seemed impossible to negotiate was now being eased into place with the greatest of care. It was a monumental a task as moving King Kong's cage with him in it. Wherever we were, we stopped and watched as our new residence, gigantic and awkward, in the form of a large double-wide trailer carefully inched along, moving in-tow on the dirt road, as if they were trying not to spill Mr. Kong's water dish.

The sisters seemed capable of doing anything they put their hands to. There was no women's work or men's work, it was just work. The next few weeks, between Mac and Teresa, bricks started encasing the bottom half of our new prefabricated steel home. The bricks matched the other buildings in the monastery's complex giving the new mobile home a look of permanence; you couldn't tell it was an addition. Still, the long wide trailer would never look like a country cottage. In keeping with the Cistercian way, it would be devoid of ornamentation with not so much as a discarded pine tree on the side of the road after Christmas to make anyone think otherwise. It would be sturdy and sound enough to withstand the worst of Arizona's elements but plain and undecorated so there would be no mistaking a group of hard core ascetics were making their home here. A fireplace wasn't included in the plans, or a Jacuzzi, nor was a diagram penned for a labyrinth as a meditative walk in back.

They did however build an uncovered, unpainted wooden porch with three narrow steps to the front door. A mail slot hadn't been cut in the front door or a pull-down mailbox with flap in the design of a rooster secured in front that had a flag letting postal workers know there was outgoing mail because of course, novices didn't routinely send mail.

All prospective members are sent a small booklet by Thomas Merton entitled *The Desert Shall Bloom*. He describes how the Temple of Solomon was built of quarried stones that were shaped underground so the sound of hammers and chisels wouldn't disturb the sacred silence. I sympathized with him. He often wrote how constant construction was the 'norm' at his monastery in Kentucky. It made me appreciate the short preparation time and minimal amount of work needed before our novitiate trailer was ready.

While we waited patiently for the mortar to dry on the bricks, when no one was around I couldn't resist scratching my initials in it with a stick. Every time I passed that corner, I checked to see if they were still there; somehow seeing them gave me a sense of permanence.

In the meantime, life went on as usual as we waited for the brick work to be completed—choir, work, classes and meals. Taking her position as Novice Director seriously, Drusilla conscientiously gave Repetition classes right up to the time the mobile home was ready for us to move in.

We were all in our desks when the Director started a routine talk. "A monk must be a well-balanced person. Monks must be able to live sociably and live charitably with others." It sounded like a pep talk to help us adjust in our new location. Why? We never had arguments, heated exchanges or pillow fights in our last novitiate and pushed her *why can't we all get along* speech, aside.

Sister Patty sat squirming in her desk. It was obvious the Director's comments on hospitable and courtesy made an impact on her. To the dismay of the Novice Director, and the rest of the class, we learned different novices valued different things. This came to light when Patty asked if it was all right to bring her collection of rocks with her. She told us she had them stacked and in neat patterns under her bed.

"Rocks?" Drusilla asked, bewildered.

"Yes, I have quite a few," the novice stated proudly.

It takes all kinds, I thought, trying not to burst out laughing. I couldn't imagine dirt-filled, germ infested, filthy rocks were very sanitary. I guess she's breaking #5 on the Rules of Etiquette list: Hygiene Begins at Home. I soon learned this wasn't the reason at all; I forgot I was in a monastery where they play by different rules altogether.

As sister-wannabes, we were not allowed to stockpile or horde ANYTHING; that in itself was very freeing. Our bedrooms were clutter free, or they were supposed to be. Not having anything of value helped because protecting items means having to store them. This saved us from developing a pack-rat mentality. Having trails of narrow passageways through our accumulated treasures was virtually impossible because we were supposed to leave our doors ajar during the day.

This rule made no difference to me. The only thing I had to hide was a poorly made bed. I was good at throwing things out after a lifetime of practice. It was easier than packing and moving every single item I own each time I moved.

Trying to understand Patty's motives, my question to her (unspoken) was, if she knew we were moving, why didn't she fill her pockets and drop them little by little in the desert somewhere before we moved? Did she want to be caught?

This prompted a lecture about walking on the spiritual road of detachment by the Director. With her eyes fixed on the novice, Drusilla told her, "Sister Patty, you have too many possessions to be a Cistercian. How can your soul journey to God under the weight of all your possessions? Get rid of them."

"Okay".

"Right now!"

That was the end of Patty's rock collecting.

For the next twenty minutes the rest of us watched through the sliding glass doors as Patty carried bag after bag of her treasures from her room, tossing them over the side in heartfelt, helpless lobs off the hill.

As I watched open-mouthed, her hobby began looking more like an obsession. It started me thinking. What was her fascination with rocks about? Although she never brought it up during class, it wouldn't surprise learning Patty had a similar background to mine with a parent with who drinks more than they should. Never discussing the family *problem* with outsiders fit the protocol of children of heavy drinkers. Discussing it with outsiders seems terrifying, so much so, I likened it to being the first person rocketed into a black hole. Talking means transcending to a different reality too, one of communication and trust, which can be just as frightening. No wonder she never brought it up.

I knew only too well being raised by a drinker sometimes causes their children to develop obsessions. I am happy to say I came away unscathed in this respect, I didn't have *any* obsessions, other than being preoccupied with learning how living with drinker affected me, and removing the effects. I was lucky; I didn't harp on some subject tediously going over and over and over it… Anyway, for Patty, removing the rocks was a start.

I had to hand it to her. She was very creative. Out of all the obsessions Patty could have devised for herself here in the barren desert where fixations were at a minimum, rock collecting was the perfect choice… like over thinking is for me.

Of course, there was another possibility: maybe she just liked rocks.

Now that Patty had gone to all the trouble of clearing her conscience, Annette insisted on coming clean too. During the same Repetition class, we learned she had a peculiarity that was, in my opinion, weirder than having a rock lover in our midst.

I came bolt upright when Annette began explaining how she was able to be on time for Vigils each morning. We all found out at the same time, including the Novice Director. Ever since her arrival, she had been sleeping *next* to her bed, not in it.

"Why on earth would you do that?" Drusilla asked in disbelief, convinced the antics of her novices were intolerable.

I couldn't help smiling; there was no rule of etiquette to cover this!

Annette innocently explained, "Isn't it obvious? I'm so afraid of being late for Vigils I don't want to take time to make my bed. Changing into my clothes takes a lot of time."

"Obvious?" the Novice Director barked. "The floor in our old rooms is made of cement. You mean you chose to sleep on cold hard cement and in your jumper? This is not an obvious choice. From now on, I want you to sleep *in* your bed."

It sparked another lecture from the Novice Director, this time on the benefits of punctuality. "Being on time for the offices shows respect for your sisters…"

Annette had a perplexed look on her face, like she was trying to understand why all of us didn't follow her example and give up our warm soft beds to sleep eight hours on the cold hard floor too. It was the most obvious solution to her; she didn't see anything was wrong with it. She was like a baseball player sleeping in his uniform so he wouldn't be late for the next days' game. The only thing obvious about it was Sister Annette had a problem with perfectionism. In her defense, I couldn't remember her ever being late for Vigils. At any rate, I made it a point to notice if her clothes were wrinkled at Vigils tomorrow.

Moving day! At the end of the class, with an enthusiastic Sister Drusilla leading the way, we walked to the mobile home and began moving in. The move to the new novitiate was a breeze for me. I carried everything I owned in two trips. I had to admit transporting items across a field was much easier than unloading a lot of boxes out of the back of a truck in a new neighborhood under of the watchful eyes of new neighbors tabulating your value by what you owned.

Because the director was in such good spirits, I should have known something was up. I had the impression she was already picturing herself in front of the class passing on secrets of Cistercian life to us wet behind the ears novices, hungry for her spiritual counsel. I soon found this wasn't the reason at all.

It can't be, I moaned to myself, but it was true; the Novice Director had been assigned one of the bedrooms in the new residence. It turned out the higher-ups felt her presence was necessary to keep us in line. (They were right.) This was the only thing that dampened my excitement on moving day. *It just can't be*, I whined again, seeing the promise of carefree, relaxed times, making sign and laughing, change into tense, strained intervals of rigid concern. I felt my breathing change into shallow, short, quick breaths immediately.

My good spirits were restored remembering she thought we will be united with our pets after we die, and cut her some slack. I still hoped her bedroom wouldn't be next to mine. (It wasn't.)

Stepping up the three steps, I was surprised seeing how big our new novitiate was in comparison to the last. There was a wide open space for a living room with a beige throw rug with a few oversized throw pillows to be used for meditation purposes *only*.

One thing stood out right away—NO television set. I remembered how traumatic it was leaving the noise of my television set. But what was a hardship at first, turned out being a blessing later. Instead of hearing blaring commercials promising relief from one problem or another, we were now in an ambience of peace that was doing more for our souls (and health) than we knew.

Giving the place the once over, told me Norman Rockwell would have been hard pressed to find any nostalgic subject material to paint here! On the right side of the room, our four one-piece wooden school desks had been brought over for Repetition classes. Besides a standing blackboard and a desk for Drusilla, there wasn't much else; no world globe, no pull-down maps, and no microphone and speaker system for her. We couldn't even look forward to seeing a cute kitten or a different scenic view on a calendar every new month.

Like before, all electronic gadgets were out of the question. As Merton put it, *the ceaseless flow of words, sounds, images, and crude noise constantly assailing our senses was a serious problem. It threatened our nervous balance; it made us sick, along with the overproduction of words and concepts that were damaging to our spiritual health as well.*

Lamenting the fact we lost our spectacular view at the new location, I realized the desert, in itself, had been a huge distraction. Here, there were windows, but they were smaller, standard sized windows, not large glass sliders. A screen door opposite the front door faced Mount Enright.

When I joined the monastery I thought my moving days were over. I was somewhat put out having to move my stuff yet again. As long as this was my *last* move, I'd gladly carry my few worldly possessions over.

Standing in the living room unavoidably brought memories of my father and the absurd solution he had for every problem—MOVE. Unable to change anything about himself, he did the next best thing by starting fresh in every conceivable way, locales, jobs, houses. And for a time, the new challenges were enough to keep him occupied: where to put the television, where to put the couch, when to have the water and electricity turned on. The problem was: he dragged his family with him. After years of moving and starting over, I didn't get excited over a bigger backyard or how our new rose bushes framed a side window like he did.

Looking at his moving objectively; my family moves were fun fun; we ate out, we road in big trucks, we were forced to interact; we were never closer. Best of all there was one huge practical consideration that came with each move: maybe it will be the last.

Moving a throw pillow on the floor out of my way, I was glad novices didn't have a say in the decorating end of it. If we did, we might have color TVs, electric blankets and small student size refrigerators, fully stocked, in the bedrooms. Where is the ascetic challenge in this?

I walked to a hallway devoid of pictures. I ripped off a piece of masking tape with my name written on it and opened the door. I knew I'd be spending the rest of my life in my new sleeping quarters and hoped I could live with the décor. To my delight, I was pleased with what I saw. If the best decorated windows are the least decorated, this one was somewhere in-between. Heavy burnt orange drapes hung in panels from hooks in front of 'real' imitation sateen lining for more privacy. The flimsy lining would allow the room to breathe in the summer, adding comfort, and the thick fabric of the drapes insulating the room would protect us from the cold in the winter. New twin beds and bedding had been delivered saving us (Mac and Teresa) from lugging over the old ones by truck.

I knew the bedspreads would give the room a nice orangey-red glow at sunset. Burnt orange had always been a favorite color of mine so I felt comfortable as soon as I walked in. My new bedroom faced the opposite direction—north. And now instead of having two large square windows, my new view was long and oblong. I pushed my twin bed against the lining so I'd be able to drag the curtains open without getting up. I smiled to myself realizing I'd be able to see the spray of the Milky Way whenever I wanted. I had a feeling I was going to like this room.

My new sleeping area came with a pull-down desk making it handy to sit on the side of the bed and write. And instead of a cardboard box under the bed to use as a drawer for nylons, tights, gloves, scarves etc., my new room came with five shallow built-in drawers that would let me find items more quickly; a definite improvement. I had always been a fireman's child in that I put things on in a hurry, not caring if they were inside out, backwards, or if colors clashed, never foreseeing this quick-change routine would come in handy later in life.

I didn't have to share a bathroom with Sister Dorothy any more. Now everyone shared a large communal rest-room with four showers and four toilets; plastic as far as the eye could see. Dorothy wouldn't need to jump awake if she wanted to be the first one in the chapel every morning. Somehow I didn't think this would slow her routine.

Our move proved more of a challenge for the bell ringer—me. I would have to get up at 3:00 (15 minutes earlier), leave the warmth of the novitiate and step outside into a faster heart rate. It took courage to hike across the field this time of night (or morning). To help, novices were given her own flashlight to light the way and scatter creatures we might meet crossing to the chapel with us. Arizona at high altitudes, I knew only too well, is bitterly cold at night. The battery operated light was as far as we were spoiled; no new fur-lined parkas were handed out to help with the cold.

Now each morning, as the official bell-ringer, instead of looking out my bathroom window at the stars, I had the exhilarating thrill of walking under a sky that seemed so close I could reach up and grab a star.

Another good thing about my nightly crossing, by the time Vigils started, like it or not, I would be wide awake, like all the novices. I avoided thinking what it would be like in the winter and seeing my breath in cold puffs as I walked through accumulated snow.

Life was good in our new home. Dorothy was still the first one in the chapel; Patty was always the last; as promised, Dolores never used the throw pills for, resting; we soon found Annette was a much better worker than an oboe player, and I felt I had finally found a home. All was right with the world.

Unfortunately, we discovered another dreadful peculiarity Annette had; she wasn't afraid of snakes. The opportunity for her to prove it presented itself directly when I almost stepped on a medium sized rattler while walking to the glass shop for the afternoon work period. It was minding its own business curled up on the dirt path when I nearly stepped on it. I don't about others, but even though I was taught to love all creatures great and small, my snake phobia was in good working order. I jumped out of harms' way at the very last second.

To say the least, I didn't like these close calls. The shock of nearly putting my full weight on one left my heart thumping for some time. I was well versed in the drill by now: shovel, chop and bury the head to keep it away from animals, namely our dogs from eating the poisonous head. Avoid looking at the long mortal coil if possible. I picked up a shovel leaning against the glass shop, tip-toed back to the snake and brought the tool down hard. In one stroke, the danger was averted.

Because the new novitiate was near the glass shop, Annette, on her way to the garden, ran over to see what all the commotion was. She paused briefly to estimate the snake's length.

Speaking is permitted during an emergency and kill or be killed, qualified. As a newly transplanted city dweller, I was sure Annette was repulsed seeing her first dead snake. The thing to do was teach her about snakes so she wouldn't be horrified. I relayed the same facts the gardener told me after she killed the large rattler in the cabbage patch: smaller snakes that don't look as threatening, are *more* poisonous than their larger counterparts; even if their skin is banded, blotched, colorful or colorless, their shiny scales are made of the same protein as our fingernails, keratin; rattlesnakes have great sensitivity to heat. In a very real sense, they can smell fear.

This was old news to her. In fact, she acted like she could care less hearing snake trivia. What's more, she 'signed' how she belonged to a club called Snake Eyes where they regarded snakes with appreciation. Before I could stop her, she signed her favorite snake recipes: 'roasted, their skin is easy to peel off and can be barbecued; gravy with pieces of snake is delicious; snake kabobs are tasty; as one long sausage, they can be stuffed with a favorite topping under lots of cheese.' I wouldn't want to go through her series of signs again—ever.

I gagged, but not before saying "There isn't enough cheese in the world to make me want to taste… Why would you think…?"

Then the truth came out. She told me blood and guts were second nature to her. Before she entered she was a nursing major in college and had to dissect many a frog in her time. This explained a lot.

As gruesome as the scene was to me, Annette wouldn't let me bury the remains. She stooped, and using both hands, dragged the lifeless body through weeds near the wire fence surrounding the property. With effort, she managed to drape the limp snake over the fence before hurrying back to me.

On really hot days, days I knew a scarf wouldn't provide enough protection for my head and face, I always wore my cowboy hat even for short distances. Today was one of these extremely hot days that made mercury bubble over its glass tube.

Pointing and gesticulating, she was trying to tell me something that had to do with my hat. Knowing exposure to intense sun light affects us all, I was aware people like her with fair complexions and blue eyes, were more susceptible than others. I figured she was trying to tell me she wants my hat, the sun was bothering her. I handed it to her immediately because heat stroke is nothing to fool around with, I would be working in the glass shop anyway. She grabbed it, reshaping the brim somewhat. I responded with a smug nod that conveyed, 'I remember when the heat used to bother me too, but when you've been here as long as I have…' I wanted to tell her having so much work wasn't always the case, but I was hard pressed to think of a time when we experienced a lull in the work load. If heat exhaustion was going to happen to her, it would be now when she was unused to the desert sun. As the responsible *senior* novice, I moved about her checking her physical condition. Her face was flushed but she didn't look wobbly, nor was she nauseous or dizzy. With relief, I watched as she headed off in the direction of the garden wearing my hat.

Two weeks under the scorching rays of the Arizona sun acted better than formaldehyde to preserve the now rippled skin. It was when I was walking across the field linking the main complex of the monastery to the glass shop that I noticed the limbless body had been removed. I thought in all probability, the Novice Director, sick of seeing the snake dangling over the fence on the way to breakfast every morning ~~took it down herself~~ asked Teresa to bury it. I assumed it was given a proper burial. Now that it was dead and gone, I forgot about the snake incident until...

One afternoon I noticed Annette waiting for me at the glass shop door. When she saw my slightly burned nose approaching, she walked straight to me in a deliberate gait. She was carrying something on a tray. The closer she came I was able to focus on the object that looked like a cake. It was my hat! With the recognition, came the thought, *God Almighty, the sun really* did *do something to her mind!*

Moving closer to me, she couldn't contain her excitement. She held the tray level with my eyes so I could see her handiwork, displaying the hat like it was a main course. My eyes opened wide seeing the snake skin, flattened and withered, wrapped around the crown of my hat!

My hat was new when I was new, by now it looked as if it had been trampled by a heard of cattle, old and worn. Adorning it with *anything* wasn't going to help, especially a snake. Even dead, I was afraid of it. I didn't want to look at it, much less inspect at close range; I didn't want to see the clever way she attached it, I didn't want to see its pointy fangs, I didn't want to see it period! My head was already itching, imagining snake germs jumping off the hat into my hair.

Sister Annette took my hat off the tray and held it in front of my face, shaking it hard like a maraca making its menacing rattles come to life. With a burst of renewed shaking, I wondered if she was waiting for me to show my appreciation. She's still waiting.

Instead, thinking of all the work she must have put into it, I said, "I must admit, you put a lot effort into this." Then the inevitable question surfaced, "Why don't you try it on?" I didn't want to appear I was ungrateful for her present, and was about to decline her request, but before I was able to verbalize my negative response, her hands were on the hat, fiddling with one of the snake ends.

"There, that's better," she said, adjusting it, lifting it over my head.

Again there was hesitation as she checked the finished product for flaws. "Wait a minute, the tail's crooked." She fiddled with it, straightening the body so it wound evenly around the hat so there were no kinks.

I finally asked, "Why don't *you* try it on? That way I'll be able to see how it looks." I hoped this would satisfy her sense of the macabre. But really, why would I want the skin of a dead snake to remind me of my time in the desert? A dried prickly pear or a bloom off a saguaro cactus, Arizona's state flower, would be more appropriate.

She took it willingly and placed it on her head at a jaunty angle. Beaming with pride, she asked, "Well, what do you think?"

I backed up and eyed it from all angles before saying, "Take my word for it, it looks perfect, just *perfect*. In fact, it looks so good on you I want you to have it as a gift." I didn't think it was possible, but she really *was* smiling from ear to ear.

That week while I was sitting in the novitiate with the others, it occurred to me, *what a fine bunch of novices we were.* I slumped forward in my desk as I thought about Dorothy's neurotic need to be first in chapel, Patty's obsessive behavior as a budding petrologist, Dolores's' need to know it all, Annette's perfectionism, and my thinkaholism. Even my unscientific mind could see a connection. We were all feeding off some rush caused by the problems we made for ourselves. The truth hit me: we were like hard core junkies squirreling away dime bags of endorphins, waiting for our next fix to make us feel good.

Not only that, people who drink themselves silly, probably feel the same high as my novice alumnae. I was taken aback and sunk lower in my desk: I was no better than a boozing bum.

All this thinking left me with a slight ache in my head. I stretched my legs in the isle and made myself look on the lighter side. Our move to the new novitiate read like a bad soap opera: would Dorothy ever let somebody else muscle her way in the chapel before her? Would Patty continue to secretly pile rocks in a quiet hollow of the desert somewhere? Would Dolores ever admit she didn't know an answer? Would Annette change her ways and start sleeping *in* her bed? Would my father ever admit he has a drinking problem? Would I ever stop my over-analyzing?

God, life in a monastery wasn't only richly rewarding, it was downright *fascinating!*

CHAPTER

39

Guiding my feet over the last stretch of a particularly rutted climb, I reached the top and stopped to survey the undulating hills and the valley below. Flaxen weeds shimmered with a reddish hue in the late afternoon as large clouds tinged with purple moved silently overhead. There was no movement, only the hushed calm of a day beginning to end.

As I gazed on the countless variations of natural beauty, I knew experiencing the mystical was always worth the hike. It wouldn't take a keen observer to feel the momentary prickling of the spiritual while on the hills. A lover of aloneness only had to view the endless miles of sunlit terrain or see the picturesque monastery shadowed intermittently by clouds, its steeple shining like gold in the last rays of the sun to bring about a new outlook.

Hiking long stretches unaccompanied always filled me with peace. It allowed me to reacha different state of mind brought on by the sound of my own steadfast steps. Even if I had to change pace and suddenly slide down the scree side of a slope, jump over cacti like a hurdler, or run like a prairie dog just for the joy of running, my peace endured. As I scanned the uninhabited hills, I had a horrible thought. What if a family built a house on top of this very hill? The word chance has two distinct meanings: absence of assignable cause and the absence of design. If I found this landscape so beautiful, it wouldn't be just one family moving in, developers would build housing tracts bringing in people; parents, children, dogs, cats, schools, supermarkets, trash cans, trash trucks, cars and buses. I probably wouldn't be able to hear the chapel bells over the din of civilization. How would the monastery have any privacy? It was a run of good luck keeping developers at bay do far. My entrance here was well-timed and lucky.

Of course, roads and freeways would be first, connecting ravines and canyons to malls and shopping centers making them just an exit away. Custom signs blocking views would go up: large ring-shaped doughnuts and realistic potatoes along with glowing neon signs advertising TV repair, and arrows pointing the way to hot dog businesses. Airports with state-of-the-art terminals would be built bringing in every shopper who wrongly equates the accumulation of things with a better life.

My peace now obliterated, I imagined prospective buyers eagerly scrambling over themselves in search of that one house that demonstrates their uniqueness from the other five thousand *custom* homes. It was disturbing to think about and it didn't take me long to feel angry and overwhelmed.

These hikes, which I took on a regular basis, *usually* worked to lighten my spirit by deflating any problems I had, but now all I was thinking about was enjoying the silence while I still could.

My blood pressure rosethinking about a worse scenario. What if a mine went in that routinely used loud heavy duty trucks, caterpillars and extracting machinery? All day, and sometimes night, they would haul rocks and dirt. I've seen open-pit mines. They leave huge holes in the earth, large open wounds on the countryside. Instead of the fullness of the desert with its sweet scent of sage and luscious odors of willow, the abbey would be forced to breathe poisonous metallic dust, along with a steady stream of exhaust fumes. Suddenly, I had a hard time catching my breath.

What were the odds of cyanide used in mining processes leaking into nearby creaks and streams, not to mention our water supply? An eyesore of a quarry taking stones, rocks, sand, gravel or slate would be just as bad. I could feel my face screwing up in disgust.

I cocked my ear hearing the pleasing sound of church bells ringing in the distance. I started running. Huffing and puffing, I walked in the chapel and went to my seat just as the office began. I brushed the hair hanging in my eyes out of the way thinking if luck is the accidental way things happen because of chance, I have always been lucky. Immediately the image of my father came to me. I was playing hooky. I was sitting at the front of my bed with my back against a wall using an open closet door to shield me. That was the day my furniture selling father decided to check the springs in my bed. Sitting bolt upright like I was a statue, I watched as he pushed down hard on the springs with me not yard away sweating bullets he wouldn't look up! He didn't. If I was a cat, I was sure eight of my nine lives had been cut from my life. It was just plain dumb luck I wasn't discovered.

Seeing Sister Lorna on the other side of the chapel wiping her brow with a hankie reminded me how lucky I was being chosen to be in on the arrangements of her Silver Jubilee. She was celebrating 25 years of rising at 3:15; 25 of chanting; 25 years of meditating; 25 years eating a vegetarian diet; 25 years of being a Cistercian. It was quite an accomplishment that deserved more then her favorite dessert at dinner. My contribution to this special occasion was helping with the seating arrangements. The community was always seated by seniority with the superior at the head of the table with novices on the other end. How could I make *where* we were seated as special as the day? I thought and thought. Finally, a fun approach popped into my head: I would let each sister be responsible for her own placement around the refectory table. Smiling to myself, I secretly went about my plan.

When the day arrived, I was happy learning the higher-ups felt the celebration of a Silver Jubilarian shouldn't be just another run of the mill celebration either. When I walked in the refectory, to my surprise, there was silver glitter on just about everything: the centerpiece, cards, flowers, presents and balloons. The refectory table was set with a silver paper tablecloth and silver plated china and glasses with silver trim set the celebratory mood. Cheese and wine were served on silver trays. The sisters placed flowers in silver colored vases, and silver candlesticks lit up the room. They didn't blow a "ram's horn" to celebrate, but we did sing a new song to mark her *first* twenty-five year interval.

When it was time to be seated, I held a bowl fill of quotes high enough so the quotes couldn't be seen and no one could pick one she already knew. (I put the ends of the quotes at the settings beforehand; the end off a quote was where each sister was to sit.) Everyone reached in my foil bowl and pulled out the first part of her quote.

To liven things up, I didn't pick 12 everyday run of the mill quotes like: *In the beginning... God created heaven and earth,* or, *Happy is the man is the man... who finds wisdom.* The problem was I used quotes I never remembered hearing before and were *way* too obscure. They were easy to find, all I had to do was look in the Old Testament where there were literally hundreds to choose from in Prophets, Proverbs, and Revelation. Lines like: *"For night and day your hand was heavy upon me... my vitality was turned into the drought of summer."* And, *Your mother was like a line in your bloodline... planted by waters, fruitful and full of braches.*

What started as a parlor game ended up with everyone walking around scratching their heads, circling the long refectory table many times; bumping into one another, racking their brains, trying to find their matching quote so they could sit down. In this game of spiritual musical chairs, no one wanted to be the last one standing. I had done a thorough job in my choosing, all right; too thorough.

What made it worse, because I knew the end of the quote I picked, I was the only one sitting, watching the parade of spirituality diligently making their way around and around the table, with the occasional sister, worn out, collapsing in a chair having found the end of her missing quote. As tedious as it was for them, I didn't hear one vulgar expression made in frustration or one impatient tone of exasperation. In fact, because this was a contemplative community under a vow of silence, no one said anything. All I heard was the swishing of habits as the sisters passed me time and again, along with the intermittent cawing of ravens as they flew past the windows like congratulatory cries to me for a job well done.

It seemed an interminable amount of time before everyone was seated, but finally it was time to cut into the large sheet cake with the number 25 written in silver icing for dessert that had been filling the refectory with its mouth watering smell all morning. I sat back taking it all in. A delighted Sister Lorna, knife in hand, cutting big pieces of cake and passing them out to everyone; the sisters trotting to the coffee urn in back grinning as they filled their cup with *real* percolated coffee. There were no long speeches of admiration by Esmeralda; no retirement plan starting with, as a member in good standing, here are the symbolic keys to the kingdom. No silver watch for faithful service.

At one point, I happen to glance at the other side of the dining table, all the way to the very end of the long wooden table. There, instead of seeing the smiling faces of sociability and fraternization, was the disgruntled face of the Novice Director sitting next to the lowly, unprofessed novices and realized, yes, I have always been lucky.

CHAPTER

40

"I have a bone to pick with you," the Novice Director began, her brow wrinkling as she spoke.

This is not something I wanted to hear at the start of the day, or anytime really. With the sudden feeling of 'what have I done now?' I tried recalling any objectionable actions I may have done, or anything I forgot to do, but my mind was drawing a blank. I settled into a wobbly chair in Drusilla's office feeling as unsteady as the chair.

She was sitting perfectly straight as usual. I had to look up slightly to meet her eyes.

I kept wondering what she had on me. Did she see me talking to Lorna in the garden? Did I accidentally let a sneer slip out in her presence? My guilty mind boggled. Did I take cuts in the food line without realizing? God help me if she finally wanted to talk about our ongoing discord; I wasn't up to that kind of emotional wrangling so early in the morning."Sister Anne, I'm talking to you," Drusilla politely interrupted my thinking.

"Sorry what were you saying?" I apologized. I racked my brain again. Maybe I wasn't spending enough time in the music room practicing the modes, or, were the other novices complaining I was hogging the music room practicing too much?The voice across the desk spoke, "It has come to my attentionyou have been stretching the enclosure borders well beyond the limits."I looked at her thinking, 'is that all?' Of course, I was, but I wasn't going to tell her that. Even as she explaining the dangers of walking long distances by myself, I was recalling the sun light filtering on one of my most surprising desert finds yet.

The ground was covered with tough little plants on the elevated ridge in back of the monastery that had few cacti to snag my jeans. I was on a casual walk with no destination other than north, stepping over seemingly lifeless ground cover like the astonishing tandem symmetry of shadowed cactus spines, or the or the delightful blue leaf coloration of the Echeveria.

After an hour, I stopped and took a swig of water from my canteen. I had never been up here before, miles from any populated area. I looked over the desert in all its' glory, empty and wild; the simmering heat, the motionless calm, the continual flush of bright light.

I turned to go and almost stumbled over a pillar of small rocks. The little stack of human endeavor took me completely by surprise. It was hard thinking anyone else would want to hike this far.

At first I thought Sister Patty was getting creative in her rock hounding ways. On further inspection, undisturbed weeds were growing close to it and dust had settled on thin spider webs interconnecting the pile and there were no telltale footprints anywhere in the area. It was evident the pile had been here for a long time.

I stepped closer. It was over a foot high with rocks that had been painstakingly piled one on top of another. The longer I stared, the more my curiosity grew. It wasn't long before the impulse to 'accidentally' knock it down came over me. I gave the stone pillar a little nudge with my boot and watched the rocks topple to the ground. To my surprise, and delight, a plastic tube rolled out with the rocks. I picked it up and saw something *inside* the yellowed cylinder! I pulled off the plastic top and tried to pinch the top of a tight scroll. On my third try, I pulled out a little roll of paper. The scroll was old and crinkly as I straightened the tight curl. The handwritten note read:

April 23, 1909
Bowdrie Law
1824 Oak Street
Tucson
RESPECT THIS HEAR CLAME!

I knew what it was right way, an authentic 'X marks the spot' holding the location until the miner registered it officially with a surveyor's office. For someone to spend so much time forming the pile, the land owner must have had high hopes on what could turn out to be a rich find, perhaps the mother lode! The earth had a reddish hue suggesting gold or copper deposits so it was possible. The fact the wobbly pile of rocks lasted through driving snow, monsoons and blizzards from prospecting times, was amazing.

All of a sudden, fear gripped me. The holder might be taking his pistol out of his holster and drawing a bead on me this very second! I backed away, jumping at the slightest sound. Anxiously, I wondered; were those dark spots drops of blood on the ground at the base?

The stack was too odd to leave alone. Looking over my shoulder, I carefully took a stone from the base and fingered it with care, hoping to get a sense of what the owner was like from its energy. Was he a good-natured old coot with a beard and a gold tooth who offered coffee to anyone who passed his camp? Or was he an ill-tempered curmudgeon with an eye patch who had a double-barreled shotgun at the ready? I didn't want to be accused of jumping his claim, so I put the stone back where it was when I discovered it before leaving.

Knowing there could be a mine with miles of shafts below the surface cutting through the land like rabbit burrows, I stepped lightly walking back to the abbey. Maybe Mr. Law's mine was worth millions! Why, this whole area could be a rich gold-producing region! From then on, I kept my eyes open for picks, axes, tin cups, iron skillets, tarnished lanterns, or blackened coffee pots. I might even find an entrance to his mine!

When it occurred to me there were a number of washes flowing in the area, a prospector could spend his life sloshing water back and forth in a pan sorting gold from gravel. I added more items to my scavenging list: dented pans, remnants of sluices, wooden planks or an old gate used for channeling water. I could almost hear his excited calls of EUREKA seeing nuggets at the bottom, in a gold fever of my own making.

"Well, have you?" the Director asked, interrupting my reminiscing. Suspicion showed in her eyes, glowering at me from her dark framed glasses.

Drat, someone must have seen me on the far end of the ridge yesterday, I thought, avoiding her searching look. I had to phrase my response in such a way future explorations wouldn't be denied."Yes, I have been taking hikes, but I haven't gone out *that* far," continuing the thought in my head *in my estimation.*

"I'm always careful not to go too far because I want to make it back for the Offices. I never take unnecessary chances." It was the truth; I *didn't* take chances and told her "No hike was worth returning delirious, staggering from fatigue, dehydrated and in a state of shock." She regarded my face in-between her long blinks. She must have been pleased with my common sense answers because she said, "Make sure you don't venture too far." What else *could* she say? Invisible borders are impossible to enforce.

"Okay," I promised half-heartedly. Drusilla *had* to trust me because she wasn't a hiker and the only way she could follow me was with a pair of binoculars. I admitted to myself, the farther I went, my curiosity took me even farther the next hike because not knowing what I'd find made going the extra mile hard to resist.

There didn't seem to be much point telling her I found the miner's marker even with the assurance, 'Don't worry, I kept my head down to avoid a bullet from the owner'. No, I didn't think it necessary to tell her I dragged tumbleweed behind me to cover my tracks so I wouldn't lead an outraged prospector to the abbey if he wanted to have it out with me at high noon. Nor did I think there was much point mentioning to her I had been searching for deserted mine shafts, not if I wanted to inspect the marker again.

"Don't worry," I consoled her again as a parting remark, "I'll be careful," hoping this final reassurance would convince her that my long treks were nothing more than harmless strolls in the park.

How could I admit to the Novice Director at times I did leave familiar trails after finding a much better way? I had soared to the heights of faith and it had nothing to do with hiking. Step by step, I had moved up the hills beyond sense and reason and into the calm of the hills, I had tasted the desert's dessert, an explorer's reward. What I had found was much more valuable then nuggets. By accident, I had discovered incomparable wealth; my own inner gold… and had every intention of returning.

CHAPTER

41

We were finally away from the monastery bumping along the back roads to the main highway on our way to Tucson. It was time for another visit to her head doctor for Sister Lorna, and like always, the trip was combined with as many other appointments as possible. I happened to be next in rotation. A periodic oral evaluation had been scheduled that would keep me smiling with sparkling clean teeth for years. I looked forward to this trip to the dentist knowing it wouldn't involve needles.

This time the Superior, Sister Esmeralda, had decided to take her turn as driver and navigated the car through the wash filled with dead branches and rocks on our way to the main highway. There we leveled out and the ride because smoother. The air continued to be silent, and still oh, so hot. I looked out from the back seat on both sides of the highway bordered with shrubs and countless groups of saguaro cacti dotting the land, their emblazoned limbs standing tall over the parched land heavy with a crimson heat.

Our car traveled safely through the clean scent of the high desert away from stillness on the two lane highway to Tucson. Gone was the natural beauty of mesquite trees and scrub oaks. As the land broadened with a wide expense of stunted growth, I knew it wouldn't be long before we joined a fast and furious freeway up ahead for the next part of our journey.

Maybe it was nervous agitation knowing the busy multi-lane divided freeway was fast approaching; maybe it was the searing heat; maybe I was just unused to traveling. Whatever the reason, it became apparent all of a sudden I needed the car to pull over. I emphatically brought this to the attention of the driver, who, seeing the odd color green on my face, steered off the highway onto the edge of the road immediately.

There's nothing like getting sick on the side of a road with others watching. No water handy, no towels, and no dignity. Leaning over in the dirt, my peripheral vision was alerted to a bunch of delicate lavender colored wildflowers growing on my right to fascinate me; a colorful diversion God put on this very spot, I was sure. A second later I was back to the upheaval at hand.

After depositing my breakfast, I staggered back to the car wiping my mouth on my sleeve of my habit. I was convinced my upset stomach was due to carsickness and instructed the Superior to drive on, moaning softly that I was just fine. She turned and looked briefly at my face. Reassured by my smile I was alright and it was only a slight case of car sickness, she pushed the car forward.

And I *was* fine for the moment. It was a mystery. My body had *always* been fine in heat. For me, it was always *the "hotter the better"*. I couldn't believe this strange turn of events was due to the staggering heat! It had to be motion sickness brought on by my not my being accustomed to traveling. Right then, I decided resolutely that for the next trip to travel lighter and skip the two bowls of oatmeal, toast, and tangy homemade orange marmalade for breakfast.

Nausea is powerfully disconcerting. I made sure I wasn't reading anything as we traveled. I kept my eyes on the on the motionless interior of the car—the fine grey dust covering the dashboard, the closed louvers on the air conditioning and heater vents, theunused stereo. When we finally reached Tucson for our errands, I was forced to look between the tall buildings. I felt sorry for the two sisters who had to witness me clearing my stomach. What must the Superior think of me now? Did the traumatic incident instantly lower her opinion of me spirtually? Did she see me as really weak and not the caliber of novice she hoped? And what about poor Sister Lorna? Knowing how responsible the gardener was, I hoped she didn't blame herself by wondering if she had worked me too hard.

I was still silently debating the causes in my mind when we turned onto the monastery's dirt drive. Our journey over, I wasn't too weak to notice the beautiful thick brown weeds, the sunny hillsides around us, and the sweet scent of sagebrush blowing in through the windows; the pleasing wildness leading up to monastery.

With a feeling of incredible relief we drove up and around the last curve past the priest's residence and the empty guesthouse; I made it! I didn't become sick a second time! I felt my body physically relax after the tense ride. Finally, we rolled over the lowered metal chain marking the enclosure and I couldn't wait to see the speedometer registering zero. We parked in back of the monastery and got out. What a relief it was standing on our solid immovable plateau after more than an hour of keeping tabs on my gastric troubles. It felt so good, the thought crossed my mind, what would the passengers think if I just lay in the dirt for several minutes? Thinking of the cool interior of the monastery, I pulled my thoughts away.

We walked across the dirt yard after the Superior and waited until she slid the glass door open and entered the comfortable shade of the refectory. Now that I was home, everything was going to be alright.

CHAPTER

42

Novices are given a list of items to bring when they enter and it is a short list, believe me. Personal effects show individuality and may create separateness and are remnants of a different time, pre-vocation; souvenirs are reminders of what we left and if we are truly leaving them, a complete break is necessary.

When a person enters a particular community, it has a character all its own. Optimally the novice will choose a good 'fit' so the new community will help make up for the disowned material possession which is a part of ascetic renunciation. Renunciation as nonnattachment, is a positive act liberating us from our grasping and greedy natures.

Even though I was told to bring the bare minimum, when I was packing for my momentous move, I couldn't resist including an old costume I felt was fitting for someone living in the Wild West, an entire outfit of a Native American Indian, complete with face makeup in case the opportunity presented itself. My thinking was, you never know, it might come in handy so I stuffed everything in under my clothes.

What possible use could there be for bringing my Indian get-up into a cloistered monastery? This *should* have been an indication to the Novice Director I hadn't made a complete break with my past. Not to mention how ridiculous it was.

As long as I had the items with me, I felt it was worth taking the "chance of asking Sister Drusilla if I could "dress" up on Halloween. All she could do was say no. I approached her office thinking: "it won't hurt to try". I prepared myself to be scolded/and or laughed at by an 'annoyed' director wondering why I had my mind on secular fun. Making my case, I would tell her it "was all in good fun. The sisters were *sure* to appreciate my efforts."

To my surprise, instead of being upset when I asked for permission to dress up on the 31st, the Novice Director didn't laugh at all. She thought it was a good idea and all for my pretending to be a real trick or treater. I was even given permission to walk around to the front door and knock to add authenticity. We'd keep it *our* secret. The rest of the sisters would be totally surprised. I was delighted.

How about that? I thought, leaving her office. I pictured myself standing on the porch holding a pillowcase open and waiting for the bounty I'd receive; individually wrapped slices of sweet rolls, homemade cookies, a frozen yogurt cup left over from the last Hermit Day. They were sure to be an easy touch and I was looking forward to it all.

Then reality set in. This was a monastery. I'd probably find a packet of incense, possibly a new rosary, and one or two holy cards all jammed together in the crease at the bottom of the pillowcase.

I walked to my room and changed into work clothes. Pestering thoughts nagged me. Why did the Novice Director look the other way when she learned I brought extra items? I was a new novice; I should have gotten what for and made to conform. That, in itself should have been an indication something was up. Whatever the reason, I was just happy I had permission.

Drusilla resurrected my box of secular memorabilia from storage and my past came to life again. Skeletal remains of what was left of my past held together by bonds of secular immaturity. I removed the items thinking this is probably the only time a Halloween trick or treater dared to approach the stoop of an otherwise tabooed contemplative Cistercian monastery. (I completely overlooked the fact this was the desert and there wasn't a house or a child within miles of our buildings.

The only comings and goings here were road runners, rabbits and lizards.)

Seeing me in a costume of an Indian, not believing their eyes, I imagined their comments: "A new hairdo; braids instead of a veil;" "Moccasins instead of sandals"; "Boy, times have really changed."

It was late in the afternoon when I made my way up the hill from the garden and opened the sliding door of the Community room. Spotting the work schedule across the room with the weeks' duties with corresponding sisters, I went to the posted notice wanting to be sure who the portress was for the week. I was relieved when I checked it and saw it was Sister Dorothy, someone who enjoys a good joke.

I slipped into my bedroom to shower and change into my costume. I pulled on a long tan floor length skirt that had black wedge-shaped Cuneiform print placed randomly over the entire garment. I felt the writing could be mistaken for Navajo to sisters who have never been on a reservation. It added an Indian touch. Instead of wearing a headdress full of feathers, I pulled on a black wig with two long braids hanging to my waist. A velvety green top hung over the floor length skirt. To complete the ensemble, I pulled on a comfortable pair of old hand-laced suede moccasins I worn so often the balls of each foot were thread bare. Almost ready, I pulled on a black wig that had two long braids, and soon I was outfitted in what I thought was a costume of a full-blooded Indian. I had dabbed so much Pan-Cake make-up on my face, it alone would frighten the living daylights out of anyone unlucky enough to see me from their room making my way around the monastery.

My costume all together now, it was time! Dusk was upon us. I slowly opened my sliding glass door and stepped outside, and closed it to keep the brisk October air out. While I looked like an Indian, I wanted to get into the role; I slunk along the exterior trying to stay as flat and inconspicuous as possible, remembering not to touch anything that would leave impressions of the ridges and curves from my fingerprints in Pan-Cake make-up on the walls as I felt my way along. Getting into the role, I relied on an Indians' stealth and cunning to keep me from getting caught. I kept close to the bedroom walls. My moccasins were and quiet. They made me feel I was a real Indian.

When I reached the end of the building, making the turn, about mid way in my escapade, I thought again how surprised they were going to be. I was looking forward to making my big Halloween appearance. At the same time, I wondered what Thomas Merton would think about my antics. I hoped he'd say something like—"Good natured belly laughs are good for all Catholics," but had the feeling he'd actually say something like—"The person who is truly silent, both interiorly and exteriorly, is always open to emptiness", leaving me to still wonder what he thought about practical jokes. Creeping my along the side unnoticed, I had kept my prank a secret so far. I reached the wing with the Community room by Mac's dining area. Standing in front of it, I exhaled a long deep breath, adjusted my wig, took a cautious step forward, knocked loudly, and waited. Sister Dorothy, the portress, should be there any moment!

Everything in a monastery is done in its own sweet time and answering the door was no exception. Fortunately because I was standing in the cool dry desert air brought a measure of relief; at least the cold wouldn't melt my makeup. It felt like I was waiting for an eternity. I kept picturing Dorothy's surprised look, not believing what she was seeing. Realizing how gaudy I would look to her framed against the beauty of the hills, I wouldn't blame her if she didn't ask me in. Snickering to myself, I hoped seeing me wouldn't be too much for her.

Finally, a voice called out, "Who's there?"

Trying not to laugh, I yelled back loudly, "TRICK OR TREAT!"

Two great big eyes stared at me through a crack in the opened door like I had awakened a hermit in a cob-webby cave. The door opened a little more. It was wide enough for me to see it wasn't the novice, Sister Dorothy. It was the Superior! My mind raced. She *never* answers the door, that's the Fortress's job!

I stood not knowing what to do. In my panic I wondered if it was too late to turn and run. I could hightail it over that far ridge without her ever knowing it was me under all under all this makeup. Or should I run cowering back around the building and into the safety of my bedroom? I did nothing except stand there dumbfounded. She had scared me, more than I scared her!

I waited for the inevitable blue expletives to fly: "What is all that #&%@# stuff on your face?" "Where do you do you think you are, Hollywood?" And, "You blankety blank novices will be the death of me yet!"

Sister Esmeralda said nothing of the sort. The composed Superior gave me a cheerful smile, opened the door all the way and waved me inside where I stood before all the sisters who were sitting at the refectory table waiting for my arrival like I was the afternoon matinee.

I was invited inside and stood in front of the Community room, with all the sisters gawking in disbelief at me and laughing, I resisted the strong impulse to slide under a table where I could try to remember if there was a special ceremony for the defrocking of novices. Or plan my transfer. I could take a safe position as a church secretary somewhere dutifully answering questions about Mass times and when confessions were held.

Realization hit; I was no surprise at all! The Novice Director had to ask permission *beforehand* from Reverend Mother to allow me to leave the monastery which meant the Superior had been expecting me all along with everyone else. I felt like a first class dope.

I resigned myself to my fate. I was nudged around the long refectory table where supper was underway and sat in my seat. Reverend Mother stood at the head of the table where she announced to the community, "HAPPY HALLOWEEN!"

My ears felt like they were beet red from embarrassment. When my initial shock was over and I was getting used to them glancing in disbelief in my direction, I took my seat at the table where a prearranged Halloween supper was already underway: yams, carrot-cinnamon oatmeal, cantaloupe slices, pumpkin bread and orange frosted sugar cookies with jack-o'-lantern faces for dessert, each cookie piped with a thin line of frosting for a big smile.

I sat thinking while I ate. Taking an edifying blow to one's pride is never pleasant. It felt like my cover had been blown. It caused me to take a deeper look at myself. This is the purpose of monasteries, to bring one's character to the fore. I had been forced to take a deeper look at myself and didn't like what I was seeing.

As they watched me trying to keep my black braids out of my food, I couldn't help thinking they were on to me, seeing through my disguise. Because no matter if I slathered on two more coats of red rouge and puffed on more powder there was one indisputable fact about myself no mount of make-up could conceal: my deep and long abiding, naiveté.

CHAPTER

43

Autumn changed the air into whistling gusts of coolness. The garden was picked and withered and had that has-been look. There was still plenty of work to do in the constant renewal that circled around for next year's garden: mending fencing and replacing eroded fence posts, pulling out tomato stakes, removing rotted watermelon, cucumber and cantaloupe vines. We cleared yellowed gourds of squash, pumpkin, and zucchini and pulled up tall coarse stems of empty headed sunflower plants. We leveled corn stalks and piled everything in the wire compost bin, adding valuable nutrients.

Using wheelbarrows, we shoveled in sand from the washes and hauled it back to the garden and mixed it with certain beds, especially rhubarb, my favorite. We cleaned tools and painted the shed and threw more rocks over the fence in the never ending battle to clear the land. Planting, watering, harvesting and collapsing; gardens are a lot of work *any* time of the year. With the garden shutting down, autumn is a perfect time for self-reflection, as Father Mac told us during a homily. This time of year was a reminder that at some point we would shut down as well. He said it was a time of *gravitas,* the reflective quality that perfects the inner silence of the whole body characterized by a deep inner seriousness.

I stood looking at the wilted plants. Seeing the garden in a state of denudation prompted me to trim back, discard and get rid of my own useless attachments. This time should be an absence of the pressure of *having* to make the right impression, trying to *be* somebody, hogging the spotlight, needing to have it all, being #1 or trying to keep up with the Jones's. They were all attachments result in the soul growing fat. All these imperfections are possible in a monastic setting in different degrees. Bottom line: these overindulgences are obstacles that cause withdrawals from God.

My mortality seemed to play out like the garden: removing bad habits, pulling out things I felt were personally unacceptable; nail biting, being impatient, sucking my teeth to show displeasure, losing my temper, excessive throat clearing (this last one I knew the sisters would appreciate) and my personal favorite—grumbling. Challenging as they seemed, I knew autumn was the perfect time for me to take myself in reign. As Father put it, it is a time to take an attitude of detachment that will free us from the tyrannical need to respond to every whim, thought, urge, inclination that surfaces by developing enough maturity to exert control over oneself. Autumnal changes had this affect on everyone. I reached for the hose and took a couple swigs before pulling it to a new position on the compost pile. Lorna had drilled it into me, "We have to keep compost moist until it becomes crumbly, brown and ready to use." I wasn't about to let it dry up on my watch.

As I watered, I remembered, when Mac told us about *Gravitas*, the silence of the whole being, he told us the rhythm of the seasons means a constant turning known monastically as *metanoia* too, *a* fundamental change of mind, like a spiritual conversion that has to come from one's own heart and from one's own personal view of the cosmos. Taking one last swallow from the hose, reminded me how people who drink too much have their own metanoia that starts with staying on the cycle of sobriety.

I dropped the hose on the ground. I remembered how surprised I was learning there were inspirational programs (non-theistic programs) as well as the traditional 12-Step program of *Alcoholics Anonymous* that has God at the center, to help drinkers stay on the road to sobriety. This was news to me. It made me wonder if drinkers who aren't churchgoers, know there were other programs they may find more to their liking. Of course, all the different programs are concerned with helping drinkers stop drinking. Programs like these offer help: on one condition, drinkers have to *pick* one! For according to Jung "everyone has Buddha nature."

'A Buddhist's View of the 12-Steps':

1. Having examined our body, speech and mind through the practice of meditation, we realized that our lives had become unworkable due to excessive use of alcohol.

2. Realized through the discipline and practice of communication with others and the realization of our own basic goodness that we could rediscover our brilliant sanity.

3. Through refuge in and devotion to the Three Jewels [Buddha, Dharma, Sangha], made a decision to cultivate and practice mindfulness and egolessness regarding alcohol in our lives.

4. Exercised exertion and fearlessness in our honest assessment in ourselves through meditation, contemplation and the study of the teachings.

5. Engaged with our world, ourselves and another person openly and straightforwardly our use of alcohol and how it has affected our lives.

6. Were entirely willing to surrender to our basic goodness.

7. Became willing to work on ourselves.

8. Through working further with our minds, recognized the past, present and future potential for causing pain to others inherent in our misuse of alcohol.

9. Made a firm commitment to work with others, exchange self with others.

10. Exercised further effort and fearlessness in the exploration of our minds, a yet more thorough, ongoing practice of the dharma, driving all blames into one.

11. Took every opportunity offered by our fortunate births to actively practice and live in the dharma with devotion, love and respect for the Three Jewels and our own sacred world.

12. Having gained unspeakable insight as a result of this process, we committed ourselves in a spirit of non returning generosity to work with others. [*Sic*]
(Reprinted with permission)

Carrying this mood from the garden, I walked through the monastery as if I was in a trance. The day had ended and it was the time right before twilight. I sauntered to my bedroom and pulled the orange curtains open so I could see the hills. They looked so peaceful, like sleeping Buddha's nothing could awaken.

As I gazed at their monotonous beauty, looking at nothing in particular, I watched my observable universe fade from rose colors to gray and black hues without moving. Then in an instant, the scene lifted to reveal a deep inner calm, a clarity which had always been there unnoticed, as if I had returned to an ancient bastion. Somehow I had awakened to the inherent energy of all things, to a limitless wholeness, to the presence of all that is essential. I was one with the universal life-force flowing through all humanity. I was elevated to new levels of harmony, wholeness and understanding climaxing in the release of my spirituality; I had transcended time. That was the moment I effortlessly experienced the center of the mandala. From then on, I was aware of a happy resignation within me and a deep peace inside that has lasted to this day.

This was the religious experience I had been waiting for. It came when wasn't looking for it, when I was completely detached in an ecstasy of indifference. It didn't surprise me it happened when I was looking over the hills on God's eternal canvas. If I didn't have another 'pure' experience while living on these high hills, I had laid a strong spiritual foundation for the rest of my life. The abbess from the east coast was right, Cistercian life does work.

The next morning at Vigils, the views were dark and ominous and had the feeling of winter as we faced one another across the shadowed chapel. Overhead, dark wooden beams gave interesting perspectives in the half light, stretching the silhouettes of our heads in odd disfigured shapes across the chapel walls. There was no wind, only a hovering coolness trying to extinguish the flame burning in the liquid wax of its former shape. The inky blackness of the desert outside reflected a deathly stillness in low-pitched tones only our spirits could detect.

It was the beginning of the Office of Vigils and none of us were quite awake yet; it felt good just to sit and be read to. The acoustics in the enclosed space of the chapel produced a quality of sound that made for easy listening and Sister Gail, the appointed reader for this week, was a good reader.

As the usual practice, the next reader picked up where the last sister left off so nothing was left out. This morning, Gail continued reading *2 Samuel 21:4-9* from the Old Testament:

"We are not concerned with silver or gold in the matter of Saul and his family," the Gabionades answered him, *"nor do we have the right to put a man to death in Israel."*

"What do you say I should do for you?" he asked. They said to the king, *"As for the man who destroyed us, who planned to exterminate us from having a place in all of territory of Israel, let seven of his sons be handed over to us, to expose their broken corpses to the Lord in Gibbet of Saul, this chosen one of the Lord!"*

"I will hand them all over," agreed the king. Then, although the king spared Mephibosheth, the son of Saul's son Jonathan, because of the Lord's oath between them, between David and Saul's son Jonathan, the king did take Armoni and Mephibosheth, the two sons of Rizpah*

the daughter of Aiah, whom she had borne to Saul, and the five sons of Saul's daughter Merab, whom she had borne to Adriel the son of Barzillai from Meholah, and gave them up into the hands of the men of Gibeon, who exposed their broken corpses on the hill in the presence of the Lord. The seven fell at one time, being put to death in the first days of the reaping, at the beginning of the barley harvest.

"Rizpah the daughter of Aiah then took sack-cloth and spread it out for herself on the rock, from the beginning of the harvest until rain came pouring down on the bodies; by day she let no bird of the air alight on them and by night no animal of the field."

After Sister Gail read her selection, she sat in her seat. A period of silent reflection followed so hopefully we would gain insight into our own lives with a serious regard for our own perfection. It was an opportunity for redefining our intentions in each ones' personal path, one that may or may not include sleeping on a rock in the rain like Rizpah.

At this very moment, when we were settled, quiet, and still, that the howls of a wild pack of coyotes shattered the silence in voices of bass, soprano, and tenor combined producing mournful howls that seemed almost within petting distance. I gulped. Remembering Ripzah's plight, their wailing was as if the coyotes had heard and were saddened too. Goose bumps spread uniformly over my forearms. We were all familiar with their lonesome howls, but we were used to them being farther away; yelping from their den way out in the desert, far from the monastery. This pack of about twenty sounded ominously close to our sheltered choir.

I looked at the sisters on the other side of the choir to see if they were concerned about the closeness of these wolf-like animals as I was; Dolores had dropped her book, Viola was marking her bookmark to the place we stopped, and Patty was half-way out of her seat. My gut instinct was to leave the chapel in fear. It was better than being sitting ducks encased in glass. While I sat afraid to move, it was very easy to visual the image of Rizpah sleeping on a rock under the stars, madly delirious in her valiant effort fighting off wild animals with a club all night, swatting hungry vultures away, protecting the pile of bloodied corpses. I sat tingling with tension, intimidated by the closeness of their howls, praying they would bypass our chapel while traveling through the countryside. The prickling of hair on my arms from my agitated nervous system made me thankful there was a brick wall, a corridor, and another brick full of windows, between us and them. Even so, I worried one crazed coyote, wild with hunger, would crash through one of the windows in an unprovoked attack.

Sitting in the safety of the chapel contemplating Ripzah's actions, I thought not only of *her* bravery, but the bravery every person needs to follow their own inner path. Would it help drinkers too scared to join a program to know about Ripzah's brave actions? She too had to act alone, but with one big difference, she was protecting a pile of bloodied corpses while people who drink too much have the opportunity of protecting the *living*, in the form of children and spouses. With the full cries of the coyotes in mind, I knew I had hit on something; the reason had to be nothing less than sheer terror keeping drinkers from looking at themselves and getting help.

Exiting the chapel, I thought of another possibility, one that was the most plausible in the mind of a drinker where one excuse is as good as another; maybe like Rizpah, drinkers were waiting for the beginning of a barley harvest too.

CHAPTER

44

She blew in like a kite on one of the most blustery days of the year. I noticed her on a hill beyond the enclosure limits leaping over tumbleweeds in a nimble game of nature's dodge-ball oblivious to the strong winds whipping about her. She was in her own private limelight of perfect pirouettes and precise plies, reaching new heights when she caught the wind just right.

The scene was surreal. Her improvisational dancing had not been hard to miss in the field to the right of the monastery. Hopping, skipping, and jumping about, carrying herself with all the elegant posture of a dancer, graceful and light-footed. I wondered silently, good God, could this be a new novice? If it was, my guess was she was hoofing off last minute jitters about entering by dancing in the dirt, trying to get as many jumps in as possible before finding there was a rule against expressing herself in arm and leg movements.

Glancing at the other novices slumping round-shouldered at the reading table like I was, I sat straighter in case she was here on official business; like starting her observership.

Novices are always kept in the dark about such matters; a practice predicated on the idea of renunciation, and as novices, we needed to be kept away from the world of distractions and its concerns for the good of our inner peace. This is another side of monasticism; not knowing what's going on is difficult at times. How will she handle being kept in the dark, uninformed, her opinion passed over, and disregarded?

About a half hour later, there was a slight knocking on the side door we barely heard over the buffeting wind. Reverend Mother headed off the portress quickly walking to the door in the Community room ahead of her.

The Superior asked loudly, "Who is it?"

A voice answered—"It's me, Jan, I made it."

In one movement, the superior, bracing herself against a burst of wind, opened the door and pulled the visitor inside, closing it without delay.

I was sitting at the reading table with the other novices. All of us were within earshot. Remembering my own grandstanding entrance in middle *of the* night, I thought, *Sure, anyone can enter a monastery in the middle of the day, where's the fun in that?* I suppose it was my impetuous nature, but I wouldn't trade my exciting entrance for anything.

Ignoring the custody of the eyes rule, I turned around to see the person attached to the voice just as Reverend Mother clapped her hands to get everyone's attention. "This is Jan, our new novice. She's a ballerina," grinning like a mother attending her daughter's first ballet.

So it was true, another novice was joining our company. I got up from the magazine table straightening my belt and walked to the Community room stepping through circulating specks of dust disturbed by the rush of air from the opened door on my way.

I was amazed when I saw Jan. She really did look like a ballerina; skinny with pipe cleaner legs. Her anorexic frame didn't matter; *anyone* entering our community was welcome because it happened so infrequently. Jan had shoulder length brown hair, mussed and wind blown. She was wearing tan leggings under an oversized brown sweater and stood on the tiniest feet I'd ever seen. She wasn't very tall, about five feet five or six and looked like she needed guide wires to keep from blowing away. We kept all the windows in the Community room tightly shut as a precaution.

As far as I knew, no one like her has ever graced our desert monastery before. Her entering fit somehow. Joining our drastic way of life with the sole purpose of living for God as a contemplative nun, is about as dramatic as wanting to be a prima ballerina. I wondered if she knew what she was getting herself into because this life was different from any other presentation; guaranteed. Like all of us, Jan will learn desert monastic dancers will spend the majority of time dancing to Saint Benedict's own peculiar tempo.

Reverend Mother's clapping brought the rest of the sisters in from all directions and the room filled with contemplative dispositions. We quietly went to our particular desk.

Reverend Mother stepped to the front and picked up a tin container already on Mac's little dining table. "Jan will fit in nicely here," she explained. And not wasting any training/teaching time, said with quick instruction, "A dancer's mastery of their body in posture, breathing and concentration is similar to yoga, with or without a mantra. In this respect she is a step ahead of those in the novitiate because her training as a dancer helps in the discipline of meditation."

I knew this was true. But instead of training muscles, the monastic routine trains the will by teaching it to move in ways other than its own likes and dislikes. I hoped Jan knew that training the will is done through the practice of obedience, even if it's through clenched teeth at times; I thought of my hair cutting episode.

Esmeralda pulled off the lid on the metal cookie container. We each smiled and said hello to her as the superior passed it around while stating our names. Right away I noticed the new novice was different from the rest of us in one respect; she passed on a cookie. When she waved it off, I noticed her unmarked and unscarred hands and thought disappointedly, they look liked they've been soaking in Ivory liquid all her life. They were in every way contrary to garden work. I smiled at her anyway.

Jan, as a new desert dancer, will learn the walk into the desert, is a walk into the heart. The rest of us took a celebratory cookie acknowledging the fact that on this windy day, Jan's desert dance had begun.

After the cursory introductions were over we went our various ways. Before I left, I saw Jan casually looking over the place; at the large rock fireplace, the long hand-crafted refectory table, and at the wild countryside through the windows on every side. I wondered if seeing the rustic interior made her feel like I did the first time; did it please her too? Did it let her, like me; know this was the right monastery for her? I couldn't tell from the looks on her face that went from happy, to doubtful, to *as long as I'm here, I might as well stay;* it was anybody's guess.

The excitement over, I walked to my bedroom and put on my work clothes. The newest novices' presence started a chain of reflections I couldn't control. Maybe it was guilt due to my own lukewarm efforts. Whatever the reason, the tidal wave of serious deliberations flooding me was immediate. While changing into my jeans, I hoped Jan already had a good idea of what was involved in entering the fast-moving monastic dance routine. She should know it requires the practiced legwork of mental preparation to avoid a loss of footing. Knowing basic steps beforehand, will fire her stamina in the continual re-fashioning of her choice. By studying and learning the reasons behind the dance of the monastery, it will give her a solid foundation vital to every monastic vocation. It will hold her up during ordinary steps and keep her on her toes during the monotony of the unwavering monastic routine.

I laced up my boots, tied the ends of my work kerchief together behind my head and placed my cowboy hat over it. I slid open the glass slider and stumbled down the long way below me to the garden, wind buffeting me with every step.

I knew Jan was meeting with the Novice Director at the moment. Opening the gate, I realized coming in, felt Jan should already know one of the most important aspects of monastic life: God's will is recognized in obedience to human superiors.

Even though I was wearing my cowboy hat, I decided to take it off, it was too windy. I trudged to the shed. Two pieces of wood held by a nail kept the door closed; in a half turn it was open. I put it on a shelf with trowels, packets of Burpee seeds and bug repellants. The shed had a saw, a number of work gloves in all sizes (all dirty), an axe, a hammer, a large ball of string, an almost empty bag of plant food and a pair of old chinked scissors. A couple kneeling pads lay in the corner.

I tromped to the water spigot. I thought back to the first time I watered; the gate was covered in morning glory vines. I watered the beautiful blue lowers first preparing them for another hot day.

I winced when I thought as prepared as I *thought* I was when I entered, many of the things I glossed over, after more than a year now, realize were the very explanations I should have taken to heart. With regret I realized too late I should have listened more attentively to essential principles because they set the stage for monasticism. As I pulled on a pair of work gloves, I wished I had paid more attention to this most, if not *the* most important notion. If I *really* understood what this meant from the start, getting my own way would have been something of an anathema. Submitting in obedience to others in the first place would have softened many a blow to my ego.

Today I was here for watering. I picked up the black hose again, dragging it up to the asparagus shoots. It was after the growing season but a few vegetables were still hanging on, like the hard little green noses of the lily family pushing their way through the dirt. Smothered in hot cheese sauce, I found them eatable. Radishes and green onions were growing nearby. As a favorite of mine, I walked clear around their rows, while clipping the ends of carrots and parsley. As I held the hose over the scallions giving them a good soak; I thought how important it was for Jan to know the basic steps to live in a monastery.

Manual labor is very important in Saint Benedict's *Rule*. The new novice should know she should never remain idle, *even under the pretext of contemplation.* He knew when work is combined with prayer it was like watering her soul, enriching her spirit so it bears fruit. And if she's dedicated and tends to her spirituality, eventually it would bear fruit and could lead to prayer of the heart. I hope the Novice Director pointed out this possibility.

Robbed of their starchy fruit, I dragged the hose over the harvested, flattened mounds of potatoes to the withered stalks of corn. With wind blowing their silk tassels about, I held the hose near a stalk that had a few remaining husks. When I pulled back the protective outer covering of a hull, I was surprised to it was full of yellow kernels. I love fresh, just picked, corn and gave the ground around it a good long soak dropping the hose near the stalk for an extra treat.

Moving on, I dropped the hose by the green pepper plants. Because fresh green bell peppers straight out of the garden were tasty, I let the water flood the area. Our plants yielded red and yellow ones called traffic light peppers, the gardener had informed me. I hated to admit it, but their mildly sweet flavor was making a convincing *pro* argument for the vegetarian diet, almost.

I stood over the plants watching the water make rivulets in the dirt and waited for it to soak in before trotting back the work shed. I shoved my hand in a bag of plant food, went back to the peppers where I sprinkled it around the bases as an extra nourishment, being careful not to accidentally drop any of it near the withered dark green broccoli heads or the ~~white~~ yellowed heads of cauliflower. This time of year we harvested small heads with hardly any leaves. While I was at it, I watered the lettuce growing near the slow-maturing cabbages at the same time.

Grabbing the hose again, I dragged the heavy tube to the pea patch and dropped it on the surrounding weeds, squashing them. Noticing a few pods still attached to a vine, I pulled one off and opened its little case to find seven green peas in a row. I popped an edible green legume in my mouth and let the foreign body roll down my throat. As far as I knew, there was no rule restricting nibbling in the garden. My thoughts went back to the new novice. As a religious sojourner like we all were she was trying her hand in the battle of wills; aka, good versus bad, virtue versus vice, selfish versus selfless behaviors. I thought again how important it was for her to know the basic steps that are essential in joining a monastery. Like the importance of ego strength. Showing a healthy respect for oneself is a responsible preliminary step needed before she is able to value other people.

I moved the hose over. I thought again of training my will against dislikes. I popped in a couple more peas. This time I chewed. No surprise; I still didn't like the taste and pulled the hose away.

I arrived at the oak tree. It was there well before even the *idea* of having an abbey in the desert materialized. Looking up at it made me realize developing a habit of behavior sometimes takes a lifetime of practice. The novice who understands this and executes the groundwork is in a comfortable position of starting from a strong foundation.

The old tree was shading wilted stalks of rhubarb. Most of them had already been harvested but a few were leaning weakly to the ground. Sister Lorna designed the garden layout well; they were next to the strawberry patch. I was introduced to the tart taste of strawberry-rhubarb pie in the monastery. Remembering the sugar-coated lattice-topped crust, I went to the wood shed for more fertilizer immediately.

Like it or not, it was time to water the zucchini. It was a vegetable, I *had* to include it. With the hose draped over my shoulder, I walked to the far end of the garden. As I approached this section of the garden, seeing the zucchini, I glanced at the golden blossoms on the end. It was hard to be ambivalent about a food that ends up in ~~too~~ many of our meals, either dark or light green. The summer squash seemed to grow year round, I thought with dismay. And they were big; one was nearly 20 inches long; enough for the entire community; oh, joy. Sometimes the cooks used the fruit as garnish and experimented with a variety of recipes: deep fried as fritters after dipping them in batter. Or they stuffed, sautéed, baked the long appendages. Or used them in soups. I must admit, when fresh zucchini sticks are dipped in ranch dressing they were ~~delicious tasty~~ okay… due to the dressing.

The cantaloups close to the fence were next. They were another versatile fruit that often showed up on the serving counter in the kitchen in salads, melon pieces, in bowls of mixed fruit, or as dessert with ice cream or custard. The really creative cooks served the orange-skinned cantaloupes with thinly sliced prosciutto over mixed greens. I heard was a vegetarian delight.

I pulled the hose to the juicy red flesh of the watermelon section. Seeing the withered empty vines made me think of the times during hermit days, a day were allowed to help ourselves to whatever we found in the refrigerator and how happy I was finding extra slices of watermelon stacked on a plate in the refrigerator. I recalled the times during the hot, summer months, I spent spitting seeds off the back hill … when no one was around.

Next to the picked over watermelon plot were the long dried vines of yellow grapefruits. Just remembering the sour citrus made my mouth pucker. I wondered if monks of old fermented the juice to make homemade grapefruit, strawberry or watermelon wine. All it takes is fruit, water, pectin, sugar; even a city slicker like me knew how to make hooch. Giggling, I suddenly remembered the words from Chapter 40 in Benedict's *Rule* about drink apportionment:

> If we are mindful of the sick, a hemina (1/4th liter) of wine for each monk each day is adequate we believe. Those who have received the gift of abstinence will know they will be especially rewarded in heaven.

About a quart a day? If I had drank quart a day, I'd have no trouble making it through my novitiate. *Remembering* it, would be another story.

The saint continued:

> *We read that monks should not drink at all, but since the monks of our day cannot be convinced of this, let us at least agree to drink moderately, and not to the point of excess, for wine makes even wise men go astray. (Eccles.)*
> *If circumstances do not permit a full measure (or even any at all), the brothers shall bless God and refrain from grumbling.*

Bearded, grumbling monks was not an easy image to forget.

I walked up a slight dirt incline to the top level dragging the heavy hose to a little peach tree. I remembered Sister Lorna showing me how to graft a branch to the fruit tree by taking a twig (scion), from an improved variety, inserting it in the stem of the peach tree. It was a horticultural technique I was eager to learn. I watched her wrap a stretchy piece of rubber material around the rootstock from the 'unwanted' items in her work room to hold the scion in place. It took hold and was now becoming a large beautiful fruit tree.

I couldn't help seeing the similarity between me and the tree. The comparison was hard to miss. I had been grafted into a community and was hoping to bloom too. As I stood at the top of the garden, I blushed with delight.

Laying the hose to one side, I carefully stepped over the roots of the peach tree. I didn't want to traumatize it any more than I had to. Because it was responsible for many a peach pie, I dropped to my knees and used my hands to scoop dirt around the trunk for a moat. I filled it with water and let it soak in hoping it would continue to grow here for years to come. It reminded me how the mystery of a monastic vocation was for life too. Building a strong foundation was an important step for all desert dancers. Jan, as a ballerina, no doubt, probably already knew this.

The quiet, with no distractions, made it easy for me to be lost in lost in thought while working alone. I couldn't believe the bells were ringing on the top of the hill signaling the end of work. I walked to the spigot dragging the hose with me. Turning off the water, I wished I had been familiar with the term hesychast *before* I entered. It was during Repetition I learned hesychasts look for God in recollected spirits. I knew recollection didn't mean literally to 'collect again', or a recalling, or gathering up. Spiritual *recollection* means reclaiming control over one's desires by the gathering up of the self. I knew it meant detaching from all desires which clears the way for *prayer without ceasing*. I hoped Drusilla was introducing Jan to all these terms because the new novice should know the absolute seriousness of the vocation she was embarking on.

Making sure the door on the tool shed was closed tight, I climbed up the hill.

Huffing and puffing, from the top I stopped and gazed at the different vegetables holding fast against the buffeting wind. Imagining them as mature plants, I let my sight roam over the green asparagus, red radishes, brown potatoes, and tall yellow corn. I saw green peppers and peas beside dark broccoli and white cauliflowers. My sight went from the red rhubarb and strawberries under the oak tree, all the way to the green bee-bitten watermelons next to yellow grapefruits at the other end. I saw the peach tree hardy and strong, lending its enduring presence throughout the garden.

I looked down at the garden one last time knowing when I turned and walked in the monastery, I'd be leaving my peaceful mood. With the wind trying to push me off the hill and back down into the serenity of the garden, it came to me in a rush how the totality of a monastic desert experience may be summed up in one word; prayer. Jan had a lot to learn. Happily in a monastic setting, it was the dance learned in peacefulness.

I showered and dressed quickly and walked to the chapel where I sat in my place waiting for the Office of Midday Prayer to begin. As an old timer, I wanted to set a good example and do everything right. Jan would be standing to the left of me opposite Dolores, which made me happy. Now visitors and churchgoers had someone else to gawk at besides me. It felt good being a role model, a spiritual mentor to inspire the new-comers helping to shape their unenlightened and untrained minds. By my way of thinking, I'd be a Bodhisattva in no time.

Jan came in and bowed. She was lucky. This office contained the recitation of three Psalms. No chanting. Even though there is no meditation period, I regret not sticking with my debunked meditation guide. Without it, she'll have to wing it like I did.

I couldn't help wondering what kind of a voice she had but hoped it was good and strong to drown out mine. Patience is a virtue and I would know soon enough. Then again, I remembered how I struggled with the first note too, so it could be a while.

While I waited, I had the growing conviction Jan should be aware of other helpful and important considerations. Because much of our time is spent chanting the Liturgy of the Hours, I realized it is vitally important for Jan to know the Book of Psalms is Scripture because it was inspired by God. It's at the root of our community. This fundamental step is crucial because when Psalms are internalized, they can be applied to everyday experiences.

I regretted not spending *some* time before entering familiarizing myself with, if not learning how to read music, then just learning notations like what the staff means. In music, it's the foundation for everything to follow and an important musical symbol to know. The word hindsight was now situated in my long-term memory.

When the offive was over, we took our turn bowing goodbye. Jan was walking behind me now. I led the way with the other sisters out the back door to the refectory. It didn't take long before we walked into the delectable odors of a prepared meal. While having nutritious meals ready and waiting with no cooking involved, is not an important advantage to some, it is a supreme consideration to me. I *never* took it for granted.

Whatever her expectation was about the food here, I know she wouldn't be disappointed. When we walked into the kitchen and saw the counter, I knew I was right. It was full of fruit pizzas made with pieces of tangerines, strawberries, pineapples, mangos, bananas and cream cheese for the main dish. I hope she liked fruit.

While filling my plate, I reviewed the arguments supporting a meatless diet because it is crucial for the new novice to know why we *have* a vegetarian diet. *Rule 39* of Saint Benedict's Rule states, "Except *for the sick, no one should eat the flesh of quadrupeds."* Knowing why he said this will provide a good base. In past centuries, only nobles could afford to own land for hunting. The poor, the peasants, had meat only as a gift on High Holy Days. Monks, as poor ~~men~~ people we followed this custom.

Eating vegetables all the time wasn't so bad. I thought of the vegetable stir-fries, vegetable casseroles, and vegetable meatballs in spaghetti sauce served over meatless meatloaf. I *hardly* noticed the substitution of rice, bread, marshmallows, potatoes, curds, provolone, carrots, dumplings, and noodles.

I finished my meal, picked my coffee mug and went to the back to prepare a cup of instant coffee. While stirring in granules of instant coffee, powdered milk, creamer and sugar, I was sure if the Saint had known about the nervous, stimulating effect caffeine has on the body interrupting a person's calmness he would have added another paragraph to the drink apportionment chapter forbidding *espressos and double lattes.*

On my to the kitchen for a second slice of pizza, I remembered how clear the saint was concerning overeating too: *Nothing is more contrary to a Christian than gluttony.* I didn't let it disturb my meal. When I was finished, bussing my own dishes, I walked to the kitchen and left my dishes on a stack of other dirty dishes. I didn't take not being assigned to work in the kitchen either.

It was time for meridian. I went to my room for a nap, pulled off my veil and lay lengthways on the bed in my habit. My mind went into action again. It was obvious Jan needs to know it was important to be moral, decent, virtuous and modest. They are all parts of a final combination needed to preserve and maintain a vocation here.

To aid in her spiritual integrity, I hoped the Novice Director would read the writings of the *Desert Fathers* to Jan as an example.

A brother was sent on an errand by his abbot, and arriving at a place which had water, he found a woman there washing clothes. Overcome, he asked her if he might sleep with her. She said to him, 'Listening to you is easy, but I could be the cause of great suffering for you.' He said to her, 'How?' She answered, 'after committing the deed, your conscience will strike you, and either you will give up on yourself, or it will require great effort for you to reach the state which is yours now: Therefore, before you experience that hurt, go on your way in peace.

When he heard this he was struck with contrition and thanked both God and he wisdom. He went to his abbot, informed him of the event, and he too marveled. And the brother urged the rest to not go out of the monastery, and so he himself remained in the monastery, not going out until death.

That was my plan too.

Knowing how Saint Benedict himself mortified his body would raise anyone's eye brows. Believe it or not, he left his cave and rolled in thorns. I have felt the sting of cactus needles lodged in my fingers for days, and have seen what a desert porcupine can do. Self-control without any props, the new novice should know, is the best way.

The very fact I *am* living in a monastery makes me a total prude. I can say without equivocation: empirically verifiable physical phenomena described in spatiotemporal terms, is conversely juxtaposed to the vital principle of incorporeal consciousness; in other words, I can sat without equivocation, the physical ain't spiritual; it's one or the other.

Finding it hard to sleep in the day, I kept thinking.

Saint John of the Cross was an acquired taste. On he other hand, if I find him interesting, maybe Jan will get something out of his writings too. I wondered if the new novice would benefit learning what the said about giving up a sensual spirit needed to attain union with God. With all the Zen-like attributes of an extended haiku, he wrote:

> In order to arrive at having pleasure in everything,
> *Desire to have pleasure in nothing.*
> In order to arrive at possessing everything,
> *Desire to possess nothing.*
> In order to arrive at being everything,
> *Desire to be nothing.*
> In order to arrive at knowing everything,
> *Desire to know nothing.*
> In order to arrive at that wherein you *have no pleasure.*
> *You must go by a way that has no pleasure,*
> In order to arrive at that which you don't know,
> *You must go by a way you don't know.*
> In order to arrive at that which you don't possess,
> *You must go by a way that you don't possess.*
> In order to arrive at that which you are not,
> *You must go through that which you are not.*
> When your mind turns upon anything,
> *You are ceasing to cast yourself upon the All.*
> For in order to pass from the all to the All,
> *You have to deny yourself wholly in all.*
> And, when you come to possess it wholly,
> *You must possess it without desiring anything*
> For if you will have anything in having all,
> *You have not your treasure purely in God.*

I was wide awake now. I crawled out of the nice warm bed and walked sleepily to the chapel where I found Jan already at her place.

Being early is a good sign. It would not go unnoticed by the Novice Director who would now see her as eager, fervent and one step away from being held up as an example to the rest of us lethargic, lazy and sluggish novices. I could hardly wait.

From the corner of my eye I watched Jan bow when we bowed, stand when we stood, and sit when we sat, right in time with the rest of us. It goes without saying, one should already have a 'feel' for a particular community before entering through correspondence and phone calls with the abbess before starting her month observership. And although she hasn't been fitted for a habit yet, when the time comes, it will help her to know what an anonymous monk, one of the Desert Fathers, said about its significance:

The old men used to say, 'The cowl is a sign of innocence; the scapula a sign of the cross; the belt a sign of courage'. Let us then conduct ourselves in a manner consonant with our habit, wearing all parts of it with zeal, so that we do not appear to be wearing an alien garment.'

As I wished Jan luck in her monastic life, it came to me Saint Benedict's *Rule* was a stage on which the monastic dancers practice community life of religious asceticism. Surviving unchanged for centuries, it's important she know the inspired principles of communality. Knowing this is crucial in maintaining a resolute and determined spirit.

Jan as a prospective member should be aware admission to religious life is not made easy for newcomers. Chapter fifty-eight of Saint Benedict's *Rule* states: *if you can observe it, enter upon the life, if not, you are free to leave.* I hope new novice knows this very important rule, because in the unlikely event she wants to leave, she can always use it as an out.

The dance of the Trappistine hesychast is different from any other. It's like being whirled around and around a dance floor in the grasp of an invisible partner. Not knowing if a polka is coming or a tango will be next, but following the lead of her heart and trusting her inner prompting will lead to a deeper spirituality. Then suddenly one day, out of ordinary everyday experiences, a spiritual dimension arises that is so personal and profound, prayer becomes involuntary, almost like breathing; the perfect two step.

After two days her Review came in: Jan was learning the routine well; she was having no trouble learning signs and we all heard her in the music room practicing the modes. She had been assigned to the glass shop only. Everything was going to plan.

One afternoon late in the day, while I was watching leaves blowing in a flurry outside, catching on cactus and blowing away again, came the bad news.

Unfortunately, sometime during her first two weeks the desert syncopation changed for the new novice Jan and we watched as we would watch a plant wilt after being moved indoors from the outside. Once she realized the monastic life was not what she had envisioned, her lighthearted ballerina step became as labored as someone trying to roller skate in sand. After only two weeks, after all her good intentions, after all the preparations and plans, Jan had decided to leave.

"Better sooner than later," Reverend Mother said in an experienced tone. "It is much worse to try for years and *then* come to the same conclusion. Stepping back is sometimes a step forward," she said in quiet resignation, accepting the loss of the new novice so soon.

That day, the wind decided to take a long deep breath. The masses of cold air pushing back and forth across the desert had stopped, there was one long thin gray cloud hanging in the cold blue sky. It had dark places as clouds sometimes do that made it look like a face, and the longer I looked, the more I could see the slender image and the dumbfounded face of Jan staring from above. All that remained was this giant floating head staring down at us as a remembrance.

Her leaving was an audible experience; windows stopped rattling, doors stopped slamming, and tumbleweeds rested. It was as if the driving force of the wind had attempted to stabilize the disparities in her vocation with high and low pressures but it didn't do any good. Like the weather, vocations have to come from God.

I stood by myself in the field behind the monastery and watched the lone cloud as the wind acted like a spiritual mentor, faintly streaking the floating head across the sky, until it was gone.

CHAPTER

45

I experienced my first snowfall this Christmas, but whenever I think of this time, I will think of it as the time of the 'round'.

Every Saturday throughout the year, the community practiced hymns and antiphons and went over last minute changes for Sunday's Mass, and if it happened to be a Solemnity, a holy day of obligation, it usually meant we could look forward to the material being extra difficult. Christmas was something else entirely.

On Christmas day the visitor's side of the little chapel would be packed full of ranchers with their families, a few visiting relatives of the sisters, and devout churchgoers looking for a more meaningful Christmas. The 8:00, 10:00, and 12:00 o'clock Masses would overflow onto the porch next to the rock and cactus garden, and Sister Viola in her effort to make sure everyone went away with a sense of inspiration, fashioned a program that would rival the Mormon Tabernacle Choir. Months before Christmas we began our practicing, and practice we did; practice, practice, practice.

The carols Sister Viola chose ranged from the familiar to the unpopular, to ones I'd never heard before, and this Christmas we would be singing a 'catch' or a rondeau, a carol sung in rounds in which we had to learn to listen carefully to make sure we came in at the right time. Fortunately, the carol had a melody that was simple and uncomplicated, so no matter how many times we were asked to rehearse it, the melody never grew tiresome. I would walk in the hall humming… *Hark to the bells* being sure to quiet *down* passing the Superior's office… then start up again meeting one of the novices… S*trongly they chime,* stop completely meeting Sister Drusilla, continue humming crossing paths with Viola…*Telling the tale* as I made my merry way through the monastery cum music conservatory.

Knowing everyone had met the one requirement, the ability to carry a tune, Sister Viola assigned each sister with her corresponding pitch; low, middle or high. I had a medium to low tone, as did the Novice Director, so together we made up the alto section. The other eight choristers were divided until we had an overlay of timbre in four groups. A glee club could aptly describe our singing group because of the informal atmosphere and conviviality, even though our communicating was done only with hand signs.

It felt good being included in all this togetherness of laughing and singing, working on an end product as a Christmas gift from the monastery to our neighbors. And when we came in singing at our right times and held to our own stanza, it sounded great and we knew it, all of us showing a "Hey, we did it!" expression on our faces. It really was a proud moment of musical accomplishment when this happened, everyone quietly acknowledging her own part as icicles dripped from the roof to a mound of crusty white slush outside.

Christmas in a monastery is a wonderful experience. It is *the* holiday, the granddaddy of all holidays, and time to open the cookbook. Cistercians are known for their expertise in the kitchen, baking in particular. The art of bread making, both white and wheat was just the beginning of what wrapped around the wooden rolling pin in the flurry of preparations that went on for weeks for Christmas day.

We had sweet rolls and cream puffs, cobblers and tarts (made with our own garden's rhubarb and strawberries), brownie squares, date squares, bourbon squares, and rum balls. Cooling in every free space were layers of cakes, pies made out of cream cheese and chocolate, and pecan short-bread's; even our ordinary bread dough was dressed up with walnuts and raisins and split into long strips and braided, that when baked and sprinkled heavily with powdered sugar became culinary works of art. I marveled at each new creation put on the counter to cool as I walked through the refectory, all the while, the melody from singing practice playing in my head, *Hark to the bells!* "Look at that, lemon tarts!" *telling us all,* "are those coconut or almond macaroons?" *strongly they chime,* "Chocolate cream pies!" as I went on my way. With warm smells of baking hanging in the air throughout the monastery, we were all looking forward to Christmas.

Many of the baking delights were given away as gifts in return for gifts received, and we received many; various flavored honeys came in from one community, boxes of peanut brittle from another and homemade fudge from the motherhouse; we would be well supplied with fruit cakes for the entire year. Greedily looking at all the treats on the counter made my blood sugar level skyrocket. It was grand.

Into all this activity, our special winter visitor arrived, Father Wyss who we called Uncle Van, was here to give his annual retreat and work on his book in the quiet of our quest house; I had the impression he was trying out challenging material on us for our reactions before it made it into print.

Because he had a distinctive Swiss accent, as I walked through the monastery's halls it didn't take long for the *Carol of the Bells* repeating in my head to turn into: *Hark, der von bells!*, followed by *Das telling us all*, closing with *Herr Jesus is King!* By the time I finished the refrain, I was almost yodeling.

Father was invited into the warmth of the refectory to join Mac at his table in back for dinners and suppers. The rest of us sat across the room at the refectory table where we were privy to their witty repartee, friendly teasing and companionship during meals. Back and forth the banter would fly as Uncle Van picked up where he left off from his last visit, making us feel like he'd never been away. He told us this was how it felt for him too, and more, when he was here, just by thinking of the peacefulness of the monastery, it made him feel peaceful too, proving his long-standing belief that he really *was* a Cistercian at heart.

Starting his retreat during this week, we gathered in the chapel pulling our chairs into two rows facing the altar and waited in anxious expectation for the retreat director/priest in the form of Father Wyss to enter. A vigil light burning on the side of the room fluttered as a cool ventilating draft of outside air pushed an almost palpable wave of incense over us. Our cowled figures sat very still. There was no whispering between us, we were an attentive group of nuns hoping to come away with deepened intuition, a scholarly perspective and insightful knowledge. I could hardly wait.

I don't know whether it was due to the eggnogs, hard to refuse refills or the open bars at Christmas parties that prompted his topic, this year Father chose a seasonal subject for his talks—intemperance,the indulgence of appetites and perdition. I was an eager listener.

"The world today seems willing to accept addictive behavior. Don't you be one of them," Father Wyss lightly scolded from the front of the chapel beginning his retreat lectures. I sat still during his long pause. A good lecturer has the ability to make it seem they are speaking directly to you. How did he know this was a subject I was familiar with? "Don't ever let yourself lose control of your senses." He told us how even priests and nuns were not immune to the addictions of alcohol and had to enter treatment programs at times too. I thought of the bottles of wine people had donated to the monastery. Not just single bottles, entire cases were stacked in the pantry for special occasions. If priests were subject to the same generous natures of parishioners like we were, I could see how excessive drinking could easily become a problem. I moved around restlessly on the pew.

"God gives you everything you need. With an air of quiet defiance Father Wyss let his wordless silences act as his fist pounding and foot stamping which had more of an effect than a raised voice ever could because it encouraged us to come to our own conclusions.

I wondered why Father Wyss chose this unlikely topic of all subjects to explain to a group of cloistered contemplative nuns. We weren't bar flies, in fact, there wasn't a drinking establishment anywhere in the vicinity. Could it be that during his priestly life he had first-hand experience with a drinker, a housekeeper, a cook or a brother? Whatever the reason, I wondered if he'd reached the same conclusion as me, that the admission *I drink too much* was unfinished and needs an ending; I drink too much *because* I had uncaring parent or was abused as a child, or any of the gazillion other life situations needed to excuse it.

I stopped my deliberating suddenly when I realized since entering the desert monastery I really *was* away from all the trouble caused by someone who has a drop too much time and time again. It had taken over a year for it to sink in, but for the first time mentally, emotionally and now viscerally, I *knew* I didn't have to concern myself with the circular logic of the addiction argument any longer; I was *truly* free!

Disinterested in the remaining retreat talks at this point and only half listening, I heard snippets of what Father was saying, "Solitude is where inner mastery is found…", "It is important to pray for grace…" and "The path of faith leads to where God wants us to be."

I had to agree with his last directive; I *am* right where I want to be, this monastery. I was certain there was nothing holding me back. I looked forward to receiving my black scapula for final vows. I walked out the back door thinking cheerfully, *only seven years to go.*

Even though Santa and his sleigh full of presents were visibly absent and there were no stockings hanging anywhere, we did have fresh cut evergreen branches leaving a strong scent of pine in the chapel. Positioned around the crèche were waist-high statues of the Holy Family and barnyard animals standing poised in straw near an empty manger waiting for Christmas when during the night, someone came and left a rosy cheeked likeness of Jesus in the homemade wooden manger. It was a nice touch. On Christmas day our rendition of *Carol of the Bells* went off without any problems during all three Masses. The many hours spent practicing seemed like nothing now that it was over and we were receiving applause, resounding praise and distinction from onlookers.

I thought we sounded pretty good. It wasn't until Uncle Van asked for a copy of the tape recorded by Sister Viola he could play for his community of discriminating Jesuits that I knew all our practicing was worth it.

For dinner the fatted calf wasn't brought in, but just about. We actually had meat! A large donated turkey was placed on the table among all the trimmings: cranberries with walnuts in an orange sauce, mashed potatoes, stuffing with sautéed apple rings, broccoli and cauliflower with cheese sauce, radishes and green onions, homemade biscuits, topped off with a generous glass of wine for those who wanted one.

I'm sure Uncle Van and Mac were as surprised as we were when instead of listening to a refectory reader during Christmas dinner, Reverend Mother Esmeralda had a special treat for us, an opera. In-between bites of Christmas morsels I heard my first opera, the original performance of *Amahl and the Night Visitors* by Gian-Carlo Menotti that underscored the Christmas festivities around us. I was enveloped with waves of gratitude for the opportunity of sharing food and libations with this colorful group of hard core spiritual ascetics, all of us caught up in a superlative opera. And while our singing was an unmitigated success during Masses, our Christmas day was unrivaled.

While I was sitting in the refectory full of good food, glad tidings and familial benevolence, I turned my head to the window and watched as the snow fell silently outside, floating down behind Father Wyss, surrounding him in a mantle of white brilliance like a flame. I knew I would never forget this special Christmas, just as I would never forget dear Uncle Van.

CHAPTER

46

Doing the same thing over and over, the months flew by. The sound of a single cricket chirping midday told me the earth was beginning to warm. It was now spring and the land was experiencing a resurgence of scents on the broad plateau. A few gold and yellow flowers had bloomed and my second summer here was fast approaching. Soon the blue sky arching the far mountain would not be enough to protect it from the sun's continual burst of bright heat.

It was a hot, dry day in May, a day like all the others. I was on my knees weeding the strawberry patch and Sister Lorna was in the middle of the garden clearing weeds from the corn furrows so water could flow freely; it was just another typical day in the monastery some people would call monotonous, boring, or both.

Having lived under the pressure of changing addresses more times than I care to remember as a child, the dull uneventful lifestyle appealed to me. I liked knowing what I would be doing every day, when and where I would be doing it, and with whom. But nothing could prepare me for this. What started innocently with the hum of a few flying insects buzzing close to my head grew to many brown bugs lining the shallow roots of strawberries. I bent over and flicked one off my boot. It had a slender body with wings pulled in close to its three-quarter inch brown frame. I stepped over it as it lay struggling to right itself in the dirt. It would become one in a sea of thousands

It was incredible, one minute everything was fine and I was pulling weeds from the strawberry patch, and the next minute a large number of winged arthropods, too many to count, were covering everything. Within minutes, there wasn't one green leaf that didn't have an insect gnawing on it.

I took off my scarf and started swatting it in short quick movements over the vines.

This can't be happening, I complained, plagues are something I read about in the Bible! Immediately my mind treated the invasion as something sent by God as punishment. My guilty conscience took over; did I bring this on by talking to Sister Lorna? What else have I done? I began going through my actions of the past week almost knocking Lorna over as I rushed past her. Obviously I wasn't smiting first-borns or invading foreign lands, but it was entirely possible to hold someone captive by holding on to past grievances. Was I was bringing this on by my unfriendly feelings toward the Novice Director? In desperation I promised to do better. Would God listen to my bartering and end this assault or was it a case of too little, too late? Was it the beginning of the Apocalypse and nothing could help?

I watched the bugs unerringly target the potato mounds landing on top the furrows in the next section as if they could smell the sweet tubers growing underneath. Horrified, I saw the fast moving mass cover the entire garden like an ugly brown smog while I swung my scarf uselessly at them. The migratory insects weren't interested in mating; all the swarm wanted was food. There was nothing we could do but watch as more and more of them flew in from the direction of Mexico and land in our horticultural oasis.

"What'll we do?" I shouted at Sister Lorna. I looked at my stomping feet scattering the insects that were gathering in fast profusion as I waited for instruction from her.

There was no time to think. Lorna pulled off her scarf too and we both swiped at the pilferers helping themselves to our vegetables. "Keep swinging at them!" she yelled back encouragingly. But swinging at them did little as the fast moving swarm ricocheted off each other and both of us. We ran about the vegetables erratically, whipping our scarves furiously but we might as well have been using bows and arrows. It was futile. There were too many of the little creatures; if I shooed ten off a stalk, twenty more lighted on the same spot. The food we were growing for the Community to live on was being eaten and there was nothing we could do but stand and watch as the fruits of our backbreaking labor were swallowed by these tiny invaders. In an effort to control of the onslaught by reasoning, Lorna said, "Did you know although all locusts are grasshoppers, but not all grasshopers are locusts? These multi-covered plant eaters aren't grasshoppers, these pests are brownish gray..."

"It doesn't matter what kind of hoppers they are, they both *jump*. The insects here *fly*! They're totally different," I said correcting her. It was hard watching the insects bombarding the garden devouring very vegetable we had.

In deepening gloom I watched the wave grow in size, at times leapfrogging over the others in their excitement, dissatisfied with their place in line, doubling and tripling each other on one leaf in their greed for more. In less than five minutes, we knew we were fighting a losing battle but we kept swatting our scarves at them anyway. It was so overwhelming a cold shiver went through me; was it a harbinger of things to come? Shaking it off, I went back to snapping my red scarf at them.

Lorna was the one responsible for putting food on the table. The invasion meant more to her than a lowly novice like me. Where I stood pop-eyed in incredulity, I had a hunch she was visualizing the closure of the abbey due to lack of food. Not that she hadn't been trying; crashing about the plants, forearms thrashing wildly, waving her hands jerkily to scare them away, like me. Without a veil/scarf, her black disheveled hair hung in her face making her look like she had lost all control. Surely she wouldn't take the blame for this. She tried her utmost to keep the little buggers off the greenery.

I looked through warm air across the garden at the picked over corn stalks, at what was left of tomatoes, asparagus and the tender shoots of broccoli. They were all gone. It was disheartening seeing the entire garden nothing but stick-like nubs where once healthy green leaves had been; they even chewed leaves on the oak tree. It is hard to put into words what I was feeling as I looked at the total devastation knowing our nutrients were nourishing fleeing bandito beetles. All we could do was survey the damage.

When they had had their fill, just as fast as the violent crush descended, they flew away taking their little heads, legs, tiny eyes and short antennae with them. The danger had passed. Our garden looked like a bone that had been picked clean.

It wasn't over yet for Lorna. The impact of seeing this catastrophic event must have been too much for her. She threw down her scarf, ran to the shed, picked up a shovel and started swinging at anything that moved with remarkable force. She stood firm trying to put an end of their unwelcome appetites once and for all.

When the bells signaled the end of work, she had to admit defeat. I heard a last defiant cry, "Dang bugs!" before she let the shovel drop. I turned and looked at her face; it looked as empty as the garden.

I left her to her downcast thoughts and clawed my way up the hill. Stationed at the top, I watched a dejected Lorna walk through what was left of the tomato crop remembering when she placed plastic covers cut from milk containers over each seedling to guard it from frost. I told her we might have a greenhouse one day. Instead, we were looking at plants that had been picked to pieces. I hoped the gardener, in shock, wouldn't start crying.

Mumbling to myself, I thought remorsefully I'd like to go back a week; back to pushing green vegetables crowding the pathways out of the way, back to picking my way over large plants and overgrown weeds, back to the way things were. Giving a sarcastic smile, I turned and stepped toward the monastery knowing out of discipline, I'd have to ignore the compelling urge to relay our exhausting, if not heroic efforts to save the garden.

It would have been the most natural thing in the world for me to jabber excitedly, "You'll never believe what just happened in the garden! We were invaded by insects and they ate all the plants!"

Of course, I said nothing of the sort. I did the most contrary and unnatural thing imaginable. I walked in the refectory, went down the long hallway to the shelter of my bedroom and didn't breathe a word about the destructive afternoon to anyone.

Inside my room, I realized monastic life may look easy from the outside, but doing what's right takes discipline and is still hard. The same concepts handed down for centuries are carried out today. There were no 'new advances' in meditation, no new theories on how to keep still, no new ways to expedite enlightenment; praying the rosary was still done one decade at a time. Meditating was still done the way it's always been done, through practice and discipline.

I showered and changed knowing it was my responsibility to put thoughts of the stripped garden from my mind. I should forget the large wad of lively insects flying en masse, the small number of dead ones littering the dirt, and the look of despair on the gardener's face. I needed to replace it with the situation at hand; centering myself for the Office of Vespers.

I followed the scampering of feet in the hall to the chapel. After the traumatic afternoon, I settled back in my seat, looking forward to the unvarying routine of the monastery, a place where nothing exciting ever happens.

CHAPTER

47

The next morning I woke and my vision was spinning like a top. My first thought was: maybe I have an insect bite from the infestation yesterday. Or worse, maybe I was having an allergic reaction and was going into anaphylactic shock. I inspected my arms for welts. Seeing none, I eliminated it as a possible cause of my dizziness. I still wondered if I 'caught' something. Maybe I breathed in spores of listeriosis, the turning disease. I knew it affects animals but occasionally humans too.

I forced myself to attend Vigils feeling dizzier than ever. I planted my feet firmly on the carpet, holding my office book tightly trying not to get physically sick on the rug. This was difficult because wherever I looked, up, or wherever I turned my head, nothing stopped the room from moving. When I made it to the chapel, chairs and nuns, organ and player, candles and altar—they all moved about in a non-stop sickening swirl.

I was only able to keep coffee down at breakfast.

Stumbling down the hill to work with Lorna in the garden grabbing at bushes, holding onto weeds, making sure I didn't roll uncontrolled to the bottom. Amazingly, when I reached the end of the path, somehow my vision was back to normal. The dizziness was gone! This gave me a glimmer of hope. If my nauseating dizziness left even for a short time, there was a chance it would stay away for good.

I turned and looked at the ravaged garden. It was nothing in comparison to the upheaval I was fighting in my mind and body. What was causing me to be dizzy? I spent the next week concealing my maddening lightheadedness. I didn't go to the Superior and tell her what was happening with my vision, and ask for help, something I should have done in the first place. I didn't want to admit my vocation might be in jeopardy. Instead, to take my mind off this horrible turn of events, I looked for a diversion. Standing on the top of the hill overlooking the garden that afternoon, an idea came to me.

Whenever I went for a walk on the hills below the monastery, there was one place I was hit by gusts of wind blowing up from a canyon like a wind tunnel. Because it was lively air, it occurred to me the area would be perfect for flying a kite. Kite flying would be a great diversion! Would I be the first Cistercian in the history of the Order to take up the hobby? It didn't matter, anything was better than losing my vocation. I wasn't just flying a kite, I was giving a signal for what I was feeling inside, not exactly an S O S, but close; novices in monasteries don't fly kites.

Obtaining permission from the Novice Director was the first step. I could hear her now: "What? If you want a sidetrack, try grounding yourself in God. Here take this book. It will help you awaken to your life's purpose, I assure you, isn't flying kites!"

I knocked on her door and walked in her office. I was unable to keep my guard up with her by fighting my dizziness and her at the same time. I didn't tell her about how I was feeling. I told her my plan. To my relief, she said nothing of the sort. Unbelievably she said, "Okay, I don't see how flying a kite can do any harm." Pushing my luck, I asked, "I'll need a couple of things to make it with too."

"Why don't you ask Sister Gail? She handles all the craft materials."

"There's still time before dinner, I'll walk over now." I was surprised and overjoyed this monumental hurdle was over.

"And by the way," Drusilla continued, "I'm leaving tomorrow to go on retreat. I'll be gone two weeks."

That was fine by me, one less person from whom I'd have to hide how bad I was feeling.

"Have a good retreat," I told her sincerely grateful I wouldn't be under her watchful eyes.

One permission down, two to go.

When I finally walked to the glass shop, Sister Gail was ready to leave. I quickly explained my kite flying plan. I told her I'd need a couple light strips of wood, glue, and all the string she could can find." As keeper of the odds and ends needed to make crafts for feast-day gifts, she was the one who knew where to find everything I'd need."Won't flying a kite involve hours of running in the hot dry air?" she asked, her voice full of concern.

"No, not at all, I only need to run a little at first to launch it, then the wind does the rest." I pictured myself leisurely resting on the side of a hill somewhere, watching the kite sailing through clouds.

"Well, okay then, if it's all right with Sister Drusilla like you said, it's okay with me." I was surprised she gave her approval so quickly.

Two down, one to go. I could almost feel the string tugging at my fingers.

I walked back to the monastery with my stomach in a knot. I knocked lightly on the music room door where I knew Sister Viola, as intoner for the week, would be going over the music before Vespers. Because Viola was responsible for the truck, she was an important cog in my plan; the donated plastic blue bags were in the back. With no time to lose, I presented my argument why I needed one of the plastic blue bags. "There is a past-time that has been overlooked here at Our Lady of the Desert, kite flying." Building my case, while hiding the queasy way I was feeling, I reasoned, "With no traffic, no people, and no high wires or poles, the grounds around the monastery are the ideal location, don't you think? The plastic bags we collect cow manure in are the perfect material to use as a substitute for paper. I've made kites out of newspaper before and have a good idea what's involved. I think one bag stretched flat to cover a wooden frame will be big enough. May I use one?"

"I don't see why not," she said, and added with a smile as I was leaving, "Make sure you take a new one."

It wasn't hard putting the kite together. But it was hard maintaining my composure acting like nothing was wrong while I was working on it. I let the glue dry overnight.

There is nothing like the freedom that comes from seeing a kite as it swoops and sails in the deep blue Arizona sky. I watched as the large aqua blue plastic kite, dragging a tail of red rags, sailed through the sky and free-fall in the wind, soar again to lofty heights; stabilize a moment, as if making sure it was sound before plummeting again.

Feeling the tug and pull of the string against my fingers as I guided it through the air, gave me the sense of having limitless freedom too. It was really me flying over the cactus and tumbleweeds, along washes and over the chapel's steeple. From this distance, *I* was the one flying over the turning weathervane and cows drinking at the waterhole, I had a bird's eye view of the rain gutters and lightning rod, the glass shop and Novitiate. I was able to direct the kite to the left or right or pull it wherever I wanted. I enjoyed the relief it gave me of being in complete control. Seeing my new-found freedom as a vicarious representation of my spiritual journey, in the trials and tribulations of life, I wished I could be so accepting.

After days of guiding the kite through the air, I became nauseous for the first time up on my kite-flying hill. I was glad no one was around to see me except the ravens waiting for an evening meal. My vision had started spinning again; dizziness had overtaken me quickly. One minute I was fine, and the next my vision was spinning out of control. By the end of work I was staggering unsteadily, trying not to jostle my head as I walked.

I didn't know how much more I could take and brought up every conceivable reason I could think of beside the obvious swarm of bugs infecting me with some kind of weird southwestern malady. Maybe I was suffering from heatstroke? But if that were the case, then avoiding the sun should make me feel better. It didn't. Nothing was making me better. Now when I stood in choir, I planted my feet carefully so I wouldn't wobble, lose my balance, and vomit.

Maybe all I need is a good night's sleep, I'd say to myself. In the morning I'd be afraid to open my eyes. Afraid I'd see the room gyrating in some diabolical design to oust me from this holy place. I knew if the room was spinning, it meant the start of another whole day of seeing furniture, dishes and sisters flying in a revolving swirl. *Not again*, I would despair. *Maybe I'm not eating right.* Was it the vegetarian diet after all? At this point, just thinking of food made me sick, so I ate very little. It was taking all my energy just to hide how sick I was feeling. What's worse, my head felt like I needed to drink a gallon of caffeine to rid its odd right-sided ache.

Maybe it was the stress of public speaking then. I always had a hard time with the readings, the intonations and making petitions. It was hard for the other novices too only they weren't overcome with fear, foreboding and dread like I was. I should have been able to handle it like they did, I kept telling myself. Running out of reasons, I came to the reason that made the most sense to me. God was emphatically asking, *"What made you think you had a vocation here anyway?"* Nothing tricky about this. What did I expect? After two years, I never reached Nirvana *once* during any of my meditations. That should tell me something. I tugged fretfully at my neckline.

Like Cicero said, "Nobody can give you wiser advice than yourself." I decided to leave. With my decision made, I went to the person in charge. As it happened, Reverend Mother Esmeralda was in Rome attending a General Chapter so the next in charge was the Novice Mistress. I had a hunch it would come down to this. I could see her laughing in my face now. But as some grand fate, thankfully, Drusilla was away on retreat, something that seldom happened. Was it a coincidence I let my body collapse while she was away too? Somehow I didn't think so. Not having to explain why I was leaving to her was the incontrovertible ~~push~~ sign this was the right time for me to hang up my veil.

If she was here though, seeing the feeble state of my body; trying not to lose my balance, trying not to get dizzy, trying not to vomit, I felt sure Drusilla would ~~be relieved~~ understand why I had to go. Remorse set in. I felt bad that during my entire two year stay, I never let myself become her 'pal', or confidante. It was clear I would be walking out dragging a big pile of regret.

The next person in charge was Sister Viola. I found her in the refectory and hoped she wouldn't try to convince me I was imagining the whole illness. Signing to her, *I like speak you,* she motioned me into the Novice Director's empty office. I made the signs for *I big sick, I go.*

At this drastic juncture she stopped signing and spoke softly. "Are you sure?" she asked, not believing what she was seeing. She said she would contact Reverend Mother immediately and left to make the arrangements. Breathing a sigh of relief at the speediness of my planned exit, I thanked God for big favors.

She arranged a fight for the next day.

It was a good thing I was as sick as I was because it prevented me from thinking at all. This was my life, the one I had studied for for years. I felt like a tragic failure. How convenient; if I didn't know better I would think I planed it this way. It was devastating if I allowed myself to dwell on it, so I didn't.

The only good thing about the entire situation, if I had to return to secular life, at least by this time my hair had grown back. To my knowledge, bowl cuts have never been popular.

The next thing I wanted to do was explain my illness to Sister Lorna. I found her in the Community room. I was so sick all I could do, was make the sign for sickness: a fisted arm bent toward the right, perhaps showing imbalance. I signed to her—*'I go from this house'.* I had hidden my sickness so well she was convinced I was making a big mistake.

Holding back tears, I signed back, *'No mistake'.*

She looked at me in total disbelief. Seeing the rigidness in my eyes stopped her persuasive arguments. The last thing she said to me was, "You will carry your cloister within you," and hugged me good-bye.

It was a good thing I was as sick as I was, because it prevented me from thinking at all. This was my life, the one I had studied about for years. I felt like a tragic failure. It was devastating if I allowed myself to think about it. I didn't let myself dwell on all I was giving up—the little community of sisters who lived life not for the sake of living, but in celebration; quiet walks in the desert, spectacular sunsets; chanting the offices; braving the walk to Vigils under the starry sky; the howls of coyotes; never seeing uncle Van again. It was all too much.

I packed what little I had, not forgetting my cowboy hat Annette, hearing my plight, had graciously returned cleaned and brushed readying it for public viewing, minus the snake skin. I did the only thing I could do—lie on the bed till morning.

CHAPTER

48

When the plane flew over the cone shaped arches of the futuristic looking restaurant at the airport in Los Angeles, I knew I was really back home. As a native Californian, I knew the restaurant had been built so patrons could watch their loved ones taking off and landing. But today as we flew over the airfield, I wondered who was cutting into a steak or casually sipping coffee while I sat, teeth clenched, listening to the welcome rumble of the wheels lowering, praying our pilot was landing on the correct runway.

I felt better immediately. Coming from the fierce Arizona sun freckling my face, to moist salty air cooling it was like magic. But why would this have such an overall effect on the way I was feeling? It didn't make sense. Lingering doubts followed. Did I feel better because I was at home away from the demanding schedule of daily life in the monastery? If this was true, I should have started feeling sick a *month* after I entered and not after two *years*.

Whatever the reason, it was pure relief escaping the on and off dizziness of the last couple of months. However, it was replaced with a new and deeper kind of suffering; the pain of leaving the Cistercian lifestyle. It felt like God had picked me up and snapped me in half, like a dried piece of cholla. A hesychastic way of life is not a popular one, but it was one I felt suited for.

Coming back to the *real* world meant finding a job. As soon as I was feeling well enough, I interviewed and landed a teaching position in a small town north of Los Angeles. It was in a dry, unpopulated area of central California known as *"wine country"*. Instead of envisioning a region filled with the beauty of rows of purple, red and green berries, family run vineyards with grapes as far as the eye can see, I should have realized that grapes thrive in hot climates, *very* hot climates. Little did I know the area described as having over one a hundred wineries, had 110° summers too. As I began my new teaching job, I inadvertently put myself back in the same situation as Arizona, extremely hot weather and a new teaching job with its inherent stress. It didn't take long for my body to react.

Was I imagining it or were colors fading? Everything looked pale and washed out. Was I losing touch with reality? Dizziness, loss of balance and now colors fading? What's next; pink elephants? Maybe I should see Sister Lorna's therapist too.

Testing the hues on my own, I covered my left eye with my hand. Sure enough using only my right eye, I saw the color red as *pink*, black was *gray*, and brown looked *tan*. It was odd. As long as my left eye was filling in an object for me, my sight was deceptively normal. It was hard to tell anything was wrong. Losing color in my right eye wasn't painful and was easy to ignore at first. I chalked it up to the stress of my new teaching job.

Biking back and forth to the classroom in the blazing heat didn't help. My nausea came back with a vengeance.

When my vision started jumping back and forth uncontrollably, I knew I needed help. An appointment was made with an eye, ear and throat specialist or me. Maybe an ophthalmologist, a specialist in medical and surgical eye problems, would have been better but it was anybody's quess at the moment. I was driven to the medical building where trying to walk to the front door, wasn't easy. I collapsed immediately on the closest chair in the waiting room, exhausted. A secretary asked my name and helped me into an examination room.

The first thing the eye doctor did was give me a shot of vitamin B to help my chances. It began a long process of eliminating possible reasons for my symptoms. Following his finger was easy. It was about all I could do at the moment.

"You want to drop what in my where?" I asked shocked. The thought of *anything* in my ears made me cringe. I didn't put up resistance after noticing with alarm the increasing difficulty I was having articulating. He could have suggested just about anything at this point.

"I want you to take a field vision test too" Putting one foot in front of the other was almost impossible with muscles that weren't working properly. Now I was getting worried. I could hardly make it to the eye machine. I felt like I was walking like a monster, a real Frankenstein walk; I swung my hips oddly, trying to move my other leg forward, while flailing my arms for balance. It was a massive effort just to make it to the machine for the test.

With my chin in the holster helping to hold me up, I covered my left eye with a black plastic shield and watched tiny lights flash intermittently inside an egg-shaped canister. Each time I saw a light, I pressed a signal button. Then I changed the shield and covered my right eye, I went through the whole series of lights again. The test was not too long but because my eyes were strained to begin with, using them in any way was a test in itself. I was glad my chin was in the holster to steady me and very relieved I had controlled my queasiness long enough to finish both eyes without getting sick in the test canister.

He told me visual field tests were used to check for gaps or defects in overall vision as well as peripheral vision. He said it checks different functions of the eye, and measures the ability to see details at near and far distances. I was glad he took the time to explain its usefulness to me but was just happy the test was over. When he left to review the results in his office, I moved to another chair in the room, sat back and waited. I let my eyes relax while gazing over his diplomas on the wall. When I came to a mirror, my reflection startled me. Something was pulling the right side of my smile down as if it was made out of clay and someone had leaned on the right side of my lip distorting my smile. It didn't hurt, but now I had a sneer to match my monster walk. Again, I chalked it up to the stress of my new job. A few moments later he was back with the test results in hand.

"Well, I found you have two blind spots, one in each eye like mirror images," and handed me the large test paper. "The black marks indicate your misses."

The results looked like a navigational chart for a submarine. Numbers showed the exact places the lights flashed like they were hits of a torpedo. He pointed out two dark patches showing where I had blind spots that where were in about the same place in both eyes; right of the pupil in my right eye and left of the pupil in my left eye; a mirror image. I never noticedthe missing parts until he brought it to my attention. Testing it, I looked at the left side of his face. A bit of his right eye *was* missing! And vice versa; if I looked at the right side, part of his left eye was missing. For days now, they were being filled in by my mind's eye. I looked at the round clock on the wall. I saw the *whole* clock because I know what a circle looks like."You see though," he said, "at least the blind spots are out of your center of vision and are relatively small."

That's *something* anyway, I thought. I guess I should be happy. Focusing on the large sheet of paper on his desk containing the field vision test, he pointed out the false negatives, presentations and perimeter results marked with numbers. It had a dizzying effect on me and looked away.

"Tell me, why is the right side of my tongue numb?" I was hoping there was a test for this too.

"Good question," the doctor said, and watched a wave of alarm cross his face.

"I want you to see another doctor to be on the safe side, a neurologist." He handed me a slip of paper with a name on it. I was disappointed I had reached a dead end with this specialist so soon.

"What is a newergist?" I managed to get out, my speech heavy with slurs.

"Someone who studies disorders of the nervous systems."

"I'll do *anything* to find out what's wrong with me," hoping I'd have better luck with this next doctor.

The eye specialist made an appointment for me with the nerve doctor. But because he was so over booked, I had to wait a week for an appointment. I've waited this long, I can wait another week.

My non-stop vomiting wouldn't wait however. There was nothing I could do to stop it. Sitting up only made it worse. During the week in an effort to heal itself, I realized what my body was doing; ridding itself of upsetting things, past trauma and hurtful experiences, up to, and including my break with the monastery.

Day after day, I involuntarily vomited all the difficult moves and the loss of dear friends in childhood. I puked up chunks of every new school; every new strange classmate; pieces of every new teacher; and bits of unfamiliar neighborhoods. I spit up the loss of a normal life, along with the loss of childhood. I retched up guilt, nervousness and anxiety till my insides were raw and my stomach ached. In one last cathartic dry heave, I spewed out that hideous and ugly way of thinking draped in selfishness: namely, drinking behaviors of a parent, and the consequences they cause, don't affect children physically. Regurgitation of a lifetime was taking its toll, it was a wonder I could walk at all.

Still unable to keep anything down I put in my stomach, I decided; enough is enough, I want to go to the hospital. Standing on the side of the driveway in lounging clothes, suitcase in hand, a wave of relief flooded me as my transportation pulled near. Marshalling my courage, I slid onto the passenger seat with the left side of my head. In a minute, the most amazing thing happened: my nausea stopped! The relief was unbelievable! I didn't think my stomach muscles would ever be the same.

By the time I got out at the emergency room, I was feeling much better. I've heard of psychosomatic healings and wondered if just *knowing* I was on the way to get help made me better. As weak as I was on this transforming ride, I had to marvel at the power of the mind!

CHAPTER

49

On a sweltering hot Labor Day weekend in September, I entered the Emergency Room with twenty-nine holiday revelers who had been in various accidents involving cars, boats and trailers. One patient had held onto the roll bar smashing all his knuckles when it rolled; being drunk hadn't helped.

I was relieved feeling a wheelchair nudging the back of my knees encouraging me to sit. The next thing I knew I was being rolled into an examining room where an ER doctor gave me pills to help keep my stomach quiet in the likely event my nausea, he called vertigo, returned. I took one immediately, and asked why my nausea stopped on the way to the hospital. He said casually, "It was probably due to the way you were riding in the car." I let it go at that. (It would be years before I fully understood how positional vertigo works.)

As my first time in a wheelchair, demeaning as it was, it was easier than trying to get my limbs to go where I wanted. I shifted my body awkwardly up onto an exam table.

The doctor checked my reflexes, the coordination and muscle strength in my arms and legs, comparing one side with the other. He asked if I had any abnormal symptoms.

"Why, yes, as a matter of fact I do," glad that he asked.

"I seldom have headaches but the last two weeks, I've had this sick headache in the same place on the right side of my head," fingering the spot. "And for some reason everything I look at seems faded."

"Optic neuritis," he said confidently, inflammation of the optic nerve. A bundle of nerve fibers transmitting visual information to the brain has been disrupted making colors fade, but they should slowly return to normal when the nerve is back to normal. Some people experience pain with optic neuritis, this could be the cause of your headaches."

"What we have here is," the doctor said as he shined a tiny flashlight in my eyes, "is an astigmatism; symptoms include eye strain which could account for your headaches, and why your vision is jumping back and forth." I heard him, but most of what he was saying wasn't registering because I was so physically traumatized. Not being able to walk other than like a monster would change anyone.

I was learning more new words. Optic neuritis didn't happen overnight. Like a thief, it insidiously robbed me of my vision by washing out colors little by little, until one day it was apparent something definitely was wrong. I could see colors with *both* eyes but the right one had become much weaker, washed out like a negative on film. Because both eyes perceive objects, it was hard telling what was happening. It wasn't until I covered my left eye that I finally figured it out. Who would think *shades* of color could change? I was glad he had a name for it. I wasn't charting new territory that would go down in medical journals under "new and weird diseases" of the 20tieth century.

Because it took *weeks* for the inflammation to get to this point, the doctor told me it would take just as long to get back to normal, or close to it. In my way if thinking, as long as my eyesight wasn't painful, other than a tolerable ache, seeing things bleached out for a while wasn't too bad. With all the muscles weakened on my right side, why should my optic nerve be left out? I felt it was inevitable and took the news in stride.

"There's one more thing," I said, "My eyes are very sensitive to light. I have been turning away from bright light for days, even the glare of the television."

"Photophobia is an abnormal intolerance to light. This is another symptom that *should* go away in time. It's an eye irritation, another common occurrence with MS that causes an inability to look at light."

Not knowing how long it was going to last was frightening, but wondering if it was going to happen in my *left* eye as well, was terrifying. Blindness would scare anyone, even if it's partial.

"What's causing all these weird symptoms?" I whined. He said he had a suspicion. He wanted to perform one last test to be absolutely sure. I could feel the beginning of a sneer coming on, but controlled the impulse. Knowing he just set the knuckles on the patient before me, I knew I was in the hands of a very capable multi-talented doctor and gave him the benefit of the doubt."It's called a lumbar puncture, which is another name for a spinal tap."

Overpowered by weakness, my resistance at an all time low, I couldn't object to any guinea pig experimentation; as long as it didn't involve dissecting me, I was game. As barbaric as the name sounds, I should have been terror stricken, but I was too worn out to care. Tapping into my spine didn't sound like a pleasant experience, but in sickness there is no dignity. I agreed to let him perform it. He turned me on my left side and asked me to pull my knees toward my head. The attending nurse asked if I would like to hold on to her hand while the procedure was performed. A hand to hold instead of a bullet to bite can't be good sign. Now I was somewhat alarmed, but with little reason. With me squeezing the life out of her hand, the doctor inserted a long thin needle into the lower part of my spine. The initial jab felt as painful as an insect bite; that was all. It was the *thought* of what he was doing that made me feel queasy. Knowing the experienced ER nurse was expecting it to be painful, I expected it too. But it really wasn't any worse than a mosquito bite, thank God. I let go of the nurse's hand so her circulation could come back.

A short time later, the tired doctor had his diagnosis confirmed. He told me from the small sample of spinal fluid he had taken; the lab was able to analyze my white cell count. After a long day of working on holiday emergencies, the weary middle aged doctor had one more unpleasant duty, telling his thirtieth patient of the day she had multiple sclerosis.

The poor doctor, I sympathized. In the awkward silence that followed, with effort, I tried to formulate the million dollar question: "What's multeorsis?"

He smiled compassionately at me and said, "It's the deliberate destruction of balance, eyesight and muscle strength."

~~Fudge!~~ @%$#! It sounded like my body was being crucified while I was still in it. I was astounded. How could I fight what I couldn't see? How could I fix what I have no control over? There was one thing in my favor; I finally knew what was wrong with me.

The doctor started me immediately on a course of steroids called prednisone, explaining, "Tecfidera is an oral pill you take twice a day. Prednisone is powerful. It will help you manage MS by reducing relapses, delay progression and slow brain lesions. Let's see how you do on it."

Officially sick now, I was helped back into the wheelchair and admitted to the hospital as a regular patient. I was fitted with an elastic band on my wrist with my name, rank, and serial number: otherwise known as my name, birth date and illness. I was wheeled into a ward among many older patients lying in different states of medicated pain. It was much better than sharing a private room with a love-sick teenager with a boyfriend constantly visiting. No one stirred as I was helped into a bed. I lay transfixed thinking; you don't know how strong you are until you have to be.

Alone in my strange new living space, I was close to a bathroom for which I was grateful in case the vomiting returned. I had the most incredible feeling: I really didn't care if I lived or if I died. It wasn't self-pity. It was the most unique feeling of detachment, like something I had been striving for my whole life.

There is something to be said for the fetal position: back curved forward, legs pulled against the abdomen, head bowed, arms wrapped around the head; in half a minute, I was asleep.

Daily on his rounds the doctor checked my progress.

On the third day I was feeling well enough to sit up and make conversation. Now, instead of words like hesychasm and recollection and gravitas, a whole new a whole new vocabulary filled my head a medical dictionary: myelin, spasticity, and scotoma. Every day, like it or not, I learned more words. My father would be so pleased. The anti-nausea pills the doctor gave me curtailed my nausea and as long as I was sitting, I was in relatively presentable shape and could pass as healthy. Being numb on the right half of my body, and eyes that were jumping back and forth aren't obvious symptoms. Being inconspicuous again was a Godsend to someone like me who is normally shy, retiring and didn't like calling attention to myself. It gave me time to think.

"The exact causes are still unknown, but it's believed damage to the myelin results from abnormal responses in the body's immune system. *Usually* the immune system defends the body against foreign invaders such as viruses or bacteria, but with autoimmune diseases, the body attacks its own tissue. Your inability to coordinate movement is an example." It cleared up more of this horrible puzzle. Now I was worried; watching parts of my body die while I was still in it sounded like a slow crucifixion. Totally spent, I fell asleep.

Every time the doctor passed my room, he dropped in with more facts. "The presence of blind spots or scotoma may be due to a wide range of diseases. It's a classic sign of MS. I didn't want to say anything till I was sure." I pursed my lips and held them in a tight pucker to prevent a sneer. "The Bell's Palsy affecting your face should clear up in time also. It causes temporary paralysis of the muscles on one side of the face. The muscles should relax and return to normal too." He couldn't tell at the moment, but I was smiling from ear to ear.

I thought it was amazing how much stress triggers. If it wasn't happening to me, I'd be absolutely fascinated by all these weird symptoms.

"It's common for the optic nerve to be affected with patients with MS. Your symptoms may indicate damage in the brainstem area that connects the inner ear and the brain." "I'm putting you on a course of prednisone at this strength. Let's see how you do. It's a steroid used as an anti-inflammatory. It works differently for everyone. In your case it seems to be working quite well. In the meantime, continue taking the medicine for your nausea. Adding, he was hopeful I'd make a good recovery. *From your lips to God's ears*, I thought, unable to keep what I learned in the novitiate from surfacing.

Giving a simple geographical spread, he informed me, "Generally, the prevalence of MS increases as you travel further north or south from the equator, while areas that lie *on* the equator have extremely low numbers of MS. Canada and Scotland have particularly high rates of the disease and White populations are at greater risk than Asian or African societies. Almost 70% of patients manifest symptoms between the ages 23 and 40; that's why it's known as the young peoples' disease. Approximately two–thirds of those diagnosed are women; you fit right epidemically."

'Lucky me," I said, trying to control another unruly sneer. He left me among the other patients in the ward who were dealing with their own 'new' facts.

The next morning, besides my walking, there was noticeable improvement in my eyes too. Instead of my vision spinning, I was actually able to focus on one thing. I admit, for me, prednisone is really a miracle drug. My sight still continued spinning, but not as fast, mercifully slowing with every passing hour. Watching the TV up on the wall was straining because the scenes changed so often. I stopped watching.

I thought with alarm, what if the prednisone *hadn't* helped? I wouldn't let myself imagine the worst.

If I attempted to walk, no matter how hard I tried *not* veering right, I crashed into whatever was there anyway.

The doctor explained. "It's hard to believe, but your lack of balance is due to hairs in your inner ear tilting in the wrong direction. The utricle and saccule have areas called maculae that have about 40-80 hairs each, and these hair bundles release neurotransmitters. Different combinations send different messages to the brain. Yours sent the wrong messages. As he was leaving, he said with a smile, "Hang in there." It told me he knew how hard it was for me.

When my family visited that afternoon, it was a real eye-opener for them. Because of Ball's Palsy, I couldn't smile. Nor could my right hand hold a fork; it was easier eating with my fingers: salads, cottage cheese, and meat I tore into pieces with my fingers. While they were here, I walked, ate and spoke as little as possible. Trying to make light of my situation by joking didn't work when the punch line was an unintelligible mumble. It was all highly embarrassing.

Along with me, they questioned out loud, how could this happen? No one on either side of the family had a muscle disease. We were all astounded. They left scratching their heads.

Now that I collapsed, would my hospital stay prove children shouldn't be made to endure massive amounts of stress caused by living with a drinker? I doubted it. I watched my parents come and go, talking of Michelangelo.

By the fourth day in the hospital, my walking had improved greatly with the prednisone. My eyes still ached but I was encouraged with my increased muscle strength over all. If I improved this much in four days, there wasn't a doubt in my mind I could work my way back to full strength. The doctor agreed, and thought it was a good idea for me to walk up and down the hallways for exercise. He told me if I wanted more room, I could use the track on the roof.

If exercise helps my strength return, then that's what I should do. I arranged for a walker and dragged my way to the roof like the hunchback of Notre Dame. I walked around and around the small track confident my efforts were helping. I went back to my room and lay on the bed waiting to feel the beneficial results. But after a couple hours, I developed an excruciating headache. What next? I moaned. I rang for the nurse who buzzed the doctor.

"You may have a spinal headache," he presumed. "It could be the result of a reduction in the volume of cerebrospinal fluid from the sample I took. Or, since it's been several days now, it could be too *much* exercise."

"Too *much* exercise?" I asked disgusted, feeling my lip trying to curl in displeasure. Why didn't he tell me this in the first place?

The doctor advised not to try so hard. This was okay with me; it wasn't easy dragging my right leg that felt like it weighed a hundred pounds.

I sunk back on my pillow. With time to kill, I called the nurse again and asked for notebook paper. Knowing the Cistercians would offer prayers on my behalf,

I wrote to Reverend Mother Esmeralda in Arizona, and Reverend Mother Sera back east. I explained what happened to me. I couldn't hold a pen in my right hand, so I had to write with my left hand. It made my scrawl look like ransom notes: *Being held against my will, send 500 unmarked prayers & hurry!* or something similar. It was important to me to send them letters as soon as I could, even if my pleas for help looked like they were written by a five year old.

On the last day in the hospital, the doctor pulled a chair close to my bed and explained general matters relating to multiple sclerosis. "First of all, M.S. is not contagious, you can't 'catch it' by touching M.S. germs on a doorknob. It's a disease of the central nervous system which has two major parts, the brain and the spinal cord." He paused to let his meaning sink in. "Protecting the nerve fibers of the central nervous system is a fatty tissue called myelin which helps conduct nerve impulses to and from the brain. In M.S., myelin is lost or destroyed leaving scar tissue called plaques. This disruption may cause a variety of symptoms."

He looked at me with a *'you got that'* look? I really needed a tape recorder.

"Your prognosis is good. Remember, people with MS go through long intervals with few or no episodes after onset, and usually live active lives years after the diagnosis. Keep in mind too, Anne," he said in a voice fostering hope, "life spans are usually not shortened, and flare-ups rarely occur after middle age." I wondered just how much of my muscle strength was going to come back.

I thought of all the diseases and/or disorders I could have had—muscular dystrophy, epilepsy, fibromyalgia, *any* type of cancer with its side-effects—loss of appetite and hair loss. Compared to these, multiple sclerosis didn't seem so bad. I wouldn't need to undergo the conventional therapy used to treat some diseases either, chemotherapy. And so far, other than headaches and eye strain, I was pain free. I was happy knowing I would be getting up from the wheelchair and walking out of the hospital on my own volition.

"Why does it happen to only to some people?" I asked, wondering why I was one of the chosen few.

While he was talking, I was opening and closing my hands to see how much my strength had been affected. My right hand was definitely weaker. Career-wise, I knew my typing would suffer. Oh, well, I was never much of a typist anyway, making me turn to practical matters; who is going to hire someone who just spent a week in a hospital relearning how to walk and talk? One thing was sure, getting back in the job market this time wasn't going to be easy and couldn't envision an occupation for myself. My musings were interrupted by the doctor's voice. "Two things you should be aware of before you are released: heat and stress have been shown to worsen symptoms of MS or even trigger flare ups. Try to stay out of the sun while you're on prednisone, and try not to aggravate your condition with undo emotional difficulties if at all possible..."

"What did you say?" I asked, amazed. Did I hear him correctly?

"Yes. Severe trauma can alter the very chemistry and physiology of the brain, especially before the age of six."

This was the capper! The results were in. I had empirical proof. I looked at him, hardly believing my ears. *Try not to aggravate my condition with undo emotional difficulties?* Too late, not when moving is considered as stressful as going through a death. It was 20 years too late! Moving every few years *has* to be the cause of my M.S.!! It made perfect sense.

"Yes, thoughts and emotions are translated into chemical expressions or codes, and communicate the affects to our biodies. Emotions such as grief, anger, fear, or joy can impact our mental states and biochemistry."

I must have had a puzzled look on my face because the doctor patiently paraphrased it for me: "There *is* a physcal connection between our feelings and thoughts that help make us sick. Molecular messages can dramatically impact physiological functions at the cellular level."

Immediately, the emotionally charged event of being made to look at a bloody head wound when I was four came to mind.

All the other factors he discussed, took a back seat. If M.S. needed a toehold, this was it. It felt as if a heavy weight had lifted off my shoulders. It hadn't been the monastic schedule or the vegetarian diet after all. It was my upbringing! It is hard to relate the relief I felt at first, relief that quickly turned into anger as I realized: it's easier for some people to go along with their sick behaviors rather than get help. Anger and resentment set in. Because of this cowardly way of thinking, I lost my health, not to mention my vocation.

As one angry x-nun, now that I had actual proof, I knew if I blast my parents with blame, it should be when they were sure to understand my pronunciation. Anyway, one contentious situation at a time was enough.

I was brought back to the present when the doctor, with genuine concern, wished me well in the future and said good bye.

So that was it. It was up to my body now. I lay in bed thinking of the doctors' attentive farewell.

Maybe it was divine intervention that brought his antithesis to me. It was a scene I'd seen my father play many times before. With a dramatic entrance, it was obvious he had something important to say. Standing before his family in complete confidence, he'd announce, "This is my last cigarette."

"Not *again*," everyone would groan; some days he did this three times. Lying here, it finally dawned on me he never made the announcement *once* holding a can of beer. The only hint of his quitting came in a farcical poem he liked to recite:

Light me up to kingdom come
with bourbon, scotch and a little rum;
the mushroom blast is me sky-high,
the ash you see, is scattered me.
From now on, there is no maybe,
I'll drink '*fried ice and apple gravy.*'

There and then, I knew he'd *never* stop drinking; selfish to the end.

I didn't blast my parents with blame because I wanted to spare my poor mother. She had her own problem. His obstinate refusal to acknowledge he had a drinking problem was like a huge stump whose roots were clamped to the other side of the world stubbornly refusing to be pulled free.

I hid my face in the pillow shutting out the world. I believed a hesychastic way of life was the *'right'* way for me to live and having the dream die was just as painful. I was left with an overwhelming sense of loss that made me shudder; I didn't think I'd ever get over it. I was changed forever.

In the pungent odor of hospital disinfectant, so different from incense or sage brush, when I was at my lowest, the parting words of Sister Lorna came to me, "You'll carry the cloister within you," and knew they were never truer.

I missed it all: the entire Cistercian way of life: growing vegetables in the garden; the snow at Christmas; exploring on long walks alone; the glorious Arizona sunsets, the intoxicating scents of the high desert. Uncle Van! And especially the support of the sisters who I hoped realized the severity of my condition, and why I had to leave in such a rush. Maybe the illegible scribbling in my letter would convince them. It made me look intoxicated. I had to laugh; now *this* was irony!

Silly me; when I left the fast pace of the monastery, I thought all my troubles were behind me. It turns out they are in front of me on an unfolding road that was filled with sadness, worry, fear, doubt and dread with no end in sight.

I rolled on my back. My eyes popped open when I realized it was start of a new pursuit, seeing how much I could do before worsening or becoming totally incapacitated. It was journey that promises to be even more adventurous than my time in the desert.

During my hospital stay, besides from my family, I received not one, but three get-well letters: one from Reverend Mother Esmeralda in Arizona, one from the abbess back East, and one from, of all people, Uncle Van in the form of a short message on the back of a postcard: *Writing to you from a desert House of Prayer in New Mexico at an elevation of 7,000 feet. You would love it here. Authentic Indian hogans. Uncle Van PS. Get Well!*

Hope gleamed from my tortured body. Uncle Van was staying in a retreat center filled with peace and quiet conducive to prayer and contemplation? Well, the picture on the front of the postcard *did* look beautiful—desert seclusion framed in sunset reds. The more I thought about it, the more I could picture myself walking over the hills and into a whole new life.

Yes, this might be just what the doctor ordered! What an adventure retreat work could turn out to be! My excitement grew and my spirit soared; now I have a reason to get well.

The End